A GREAT AND RESTLESS SPIRIT

The incredible true story of Harry Hawker—
Australian test pilot, aircraft designer,
racing car driver, speedboat racer, world-beater

D.R. DYMOCK

Author of *Hustling Hinkler*

A great and restless spirit:
The incredible true story of Harry Hawker—Australian test pilot, aircraft designer, racing car driver, speedboat racer, world-beater

© D.R. Dymock 2022

Published by Armour Books
P. O. Box 492, Corinda QLD 4075 Australia

Cover images:
Airwolfhound, CC BY-SA 2.0 <https://creativecommons.org/licenses/by-sa/2.0>, via Wikimedia Commons. By courtesy of Tim Felce.
The Queenslander, 21 June 1919, 28, State Library of Queensland, IE1791808_FL1796104.

Interior Design and Typeset by Beckon Creative

ISBN: 978-1-925380-415

 A catalogue record for this book is available from the National Library of Australia

All rights reserved. No part of this publication may be reproduced, stored in, or introduced into a retrieval system, or transmitted, in any form, or by any means (electronic, mechanical, photocopying, recording or otherwise) without the prior written permission of the publisher.

Other non-fiction by D.R. Dymock:

Hustling Hinkler:
The short tumultuous life of a trailblazing Australian aviator

The Chalkies: Educating an army for independence

Extending Your Use-by Date:
Why retirement age is only a number

A special and distinctive role: WEA Sydney 1953-2000

A sweet use of adversity:
The Australian Army Education Service in World War II

What reviewers said about *Hustling Hinkler:*

'Hustling Hinkler' is mandatory reading for everyone who loves flight. Superbly written (with a surprising end-twist), 'Hustling Hinkler' shows how unbridled passion for man, machine and humanity trumps fear, doubt and complacency.

~ Richard de Crespigny, Qantas pilot, author of 'QF32'

'Hustling Hinkler' is a fantastic book and an absorbing read.

~ Dick Smith AO, Australian entrepreneur and aviator.

Contents

Introduction		vii
Chapter 1:	'His one dream was speed'	1
Chapter 2:	Genius unleashed	11
Chapter 3:	'A sort of inspired light'	27
Chapter 4:	Like a will-o'-the-wisp	39
Chapter 5:	No respecter of fools	53
Chapter 6:	A post-war proposition	65
Chapter 7:	Waiting for the future to unfold itself	73
Chapter 8:	'Mildly surprising to downright unpredictable'	91
Chapter 9:	'Possess our souls in patience'	103
Chapter 10:	A game of cat and mouse	113
Chapter 11:	Not without a struggle	123
Chapter 12:	'Many a prayer was breathed for their success'	133
Chapter 13:	'Making the night less terrible'	143
Chapter 14:	Close to boiling point	153
Chapter 15:	'And vanished into the blue'	161
Chapter 16:	Three magic letters	171
Chapter 17:	'The sweetest and most wonderful thing'	183
Chapter 18:	Wild about Harry	191
Chapter 19:	A restless spirit	199
Chapter 20:	Feelings of qualm	209

Chapter 21: Finished with failures 219
Chapter 22: 'Precarious activities' 231
Chapter 23: 'We're really beginning to go now!' 243
Chapter 24: Brave and ageless 253
Postscript 267
Acknowledgements 279
Bibliography 281
    Books 281
    Newspapers and journals 282
    Selected websites 284
Notes 285
Index 295

INTRODUCTION

William Shakespeare once wrote: 'Some are born great, some achieve greatness, and others have greatness thrust upon them.'[1]

Harry Hawker was not born great. His father was a suburban Melbourne blacksmith, his mother a dressmaker. Harry left school at age 12.

Nor did he have greatness thrust upon him. He spent his growing-up years mostly in rural Victoria, working as a chauffeur-mechanic on grazing properties and honing his mechanical skills.

However, when he found aviation as a young man, he soon *achieved* greatness.

For all the wrong reasons, the aviation industry blossomed during World War I. Harry Hawker not only survived the war, he thrived. He found a home with Sopwith Aviation in England and became one of its top wartime designers and test pilots. CEO Tommy Sopwith thought Hawker was a genius.

Even before the war, Harry was a legend. He earned his pilot's licence in double-quick time. Not long afterwards he flew faster, higher and for longer than anyone else in Britain. His fellow pilots could see he was special—they reckoned he had an intense fire inside him and an inspired light in his eyes.

In a classic boy-meets-girl scenario, Hawker met Muriel Peaty in a London park when her car broke down. She provided the stability he needed in his life while he pursued his dream of

---

[1] Twelfth Night.

speed. If it wasn't in planes it was in racing cars and speedboats. No wonder she became anxious about his never-ending urge to go where no one had ever gone before.

And when Harry disappeared attempting the first transatlantic flight, the whole world held its breath.

On the surface, Hawker was the epitome of his age—daredevil, competitive, pushing the boundaries, intensely focussed, ready to take on any challenge. A great and restless spirit.

Yet beneath his larrikin exterior and public affability, there bubbled away an underlying weakness he seemingly discounted or denied. It was an heroic pose that would eventually result in a devastating outcome at a relatively young age.

I came upon the story of Harry Hawker while I was researching for my book on another Australian aviator from the same era, Bert Hinkler. The two came from similar backgrounds, but their life journeys were quite different. Nevertheless, they shared the same sort of restlessness.

This was partly due to their temperaments, and partly to the sort of world they found themselves in. Aviation was an exciting if precarious development in an increasingly technological universe, spurred on by the pernicious demands of 'the war to end all wars'.

In *A Great and Restless Spirit*, I have tried not only to portray Harry Hawker as an outstanding pilot and designer, a person of great technical skill and intellectual capacity, but also to show how his relationship with his wife Muriel was integral to what he achieved, right to the end.

It is the complexity of this Australian-born adventurer and his 'need for speed' that drew me to write about him. I invite you to explore Harry Hawker's short but eventful life, to see where his great and restless spirit took him. And to wonder.

D.R. Dymock

Within a small exterior he had a great and restless spirit, a driving force which made it imperative for him to be up and doing.[1]

They knew that except for that one hidden moment they were invulnerable.[2]

Once the two men were out of sight, Muriel went once more to the front of the car and gave the starter handle another quick twist. Still no luck. She checked the carburettor again, and discovered fuel dripping from it onto the ground below. Curiously, however, the petrol was pooling on top of the gravelly surface, not soaking into it. Muriel likely put a finger under the carburettor and first smelled, then gingerly tasted the droplets. This wasn't petrol—it was water.

The boy at the place where she'd thought she'd bought petrol had given her a can of H_2O instead.

Ever resourceful, Muriel managed to drain the fuel tank. Then she and her friend sat and waited for another car to come along. They had plenty of time to watch the families picnicking in the park and the shy groups of almond-eyed deer on the lookout for early shoots of grass. Eventually the women flagged down two other motorists, but neither had any petrol to spare.

A short time later, a familiar blue car pulled up alongside. It was Harry and his flatmate, Basil Watson, in the French convertible. Before Muriel could explain about the fuel mix-up, Harry said, 'So, it was petrol after all?'[3]

The two women looked quizzically at him, and asked how he knew.

'If a girl breaks down,' Harry said with a smile, 'she will invariably take down everything that is detachable before she looks in the petrol tank.'

No doubt the 'girl' quickly set him straight about the can of water as he proceeded to transfer the needed fuel from a container in his car. He didn't explain how they happened to be passing by once again.

Apparently unfazed by their rescuer's sexist comment, Muriel and her friend were persuaded to swap phone numbers.

Harry diligently turned out every pocket of his suit, like an early version of Mr Bean, but couldn't locate his calling card, so scribbled his details on the back of Basil's card. Nevertheless, Muriel didn't think she'd made too much of an impression on the Australian.

'He had a nervous, off-hand manner all the time,' she said later, 'and, although he made one very unconvincing effort at a compliment on my knowledge of motor cars, he seemed genuinely relieved when I let in the clutch and with many thanks drove away.'[5]

Hawker was 26 when he first met Muriel Peaty in London in 1915.[4]

The 18-year-old didn't expect to see either of the men again. But soon the destinies of Muriel Alice Peaty and Harry George Hawker would intertwine in ways she could never have imagined.

When the young Englishwoman met the brash Australian in London that sunny April day in 1915, the Central Powers (Germany, Austria-Hungary, Bulgaria, the Ottoman Empire) were arrayed against the Allied forces (Britain, France, Russia, Italy) in the world's deadliest chess game—the war to end all wars. Former colonies Australia, South Africa, Canada, and

New Zealand had answered Britain's call to join the fray, along with Indian troops.

The United States at this point was staying aloof. For months French and other Allied soldiers in Europe had been digging themselves into the network of increasingly miserable and muddy trenches that would come to define the Western Front. German troops in Belgium had used choking chlorine gas for the first time. At sea, the Royal Navy with its fearsome fleet of dreadnoughts and cruisers had imposed a total blockade on Germany, although lethal U-boats still prowled the Atlantic.

On the Gallipoli peninsula, British, Australian and New Zealand troops were poised to storm ashore to take on the Turks defending the heights. The reason Harry Hawker was not among them was that he was making a significant contribution to the Allied cause in a very different way.

Harry had come to England from Australia four years earlier, chasing a dream. His father George, born in Harcourt, Victoria, had a blacksmith-and-wheelwright's shop on the Nepean Highway at South Brighton (now known as Moorabbin) on the outskirts of Melbourne. In 1883 George had married another Victorian, Mary Anderson, a dressmaker, and the couple had produced four children—Maude, Herbert, Harry (b. 1889) and Ruby. The family was generally self-sufficient—they kept a couple of milking cows and a few horses, raised chickens, grew vegetables and baked their own bread.

George Hawker was also a Farrier Sergeant in the Victoria Royal Artillery, and represented Victoria in international rifle shooting competitions in the late 1890s, a skill he passed on to Harry. He was also a keen member of the Methodist Church, and helped with Sunday services in churches on the local circuit, including Mordialloc and Brighton. With his brother Bert and sisters Maud and Ruby, as a boy Harry would hand out hymn books and help with tea on these occasions. Although it doesn't seem that Harry carried on that particular religious tradition as he grew older, he does appear to have inherited the 'Protestant ethic' of hard work and the belief that achievement came through sustained effort. One Methodist trait that Harry also followed was lifelong abstinence from tobacco and alcohol.

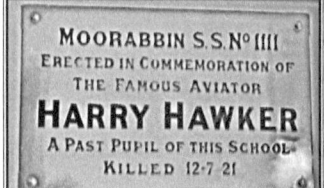

As a child, Harry struggled to find a school that suited him, and after three tries (when he reportedly continually ran away), he ended up at nearby Worthing Road State School. There he joined the school cadet corps, an organisation intended for developing discipline in children. Today his alma mater is known as Moorabbin Primary School No. 1111, which proudly proclaims itself as 'The Place to Excel'.

Harry Hawker eventually came to personify that motto but, at the time, he reckoned he'd rather have his hands in an engine than his head in a book. It was a decision he would later regret. So, after completing the basic requirements for the minimum leaving age of 14 years, he left school at age 12 and started work.

As well as being a craftsman in wood and metal, his father George had a talent for good engineering and an eye for invention, and over time built

Hawker as a 12-year-old school cadet at Moorabbin Primary School.

A key aim of the cadet corps was to instil discipline.[6]

a variety of engines and boilers, and extended his creativity to a steam-powered car. So, even as a child, Harry knew his way around a workshop and grew up in an environment where technological experimentation was encouraged and idleness frowned upon.

On leaving school he moved into a world where cars were increasingly beginning to putter along the streets and motorbikes darted down the lanes, gradually replacing the plodding horses and carts of his childhood. Nevertheless, one of his friends from this time, Andrew Lang, recalled that 'cars were so scarce that should you meet one the natural thing to do was to stop and have a quiet chat with the other motorist.'[7]

As he would do all his life, Harry snapped up any opportunity that came along that needed technical expertise: first at a Melbourne manufacturer of bicycles and wheelchairs, then at a car sales company. In his late teens, he headed off to the country as a chauffeur and mechanic for well-off graziers—initially just across the New South Wales border at Deniliquin, followed by a stint at Skipton in the Western District of Victoria. All the time Harry was building his skills and expectations, always on the lookout for new challenges in tuning engines and driving cars.

Not yet 20, he finally found what he was looking for at Ernest de Little's grazing property at Caramut, 100 kilometres west of Skipton.

Harry's competitive spirit was evident in everything he did—he was handy with a cue at billiards, and fast on his feet as a boxer, with a devastating punch, despite being only five feet three inches (160 cm) tall. But he was most at home behind a wheel, and the determination and aggression he would show throughout his life came to the fore when he took charge of de Little's Argyll 12/14, a four-seater Scottish-built open wheeler.

Argyll cars had already made a name for themselves internationally for speed and quality, and Harry worked his magic under the bonnet to get the maximum from the grazier's four-cylinder model. His main task was to ferry his employer, a top polo player, and his fellow sportsmen to shooting, polo and horse-racing events.

'His one dream was speed,' Lang said. 'As soon as the events were over, if there were any cars on the road anxious for a dusting-up, they got it from start to finish at the hands of Hawker.'[9]

At the time, Lang himself was driving a new 1907 12/16 Talbot, and there was tension between him and Harry over whose car was faster. Lang's description of the resulting tussle

Hawker's competitive spirit and technical skills came to the fore in tuning Victorian grazier Ernest de Little's Argyll 12/14 for maximum speed.[8]

on the road after one of these sporting events reveals a lot about Harry's ruthlessness in competition:

> Getting away from the gate there was a huge pool of mud, and just about 50 yards ahead I caught sight of Hawker forcing a machine off into the mud. A few seconds later a vehicle forced me out at the same spot; but by sheer luck the Talbot pulled through, and I got back to the road, with Hawker by now about a hundred yards ahead. Getting clear of the town with nothing lost or gained, we settled down to it properly, and fairly flew along. My mount was fitted with four gears; Hawker had only three. Coming to a longish grade a few miles out from the town I made an early change into third, and by degrees gradually began to bring the Argyll back.
>
> The grade did not last long enough, as when within about forty yards of Hawker's tail he topped the summit, still on top, and was off. But my advantage still held, and things looked rosy except for the problem of how to pass him when he was caught.
>
> Suddenly a reddish streak appeared from under the wheels of the Argyll. I caught the flash of the kicking legs of a calf, and I swerved. My lady passenger screamed, and with great difficulty — but with the throttle still open — I managed to get the machine back on to the road without shedding a tyre. However, this had cost me at least fifteen yards. Suddenly a mongrel greyhound darted out, too late for Hawker, but got me. One calf and a dog — both killed — in 400 yards was not bad going.
>
> It transpired that the calf insisted upon lying across the road, and Harry feared that if he swerved to avoid it he would be giving me the chance to get in and pass him! That was Hawker on the road when it came to a matter of a real dust-up and the reputation of the Caramut Argyll was at stake.[10]

On his frequent visits to Melbourne, Harry teamed up with his mates Harry Busteed and Cecil De Fraga to build and race motorbikes from their own often radical designs. At first they tried them out on a steeply banked bicycle velodrome near Flinders Street Station, but the manager banned them when he discovered the wooden structure was starting to come apart under the pounding. So they took their rough-and-ready machines on to country roads, no doubt to the chagrin of local farmers still in the horse and cart stage.

Harry became obsessed with building a motorbike that could beat all-comers. He set up a lathe at Caramut House and invented a bike that could reach 70 mph, a remarkable speed for the time. Typically, however, Harry wouldn't settle for less than 80. He was still working the engine up to full throttle when he had an altercation with a small animal on the road (another calf, a dog?) and smashed the machine beyond recognition. He decided to give up building his motorbike after that, 'not on account of having nearly killed himself, but because of loss of time and sleep.'[11]

It was an attitude he would always carry with him, whatever he did.

From the time he left school it seemed all of Harry's interests revolved around speed, the faster the better. It was a symbol of the restlessness, the urge to move on to new challenges, that would shape his life. According to Lang, 'Hawker as driver, tuner, or mechanic was always intense, and living in the sporting atmosphere of Caramut House helped him a great deal in the matter of finding himself.'[12]

The Melbourne household he grew up in and his subsequent experiences in rural Victoria might have helped shape and sharpen Harry, but it was a Frenchman who set him on a new path, one that would soon help define him.

CHAPTER 2

Genius unleashed

The year was 1909, and Harry Hawker was twenty years old. It was only six years since America's Wright Brothers had cemented their place in aviation history with the first powered flight. But it was in Europe that the tiny industry was beginning to blossom.

French inventor and aviator Louis Blériot had already established a company to build and market the flimsy machines. In July 1909 he went into the record books when he took off in his 25-horsepower monoplane from near Calais, France and piloted it across the English Channel to make a pancake landing in a field near Dover—31 miles and 40 minutes later.

It was the first crossing of the Channel by air, and Harry and his friends Harry Busteed and Harry Kauper were captivated by the boldness of the feat. Suddenly they could see their futures.

'From the day that the Frenchman pulled off this world-startling effort,' Andrew Lang said, 'the lives of the three Harrys … had a new outlook. Here was something new, and we knew deep down in our hearts that this new form of sport was to prove the metier of all or some of us.'[13]

In an instant aeroplanes took over from cars and motorbikes in the trio's imaginations. They devoured magazines and books on the topic, even though at this point they'd never actually seen a plane. That is, until the world-famous escapologist, Harry Houdini, arrived in Australia nine months later with a Voison biplane. Along with his uncle, Bert Chamberlain, and the other two Harrys, 21-year-old Hawker camped for a few days in March 1910 on the railway station at Diggers Rest, on the outskirts of Melbourne. There he had the thrill of seeing the American entertainer make what was arguably the first powered flight in Australia.

The self-promoting Great Houdini (born Erik Weisz, changed to Ehrich Weiss) almost clipped a gum tree on take-off, but managed to fly a two-mile circuit over drought-parched paddocks in two-and-a-half-minutes in his box-like biplane to claim the record (although debate continues today on whether he really was first).[14]

Whatever Houdini's ultimate place in Australian aviation history, his flight that day sent the imaginations of the three youthful Harrys soaring into the stratosphere. The trio of mates, dubbed 'the Eternal Triangle', had grown up alongside remarkable technological developments—the internal combustion engine,

Hawker was at Digger's Rest, Victoria, on 20 March 1910, to see Harry Houdini lay claim to the first powered flight in Australia.[15] *The event changed Hawker's life.*

washing machines, vacuum cleaners, radio broadcasting and the Model T Ford. Now aviation offered exciting possibilities for a future they could hardly comprehend.

The three booked themselves a passage to England on the White Star Line for the following year, full of youthful hope. They were escaping what they saw as the limited aviation opportunities in Australia to seek their fortune in Britain, heading in the opposite direction to the convicts and free settlers of the previous century.

Youthful enthusiasm wasn't enough to secure them jobs in the Old Country when they arrived there in May 1911. They hadn't thought to take references from Australian employers with them. They were also up against the thousands of British locals competing for jobs.

In desperation, Harry Hawker, now 22, offered his labour for a week for free to prove his worth. However, the sort of general engineering work he could do wasn't readily available, and he had no takers. After two months without a job, his finances were dwindling, and he seriously considered heading back to Australia. Just in time he managed to pick up work with Commer cars, then went on to Mercedes and Austro Daimler, all infant automobile companies whose names would soon become internationally known. Each time his pay went up a few pence an hour, but there was no way he could afford the flying lessons he was so desperate for.

All he could do in his free time each week was head to Brooklands, just outside London, where an airstrip built inside a car racing track had become a magnet for small aviation companies and flying enthusiasts alike. There he longingly watched flimsy biplanes take to the air in the hands of other, luckier, pilots. After ten years of development, designers were still struggling to tame the forces at play with these lighter-than-air machines. The death rate for early aviators was high. Yet young men (and an occasional woman) kept coming forward, eager for the challenge, as if this was what they'd been waiting for.

Harry Hawker's big break came via his mate Harry Kauper, who had scored himself a job as a mechanic at one of the new Brooklands companies, Sopwith Aviation. He alerted his long-time friend to the possibility of work there. And so it came to pass that in June 1912, thirteen months after his arrival in England, Harry Hawker joined the aviation company that would quickly become a significant part of his life.

Conscious of the precariousness of his earlier stretch of unemployment, he carefully set aside fifty pounds to cover his return passage to Australia, just in case.

The sort of Sopwith advertising poster that attracted Harry Hawker's attention in 1912.[16]

He need not have worried. The Works Manager, Fred Sigrist, soon recognised Harry's workshop skills, honed back in Victoria. Harry was itching to get off the bench and into the air, however, and soon persuaded the company's owner, Tommy Sopwith, to teach him to fly. The story goes that he paid for his lessons with the money he'd set aside for his return to Australia.

Sopwith, just 12 months older than Harry, quickly discovered that the Australian was not only a first-class mechanic but also a natural-born flier. Within a few days of his first lesson, the new Sopwith employee was so far ahead of his fellow pilots he was allowed to fly solo. In September 1912, the 23-year-old qualified for his Aviator's Certificate, No. 297. '"He took a very good ticket" was the comment made at the time,' the editor of *Flight* magazine said.[17] Soon Harry was an instructor himself in this emerging if precarious industry.

He was also immediately at home. It was as if the stopper had been taken out of the bottle and had released Harry Hawker's aviation genius to the world. He must have hardly been able to believe his luck. For a man driven by a need for speed and a desire to win, almost every week there was some sort of flying competition or other. Tommy Sopwith gave him access to the company's developing stable of planes. Over the months that followed, Harry was quickly among the placegetters—second in a quick-starting competition, first in a relay race where the pilots worked in pairs, third in a speed handicap...

On 24 October 1912, just weeks after being awarded his pilot's licence, he set a British Duration Record of almost eight-and-a-half hours, a time that wouldn't be beaten for several years. Despite his competitive nature, Harry was very cool during the event: 'I had a Thermos flask of cocoa on board, some chocolate, and some sandwiches, all of which I found useful in either passing the time away or relieving the monotony by giving me something to do.'[18]

In June 1913, with only nine months experience as a pilot, Harry Hawker created a British solo height record of 11,450 feet (3490 metres). Not content with this solo feat, on the same day he set two more height records, carrying one and then two 'average weight' passengers. The following month he claimed a prize of £500 (£59,000 today) by making six 'out and back' five-mile passenger flights (including a climb of 1,500 feet/460 metres) in a seaplane, the Sopwith 'Bat Boat'. At each turning-point he had to touch down on land and sea alternately. In August 1913 Sopwith entered the two Harrys, Hawker and Kauper, in the *Daily Mail* Round Britain Race, where they had mixed success, as will be seen later.

Sometimes in the shorter events in 1913 Harry was competing against, and mostly beating, his boss. Not that Tommy Sopwith minded. His company's aircraft were selling well to the British Government, and any win was good publicity.

Sopwith Aviation was quick to capitalise on Hawker's 1913 achievements.[19]

It also turned out that this crack Australian test-pilot who had left school at age 12 and had no professional qualifications had an innate understanding of aircraft design. In 1913, at age 24, Harry contributed significantly to the initiation and design of a small, fast, two-seater 'demonstrator' biplane. Initially referred to as the 'Sopwith St.B.' (which some have interpreted as 'Stunt Bus'), the new highly manoeuvrable biplane with its 80hp Gnome engine came to be known as the Sopwith *Tabloid*. This was the forerunner of the Camel fighter which would come to play a significant part for the Allies (and Sopwith Aviation) in the war that was just around the corner.

With his new-found confidence as a pilot, Harry was also not averse to making money from his new career—if this alleged story from a Sopwith worker can be believed:

> I tell you 'ow it was with that there 'Arry 'Awker, sir; he was my fancy for anythink every time. It was like this: we were standin' there down the Solent chattin', and that there Tommy Sopwith was remarkin' as nobody 'adn't looped-the-loop on a seaplane, and mentioned a matter of 40 quid for the man as did it first on one of his machines. 'Awker, who was standin' by, got 'im to confirm it; then went across to his machine and started up the engine.
>
> There wasn't what you might call more than a couple of 'andfuls of water where it was moored; but he just bumped and splashed it into a flight, and a couple of minutes after he looped over our 'eads twice. That's 'Arry 'Awker; no 'alf measures, no stintin'; and it was the first time a seaplane had looped-the-loop. Then he brought 'er down and walked

straight up to Tommy Sopwith, 'olding out 'is 'and for the boodle. That's 'Arry 'Awker, too. 'E's there and 'as the goods to be there. I tell you, sir, 'e's my fancy every time.'[20]

In 1913 Hawker gave flying displays over Brooklands on Sunday afternoons, something he'd hankered to do from the time he'd arrived in England two years earlier.[21]

In early 1914 Harry managed to combine business with pleasure when Sopwith shipped him and a *Tabloid* to Australia for several months to show the two-seater off to Australian military authorities. Harry Kauper went along as mechanic. They arrived in Fremantle, Western Australia, on 13 January on the RMS *Maloja*. A headline in the Perth *Daily News* underlined Harry's amazing rise in the aviation world since he'd left his homeland just three years before: 'THE WORLD'S CHAMPION AVIATOR: AN INTERVIEW WITH MR H. G. HAWKER.'[22]

Another commentator noted how fame had not gone to Hawker's head, however: 'The Australian aviator... is a quiet and modest youth, who does not wear the trappings of his craft, but goes aloft in an ordinary sac suit,[23] and could be mistaken for any ordinary individual.'[24] For his part, asked about the dangers of flying, Harry said that the risks were exaggerated and that aeroplanes would come to play an important role in the world. He also hinted he might loop the loop sometime during his stay in Australia. But he never did.

Harry arrived in Melbourne in time to celebrate his 25th birthday with his family on 22 January, 1914. His father, who had passed on his mechanical aptitude and design capability to his son, said 'the thoroughness with which Harry does his work is an object lesson which young men might copy.'[25] A local paper described him as a 'quiet modest-looking young man of slight but supple build.' He was, in fact, around five feet three inches tall, and in photos can be seen wearing built-up shoes.

Harry's first exhibition was delayed when Customs took its time clearing the special oil needed for the plane's Gnome engine. In the meantime, the *Tabloid* stayed in its shed at the CLC Motor Garage and Engineering Works, partly owned by the pilot's brother-in-law. The oil was finally delivered on 27 January. Shortly afterwards, Harry amazed the locals by using New Street as a runway before rising steeply into the air over the adjacent Elsternwick Golf Course. After some low-level left and right banking, he swooped down close to the ground and hopped the plane over trees and fences before zooming back up into a clear blue sky. 20 minutes later he was back on the ground. He told excited locals he'd reached 5,000 feet, travelled at 90 mph, and that 'the air is much clearer than in England.'[27]

The program cover for Hawker's Randwick Racecourse flights, Sydney, 1914, overstamped for Albury, NSW. [26]

A few days later he dropped in on Lord Denman, Australia's Governor-General, on a pre-arranged visit. Harry descended 'in a magnificent spiral, whizzing round and round, and down and down at a terrific pace'[28] before spending 30 minutes with the G-G and his guests, who had interrupted a game of tennis to greet their high-flying guest.

Melbourne was alive with excitement for the famous pilot's visit. On 7 February 1914, a crowd variously estimated as between 25,000 and 40,000, most of whom had never seen a plane, turned up at Caulfield Racetrack to watch Harry put the *Tabloid* through its paces. 18 special trains and extra trams and buses were harnessed to cope with the demand. 'All you have to do,' Harry had said, 'is to get off the ground, keep up, and get back again—when you want to of course, and where,' he added.²⁹

He might also have also said: 'and also dodge the unruly crowds.' His Caulfield flight started well enough: 'rising with remarkable ease and gracefulness, soaring away in the teeth of a blustery breeze which does not appear to trouble him. From a great height he drops sheer for a couple of hundred feet, turns the machine right over on its side and then noses down again appearing that he will dive into the crowd. From 40 feet he darts up and over the stand buildings with an exhibition of corner turning, evoking roars of applause repeated when he lands.'³⁰

That's when the trouble started. The crowd charged over the barriers and surrounded the plane. Harry was trapped there for 45 minutes. A Miss Ruby Dixon had booked to take a joyflight with

*Hawker over Caulfield Racecourse, Melbourne, February 1914.
The crowds were unruly, making take-offs and landings difficult.*³¹

him, but Harry decided it was too dangerous to take off with her in the passenger seat. Instead, the organisers managed to clear an area large enough for him to go up solo, and he thrilled the spectators with a 15-minute flight that took him to 7,000 feet (2100 metres).

Eventually he managed to take off with Ruby Dixon on board, but when he wanted to come down, the crowd had once again flooded across the racetrack. Harry headed back to land on the golf course at Elsternwick, only to discover that crowds had gathered there too. He was forced to set down on another part of the course, but it was a bumpy landing and the propeller and undercarriage were damaged. Fortunately pilot and passenger were uninjured, but Harry's subsequent Sydney event had to be postponed a week while the plane was repaired. It travelled by train to Sydney.

In front of 20,000 people at Randwick Racecourse, 'he goes up almost perpendicularly and comes to earth in wide circles at times upside down or what looked to be so. He provokes a great outburst of applause by soaring down from heights to the straight and maintaining his flight low in full view of the spectators, alighting in front of the grandstand.'[32]

Shortly afterwards, the Australian Governor-General, Lord Denman, clambered aboard, wearing a tail coat and a wing collar but also the most unlikely headgear: a flatcap set backwards, à la Harry. On his return from the short flight, the G-G declared that Harry inspired him with great confidence.

Conscious of Sopwith's hope of selling *Tabloids* to the Australian Government, Harry also took the Defence Minister, Edward Millen, up for a flight. The experience convinced Millen of the need for better military aviation for Australia, and he called for the early completion of Australia's first military flying school at Point Cook, Victoria. Harry had already said the three aircraft purchased by the government, and held in storage, were out of date and useless for military purposes. Nevertheless, the three were finally taken out of storage and assembled.

An attempt was made to raise enough funds to persuade Harry to fly non-stop from Sydney to Brisbane. In the end, however, he and his father and Harry Kauper loaded the plane on the train for Melbourne, but stopped over in rural Albury for another demonstration (and civic reception). Once again the local racetrack was a convenient if hazardous airstrip.

On March 7 he took the plane up to 7800 feet, a new Australian record. Earlier he'd explained how he liked plenty of air under the plane. 'From choice, I don't fly lower than 3000 feet,' he said. 'You see, if anything happens when you are well up you have a good chance of making a recovery before you hit anything solid. But it's a very difficult matter when there are only two or three hundred feet between you and the earth.'[33]

Which was just the situation he found himself in as he dropped back down after his record Albury flight. After its time above the clouds, the Sopwith's engine was so cold it cut out just 300 feet (90 metres) from the ground. Twice he made short dives to try to kick it back into life, but without success. He decided he'd have to land the plane without power in the crowded paddock below.

Hawker's abrupt landing at Albury Racecourse, Victoria, March 1914.[34] *'I was never further from a serious smash-up in my life.'*

Harry tried to keep the *Tabloid's* speed down enough to pull it up quickly, but it was coming in too fast, and he feared that any minute it would smash into the racecourse's running rails. So he elected to make an emergency stop, and in front of the noisy crowd abruptly plunged the plane's nose into the ground, splintering the propeller and cracking the undercarriage.

Next day there were media reports that he'd crashed at Albury. Not so, said Harry. 'I was never further from a serious smash-up in my life... There were no brakes on the landing chassis, which was broken simply because I brought the machine up abruptly.'[35]

For him, it was a controlled crash. You do what you have to do.

And whatever Harry did, it seemed the Australian crowds loved it, if this local poet can be believed:

> An' away 'e went a-soarin',
> While the ladies all adorin'
> With us common blokes a-roarin'
> In our joy;
> An' our praise 'e needn't flout it,
> So let everybody shout it,
> For there was no doubt about it
> 'E's the boy!
>
> An' we 'ear that Mr. Millen
> Found that flyin' way so killin'
> That no doubt 'e'll now be willin'
> Straight away
> To give 'im an invitation
> To be boss of aviation
> For our young Australian nation,
> With good pay.[36]

Thousands turned out to watch Hawker in the Sopwith Tabloid on his Australian visit 1914.[37]

A month later there was another incident at Ballarat racecourse in country Victoria. However, this time it wasn't so much under the pilot's control. In front of a crowd of 7000, as Harry came in to land on the racecourse, carrying a paying passenger, everything seemed to be going well. It was clear nevertheless he was coming in very fast. It almost looked as if he was planning to jump the *Tabloid* over a brush fence on the track, hurdling it like a steeplechaser.

At the last minute he missed the barrier, however, and landed at speed on the rough racetrack. Suddenly the wheels hit a rut, the plane tipped to one side like a drunken sailor, and a wing struck the ground. The Sopwith's nose again plunged sharply into the ground. Fortunately, the pilot and the no doubt white-faced passenger emerged unscathed.

'The fact was,' the *Melbourne Leader* laconically reported, 'that the biplane landed with too much impetus.'[38] It was a verdict Harry probably couldn't argue with this time.

On this occasion the plane was damaged so badly that shortly afterwards he decided it was time to take it back to England. Before he left Australia, however, the Defence Minister invited Harry to accompany him on a visit to the new Central Flying School at Point Cook. On their arrival they came across the wreckage of a recently crashed Deperdussin monoplane—one-third of the

Australian military fleet was out of action. Nevertheless, the Australian Government ultimately decided not to purchase the *Tabloid*—they thought the design too advanced for the nation's needs at that time. Nor did they invite Harry to be 'boss of aviation', as the poet had suggested.

While he'd been away, another Brooklands pilot, Fred Raynham, had claimed the British height record with a passenger on board. Harry's eyes were elsewhere for the moment, however. He'd told reporters he was intending to be back in England in time to help develop a plane for the Gordon Bennett Aviation Cup in France in the autumn. That might have been optimistic, given the rumblings of war in Europe. Just a few months later the world would be at war. One immediate outcome would be that Australia's previously lacklustre military aviation capability would spring to life, leading just after the war to the establishment of the Royal Australian Air Force.

As Harry left Australia by ship in early May 1914 for the four-week voyage to England, there was also something niggling at him that would eventually have personally catastrophic consequences. But he was either unaware of it or in denial at this point in time.

CHAPTER 3

'A sort of inspired light'

Harry Hawker arrived in Southampton from Australia on Sunday 7 June 1914. That same afternoon he was back at Brooklands, taking up the Sopwith biplane that in late April had taken the honours in the international Schneider Cup competition in Monaco with a different pilot. An observer reported: 'His handling of that machine shows he has lost none of his old skill during his absence. He is looking very fit and well and as keen as ever on flying.'[39]

At this point international relations in Europe were on a knife-edge. But the flashpoint was yet to come, and outwardly everyone carried on as usual. Harry and Muriel's first meeting was still ten months in the future.

On Tuesday June 16 Harry put on a spectacular flying display at Brooklands. It was supposed to be summer, but it was an *English* summer, and the temperature was struggling to climb out of the low teens. No one had his shirt off today. Nevertheless, it was a clear afternoon, so the spectators would get a good look at Harry. He was flying the *Tabloid* biplane he'd brought back from Australia. However, it was looking a little odd, because he'd asked the restorers to remove the fabric covering from the back section of the fuselage, revealing the matchstick framework underneath. It looked half-finished.

Everyone at Brooklands knew Harry was in the air and they were watching to see what he was up to as the *Tabloid* climbed into the sky. Next moment the engine stopped and the half-dressed plane went into a dive. The crowd held its collective breath. In the cockpit, Harry waited for the moment, then hauled firmly back on the stick. Now it was all physics. Centripetal force was pushing inwards; centrifugal force was pulling outwards. At the same time the pilot was constantly adjusting for changing speeds and wind drift. The biplane began to curve in an arc up into the sky as if pinned to a roller-coaster track.

Harry was now upside down in the cockpit, held there firmly by his safety strap, blood pounding in his head, unseen forces pushing and pulling at his body.

The plane seemed to pause at the top of its imaginary circle, glinting in the sun like the diamond on an engagement ring. If its speed was too low, it would drop like a brick, with Harry inside. Too fast, and he risked breaking free of the circle and plunging nose-first into the ground. The crowd watched in awe, hardly breathing. Then they began to clap and cheer as the Sopwith arced downwards, on its way to the bottom of the circle. But Harry didn't hear the applause—he was too busy on his way to repeating the manoeuvre. Up and over again. And again.

That's why he had the covering part-removed—he reckoned it'd make looping the loop easier. The spectators were ecstatic. Next day he did twelve loops in succession, and over the following weeks at Brooklands and nearby Hendon airstrip, the spectacular manoeuvre became his party trick. His fee for these acrobatics was £30 a day (£3500 in today's money).

Harry trusted his skills and judgment and, in the uncertain world of aviation, his passion for flying was obvious to everyone around him. A fellow pilot suggested there was 'an intense fire of enthusiasm burning inside him to the exclusion of everything else.' [41]

Surprisingly, Harry's drive to be the best at whatever he did was not matched by robust health. Three days after his twelve loops in a row, the 25-year-old became so ill during an air race, 150 miles from Hendon to Manchester and return, that he was forced to withdraw. He was favourite for the event, but the normally indomitable pilot became sick before he'd finished the first leg and, after becoming lost in a fog over Coventry, decided to return to London. When he landed he was close to collapse. A doctor thought the problem might be a reduced supply of oxygen in the cockpit.

The 'half-dressed' Sopwith Tabloid *in which Hawker looped the loop at Brooklands, June 1914.*[40]

Although this might have seemed like a 'one-off' event, despite his relative youthfulness Harry's health was fragile. One observer described the Australian as 'a remarkably frail little man with the heart of a lion.'[42] Tommy Sopwith became constantly concerned about his famous pilot's wellbeing.

Nevertheless, a short time after his withdrawal from the race, Harry was back in the air again at Brooklands. It was Saturday June 27 and he was again flying a *Tabloid*, but in this case a military version, sometimes called the 'Scout'. The tiny plane was fully dressed this time, and the crowd was hopeful they'd see him looping the loop once more. As the month had gone on, the weather had warmed up, and it was a balmy evening as the biplane curved upwards into a still-bright sky.

Harry was focused on the task at hand, 'to the exclusion of everything else.' He'd already been trying out this Sopwith, pushing it to its limits, learning its weaknesses. A key member of the design team, Reg ('Pop') Ashfield, said, 'As soon as Hawker started to fly he had an angle we hadn't. He could tell where the shoe pinched. He was a damned annoying blighter, but he was right.'[43]

One of the reasons some regarded him as a 'damned annoying blighter', according to another Australian pilot was that

'he was a "colonial", and not all British people had yet come to accept their former subjects as equals. It irritated them to have one of the species voicing bombastic opinions and fantastic prophesies. Perhaps he sounded bombastic, too, but Harry wasn't that way. He had ideas and he had faith in them and the tremendous future of aircraft, and he said nothing till he was pretty sure he was right and knew what he was talking about.'[44]

[45]

On this Saturday evening as he reached 1200 feet Harry was confident he could give the punters below the sort of display they were looking for. He pointed the nose downwards, then it was the familiar pull back on the stick and the Scout began to climb the arc. Moments later he'd completed the first loop beautifully, an orbit of delight for the watchers below. Before he could began the next circle, however, the plane went into a dive and at the same time began to spin.

The crowd didn't know whether to be alarmed or excited, not sure if this was part of the display.

In the cockpit, Harry was fighting for control as the Sopwith headed rapidly nose-first towards the ground. Initially the plane was in a perfect 'tourbillon' spin, the wings revolving around the centre line of the fuselage as it dived.[46] Then the tail flicked out and the Scout went into a spiral. The physics had gone awry. Gyroscopic forces around the rotary engine contended with aerodynamic ones. For a split-second Harry considered shoving the stick forward and putting the plane into a straight dive, which would increase his chance of recovery, but he decided he was too close to the ground.

The margin was narrowing rapidly now, and he worked the controls furiously, managing to slow the descent and bring the aircraft closer to horizontal. But the Scout was fluttering rapidly downwards like a damaged butterfly. To the consternation of onlookers at Brooklands, it disappeared behind the trees on nearby St George's Hill.

There was a charge of bystanders over the rise to where they thought the plane came down. It was a forested area and there was no immediate sign of the Sopwith or its pilot. After some frenzied searching, they found the Scout almost hidden inside a thick clump of trees. Harry was standing beside it, his clothes torn, and his face and hands criss-crossed with scratches and abrasions oozing blood, but otherwise apparently unhurt.

He'd managed to keep the biplane's nose up but had also hit a tall tree head-on—fortunately not at great speed. The plane then slid vertically down into the copse, knocking off branches and folding its wings over the cockpit as if protecting its pilot's head from a beating. Saplings and undergrowth cushioned the final thump into the ground, but the Australian was lucky to be alive.

Shortly afterwards, he was sitting astride the carrier of a motorbike on his way back to Brooklands, while the Sopwith crew swarmed around the plane. Their initial checks confirmed that all the controls were working perfectly at the time of the crash.

As the bike zoomed past a fellow Aussie, Horrie Miller, Harry shouted to him: 'I'll get her out all right next time. Lucky I landed in a tree!'[47]

Miller was astonished Harry had survived the crash, yet alone was talking about having another go. But at the same time, he also noticed 'a sort of inspired light' in Harry's eyes.

Back at the airfield, Harry relived the experience in his head, trying to pin down how the plane went out of control, and analysing his response. The spin, the urgent moves on the control stick, the pressures building on plane and pilot, and the gut-sinking inevitability of the final plunge. He'd been working around engines since he was a boy, and his practical mind told him that every problem had a solution.

'I knew what I should've done,' he told his rescuers. They leaned forward, anxious to hear. But they were disappointed. Harry saw this as his problem, one that he alone had to sort out. Not for Sopwith or the sake of aviation, but because he was not going to let this get the better of him.

Hawker was 5 feet 3 inches (160 cm) tall and in this photo is wearing built-up shoes.[49]

'If only I'd had the guts to do it,' he said. They leaned forward again. 'I'll have a new plane ready in four days. I'll get into a spin and get out of it.'[48]

His eyes were still shining with that inspired light, but no one was any the wiser about how he planned to do it. And no one was game to ask the damn annoying blighter.

But none of them doubted that he would.

The next day, Sunday 28 June 1914, a Serbian gunman in Sarajevo, Bosnia, took an opportunistic moment to shoot dead the visiting heir to the Austro-Hungarian throne, Archduke Franz Ferdinand, and his wife, Sophie. His spontaneous act lit the touch-paper that would shortly ignite a firestorm, the like of which the world had never seen. Over the next few weeks there would be political posturings, warnings, threats, provocations and military mobilisations that would culminate in Britain declaring war on Germany in early August.

Like many others, Harry would have read the signs and would've had a good idea of what was coming. But, like the rest of the world, he couldn't possibly imagine what a fierce and fluctuating maelstrom of death that would be, nor the part he would play in it.

For the moment, he had something else on his mind. Four days after the Brooklands crash he stood beside his new plane, identical to the earlier one except for the engine. Just as a rodeo rider was determined to ride into submission the bull that threw him, so the Sopwith test pilot was about to take on the forces that brought about his downfall. In leather jacket and goggles instead of chaps and spurs.

Any miscalculation, any unexpected manoeuvre by the beast he was riding, this time he might not be so lucky.

An early-morning mist rested gently on Brooklands as Harry took a long look at the brightening sky. The only other person present was Horrie Miller, there to swing the propeller.[50] This was a private battle, not a public performance.

'I'll go to 8000 feet, get into a spin and come out,' Harry said,[51] as if there was no doubt. He climbed into the cockpit and strapped himself in.

'Switch off! Suck in! Contact!'

With a puff of white smoke, the rotary engine leapt into life. Harry brought it up to full revs, the sound rippling rapidly across the empty airstrip in the cool morning air. He gave the thumbs up and Horrie whipped the wheel chocks away. The bull was out of the pen.

At the end of the runway the newly built Sopwith arced gracefully into the air as if it was born to it. The Australian nursed it, nurtured it, climbing it steadily above the grey-white ground mist. Four thousand feet below, the dark green serpent of the ancient River Thames squirmed its way through farmland, forest and town. At six thousand feet, to his left Harry could see the city of London that William Wordsworth saw a century earlier from Westminster Bridge, wearing the beauty of the morning, silent and bare.

But if, as the poet wrote, the mighty heart of that city was lying still, Harry's heart was probably not. He was about to reach the altitude where he would challenge the beast.

Eight thousand feet. A bit chilly at this level, but at least there was room this time for improvisation. He knew the manoeuvre—control stick over, rudder around, engine off. In the sudden silence the plane slipped into a spin, nose down, wings revolving around the centre line of the fuselage, just like before. Brooklands was an oval-shaped blur far below.

Any moment the tail would kick out and the plane would spiral out of control. The bull would try to unseat the master rider.

The urge was to pull back on the control stick. It was counter-intuitive to push it forward. That would only point the nose lower, a steeper descent towards the ground. 'If only I had the guts to do it,' Harry had said after the earlier crash. Fighting against all his instincts, in the midst of the spin he leaned against the stick, pushing it firmly forward. At the same time he brought the rudder up to the vertical. And held them both there.

Harry liked a challenge. Not only as a pilot but intellectually. Despite his lack of formal schooling, he had a sophisticated understanding of aeroplane design and an unequivocal belief in their potential. 'They disliked it at the factory when he told them that their ideas of aircraft were out of date,' another Australian pilot said. 'He told them things about building for speed and endurance, building for more power, and they laughed at him.'[52]

Now, in the middle of a spin, he had to hold on to that self-belief. He was staring the beast in the face.

And then, in one transcendental moment, the plane was no longer spinning. It was still heading downwards, but under control, buoyed by the wind beneath its wings.

The beast had been vanquished. Not like a rodeo bull, but with the courage and intellect of a matador.

The Australian looked around the countryside below him until he spotted factory smoke that would show him the wind direction. He circled around, lined the Sopwith up with the Brooklands runway, and a few moments later touched gently down.

Only Horrie Miller was there to see it, but everyone in aviation soon knew that Harry Hawker had conquered the spinning dive.

This was not a world that Muriel Peaty knew. She lived with her parents, Alice and Frederick, her older brother Leonard, and younger sister Evelyn, in West Ealing, a modern and fashionable community on the western outskirts of London. Her father was managing director of a piano manufacturing company. The family was well-off enough to afford a cook, and for Muriel not to have to work.

At just 19 years of age, she was a modern miss for the times, with plenty of leisure time and a car to tootle around in.

A week after her encounter with Harry and Basil in April 1915, there was a phone call for her at the Peaty residence. It was the police, they said. As she picked up the phone, Muriel's heart might well have been beating a little faster than normal. She was not used to run-ins with the law, and probably wondered what she might've done to attract their attention. 'Hello,' she said tentatively.

She immediately detected that the male caller had an unusual accent—not the rounded sounds of a London bobby, but more like an Australian twang. In fact, suspiciously like the one she'd heard recently in a London park. And so it proved to be—the person purporting to be a policeman revealed himself as none other than Harry Hawker, the man she thought had been glad to see the last of her the previous Sunday.

'I've just bought a new car, an Austro-Daimler,' Harry said. He wanted to know if Muriel and her friend would like to come and try it out the following Sunday.

The 18-year-old had obviously made more of an impression on the Australian than she'd thought. He'd apparently decided to impersonate a policeman because he thought her parents mightn't be too impressed with her going out with a stranger she'd met in a city park.

Perhaps flattered by Harry's audacity and ingenuity, Muriel accepted. But she didn't tell her parents.

And so, on Sunday 25 April, 1915, the day Australian troops stormed ashore at Anzac Cove to a bullet-filled reception, Harry again met up with Muriel Peaty.

The reason he wasn't in the frontline with the Australians at Gallipoli or British forces on the Western Front was simple. Soon after Britain entered the war in August 1914, Harry headed off to sign on as a pilot with the Royal Naval Air Service (RNAS), the air arm of the Royal Navy. For some reason, the RNAS rejected Harry's application, possibly because the British Government believed he could make a more significant wartime contribution as a test pilot and aircraft designer than as a frontline flier. As became clearer later, it's also possible that, despite his outstanding achievements in the air to that time, Harry didn't meet the RNAS medical requirements for service pilots.

Whatever the reason for the rejection, Sopwith Aviation was delighted to reclaim their test pilot with superior flying skills and the uncanny ability to tell them where the shoe pinched. Already the company had swung into wartime production of planes for both the RNAS and its Army counterpart, the Royal Flying Corps (RFC).

Harry's presence would turn out to be a special blessing for all of them.

CHAPTER 4
Like a will-o'-the-wisp

As the war gathered pace, Harry became a key man at Sopwith. However, from the time of that April 1915 meeting he spent his Sundays with Muriel Peaty. He managed to keep secret the early sorties, not only from Muriel's parents, but also from his fellow pilots, who thought flying was his only passion.

A fellow flier later remembered him as: 'a small, dark lad, keen-featured, with eyes that had a habit of looking through a person who attempted to engage him in conversation on any subject other than aircraft. He did not mean to be rude. It was just that his mind was so completely absorbed in his work that it could not focus on anything else.'[53]

Muriel clearly had a special something that managed to distract him. The couple quickly discovered they had a shared interest—a love of speed. It's unlikely they were content to continue to meander their way through London parks. In 1915, wartime petrol rationing wasn't yet in force, and the odds are that Harry and Muriel spent their Sundays zooming around the roads on the outskirts of London in his Austro-Daimler. The British way of life was under threat, however. The Kaiser's deadly Zeppelin airships began to float across the coastline to drop bombs indiscriminately on the English countryside.

No doubt Muriel had trouble keeping a straight face at home about her Sunday excursions. Eventually the secret leaked out. Keen for her parents to meet Harry, she persuaded her mother to invite him and Basil to dinner at their Ealing home.

If Harry was nervous the first time he met his girlfriend's parents, he didn't show it. He was all manners and charm, just as their daughter had told them. After dinner, Fred and Alice Peaty and a visiting friend were keen to play whist, and needed a fourth player. However, Muriel and the friends she'd invited wanted more youthful fun. Harry generously volunteered to make up the foursome, despite the fact, as Muriel discovered later, that he hated cards and had only ever played one game of whist in his life. So while Muriel and Basil and the other younger ones went off to enjoy themselves, Harry was in another room pretending to understand the intricacies of tricks and trumps. Of course, whist wasn't the only game Harry was playing that evening.

Muriel had no trouble convincing her parents that her Sunday excursions should continue.

For Harry, roaming the roads with Muriel provided a sanctuary from the hectic world of wartime aviation. The race was on to develop planes that could outfly and outshoot the enemy. Sopwith Aviation was at the forefront of fighter-plane construction for the British forces, including the Pup, the Strutter and later, the Camel. In December 1912 Sopwith moved their main manufacturing centre from Brooklands to the site of an old roller-skating rink at Kingston-on-Thames. As the war rolled on they ramped up production, contracting out some of the work to other companies in Britain and France. It was a challenging but stimulating time for the firm and for Harry.

Brooklands remained an active aviation facility for military purposes, but was closed to the public. It nonetheless continued to be a favourite with the Australian. He flitted like a will-o'-the-wisp between delivery sites, testing newly built planes—from Great Yarmouth in the south, to the Isle of Grain in Kent, as well as to Dover and Felixstowe, and up to Dundee in Scotland. Occasionally Harry visited Sopwith's partnering company at Villacoublay in France. He also talked to British pilots fighting on the Western Front about design changes that might help their tiny aircraft combat the speed and climb of the German machines.

Harry fed suggestions to the rest of the design and production team, which included Tommy Sopwith and Fred Sigrist. Both these men became firm friends. Harry Kauper, promoted to works foreman at Sopwith, made a contribution by inventing a synchronising mechanism to stop Sopwith pilots shooting off their own propellers.

Some idea of the intensity of Harry's wartime schedule can be deduced from this selection of tasks in the early months of 1915:[54]

- 'On 4th January Harry Hawker re-delivers Sopwith "Type 806" Gunbus No.804 with a 150hp Sunbeam engine to Hendon. It is to be crated and go forward to 1 Squadron RNAS at Dunkirk.

- On 6th January the third 80hp Gnome engined Sopwith "D3 Daily Mail" landplane No.1053 is flown from Brooklands to Eastchurch Naval Air Station by Harry Hawker. It is tested that day and accepted by the RNAS.
- Sopwith "D3 Daily Mail" landplane No.1054 which had been delivered disassembled to Eastchurch on 2nd January went forward to Killingholme Naval Air Station on the Humber River estuary on 6th January the same day that No.1055 arrived there directly from Kingston. A Sopwith outwork team takes two days to assemble both machines. On 9th January Harry Hawker arrives to test them before handing them over to the Admiralty.
- On 28th January another new "D3 Daily Mail" landplane No.1056, which arrived at Yarmouth by train from Kingston two days ago, has been erected by a Sopwith out-work team and is test flown by Harry Hawker.
- On 24th March the replacement for the crashed prototype "Type 860" No. 851 is tested by Harry Hawker who has rushed down to Calshot to stand in for Victor Mahl [who is ill in hospital].
- On 25th March Harry is testing the fourth "Schneider" floatplane No.1439 at Calshot. It is to be packed and sent in three days time to Liverpool for HMS Engadine complete with deck-flying and side-movement trolleys.
- 7th April: Aeroplane magazine reports that Harry Hawker is now testing Sopwith small floatplanes, and has been seen "looping the loop". "Despite the floats, the first loop and the others that succeeded it were as perfect as those which the same pilot is accustomed to do on land machines."
- On 26th May "Type 860" floatplanes Nos.929 & 930 are being tested by Harry Hawker at Dundee after delivery there on 17th and 21st May. Harry is doing a lot of travelling.

In amongst his frenetic travel and testing commitments—to the surprise of everyone except the Sopwith team—in early June 1915, Harry had a crack at the British altitude record. At the time it was just under 15,000 feet. Flying a radical design two-seater lightweight biplane known affectionately as the 'Sigrist bus', he took off from Hendon and in 20 minutes lifted the machine to 10,000 feet.

One of the projects Hawker became involved with during the war were experiments to launch standard planes from the adapted decks of existing warships.[55]

Their necks stiff from the effort, the watchers below followed the plane's progress until it was a tiny winged insect disappearing into the wispy clouds.

Despite the intense cold, Harry continued to push the aircraft upwards, his eyes on the barograph that would record his altitude, until finally he realised he'd taken almost ten minutes to rise just 100 feet. With his gums bleeding from the near-freezing air, he spiralled back down to discover he'd created a new British height record: just over 18,000 feet. In April the next year, he would break the record again, taking a Sopwith 1½ Strutter up to almost 25,000 feet.

Also in 1915, Harry managed to fit in a cricket match at Sopwith's Kingston plant. With the third highest score of 15, he helped the Works team to a win against the Sopwith team, where CEO Tommy scored 54 not out.

Another of Harry's achievements at this time was winning over Muriel's mother. When she discovered that he and Basil would be alone over the festive season, Alice invited them both for Christmas dinner and to stay overnight. 'Don't be late,' she said. 'We have dinner at four o'clock on Christmas Day.'

Harry and Basil took her at her word—but mistakenly turned up at 4pm on Christmas Eve, 24 hours early! When they knocked, only Muriel's father was at home. Harry immediately realised their error and, thinking quickly, told the surprised Mr Peaty that it was an Australian custom to pay a courtesy call on people the day before they were due to visit them. No doubt surprised, Fred Peaty nevertheless invited them in. As Harry continued to explain away their premature arrival, he realised that if their host came out to wave them off, he would see their suitcases in the back seat. So he looked fixedly at Basil and asked him to go and turn the petrol off because the fuel joint leaked. Basil, who'd come back to England with Harry after the *Tabloid* displays in Australia, quickly caught his flatmate's drift, and ducked outside to cover the bags with a rug.

Shortly afterwards, when the two men took their leave, Fred Peaty did indeed come to the car to see them off. The winter day was beginning to cool, and they may have wondered if he was on to them when he suggested they throw the rug that was on the back seat over their knees to keep them warm on the way home. With a straight face, Harry told Muriel's father that the cold didn't worry either of them, and quickly drove off.

When Muriel turned up a little later and heard her father's story, she was convinced that Harry and Basil had the days mixed up. However, Mr Peaty assured her it was an Australian custom.

Meanwhile, the war rumbled on. In December 1915, around the time Harry was pulling the wool over Muriel's father's eyes, the Anzac force was pulling out of Gallipoli, his brother Bert among them. After 7,500 Australian deaths, 26,000 casualties and months of inconclusive mind- and body-sapping trench warfare, the Diggers had cemented a national legend but not a victory against the fiercely determined Turks.

In March 1916 the same Australians again found themselves in trenches. This time they dug in on the Western Front alongside French, British and other Allied troops, while a teeming army of rats and lice attacked them on quite different fronts. Soldiers and vermin alike endured one of the most intensive years of the war. Attack and counter-attack in the eleven-month Battle of Verdun in 1916 brought another non-result—at a cost of a quarter of a million dead and over a million wounded. At the Battle of the Somme the same year more than a million soldiers on both sides were killed, wounded or captured.

In just one year the number of casualties in these battles was equivalent to the population of a medium-size European city. Yet gains could mostly be measured in yards rather than miles. And there seemed no way forward. When salvo after salvo of screaming shells hammered the trench-lines, peppering its defenders with shrapnel and scattering the rats, no Pied Piper appeared to lead the survivors out of their muddy maze.

British industry was, of course, full-steam ahead on wartime production. Harry was flat out with his job at Sopwith, sometimes testing up to ten planes a day. Connie Webb, a young woman whose family home was on the Thames near Sopwith's Kingston factory, wrote in her diary about a test flight she saw Harry make, when his machine

> seems to be rather a failure for, after skimming along the river, it fails to rise and comes back. Hawker tries it again until at last it rises properly. I think he should wear a uniform, there is nothing to distinguish him from a slacker and he is much braver than some who swank around in an officer's uniform.[56]

Perhaps it was after a particularly exhausting day that Harry asked Muriel how she managed to fill in her time.

> 'It was brought home to me ... how little work I did,' she later said disingenuously.[57]

Stirred by the question, Muriel made a bet with Harry that she could find a job within two weeks. She wasn't sure what that job might be, since she had no formal qualifications or experience. Nevertheless, the 19-year-old took herself down to the government employment office, otherwise known as the Labour Exchange, and filled out the required forms. The days ticked by, and it looked as if she was going to lose her wager. Then, three days before the fortnight was up, she was told to report to the National Health Insurance Commission, Buckingham Gate, London, for an interview.

After the interview, Muriel was invited to start work in the Commission's office the next day. She nearly laughed out loud. She'd won the bet, just inside the deadline.

Muriel joined the increasingly feminised workforce in Britain. Male conscription had been introduced in early 1916, sending working men into the forces. When the armistice eventually came, British women who'd committed themselves to working for the war effort would discover they had another battle to fight—for the right to continue to work in paid employment.

Meanwhile, Harry had been working on his own design project at Sopwith. He'd decided he needed a little runabout he could use to dash between centres across the country. Not on the ground, but in the air. He drew a full-size outline of a monoplane design in chalk on the wooden floor of the former skating rink at Kingston, and the Sopwith team went to work to transform it into reality. Soon the streamlined lightweight yellow single-seater, nicknamed 'The Sparrow', became a familiar sight at airfields across the nation as the Australian dropped in to check out yet another plane fresh off the assembly line.

And sometime he used it for pleasure. In November 1915, *Aeroplane* magazine reported sighting Harry at Hendon Aerodrome: 'Mr H Hawker on 50hp Gnome Sopwith, speed 22mph to 84.6mph, 6 loops, tea, 6 more with tail slides, nose dives etc. and home.'[58]

Harry made a bet with fellow pilot Fred Raynham that he could fly the Sparrow under the pedestrian bridge that spanned the Brooklands racetrack. He was so confident of success that he booked a photographer to record the occasion. Aspiring aviator Cecil Lewis was impressed: 'As trainee pilots lumbering round the circuit in Longhorns it seems the most wonderful, beautiful aeroplane in the world. It is so beautifully proportioned. When Hawker flies it stylishly round Brooklands we are all enraptured. When, to cap it all, he flies the little thing under the Byfleet footbridge, we are Hawker fans for life.'[59] After the war, Harry did the same thing again, in a Sopwith Grasshopper.

At her house on the Thames, Connie Webb was also a fan: 'I do like his face, it is so pleasant and he has such a jolly expression as if he is wanting to smile but mustn't.'[60]

Despite the grey pall hanging over the world, Harry and Muriel created a little sanctuary of hope for themselves: in late 1916, some 18 months after they met, they decided to become engaged. She was not quite 20; he was 27.

Given his mates' view of him as a single-minded aviator, and the maelstrom of war swirling around them, it's hard to imagine Harry down on one knee, diamond ring in hand, popping the question. And yet, from what Muriel said later, it may well have been his idea, because she regarded it as a 'provisional' engagement. 'Still being in my teens, and taking into account the uncertainties of war, I didn't want to be tied completely,' she said.[61]

Like many other women at the time, Muriel knew that when men went off to war, they often didn't come back. There were huge casualties on the killing field known as the Western Front. Harry might not have been in the trenches, but he was at the forefront of aeroplane design, in the air almost every day, testing newly minted craft fresh off the production line or sporting untried modifications.

Muriel recognised that, despite her fiancé's outstanding skill as a pilot, the odds of a mishap in these still-experimental aircraft were high. There was too much at stake, too much personal investment and risk, for her to want to be 'tied completely'. No doubt she'd also seen that 'inspired light' in Harry's eyes, and knew what it meant—he was determined to never again let a plane get the better of him, whatever it took.

Hawker in a Sopwith 1½ Strutter at Hendon Aerodrome April 1916.[62]

The prevailing picture of Harry as the tough-minded larrikin who loved flying and any other form of speed was tempered by another side of the Australian-born pilot that Muriel saw. During their engagement, he warned her he had a 'terrible temper'. He told her that when he was in that sort of mood, he was 'unapproachable', and that she should leave him completely alone.[63] Muriel asserted herself by ignoring this advice.

'I often wonder if the early days of our engagement would have been less stormy had I been more nearly Harry's intellectual equal or else a different type of girl altogether,' she said later. 'But Harry had no time for the "take-care-of-me" kind of female, and I believe he thoroughly enjoyed our heated arguments.'[64]

Muriel didn't say what they argued about. Yet she paints an intriguing picture of the diminutive Australian and the young Englishwoman at loggerheads in the early months of 1917 as they negotiated their 'provisional' engagement. Whether this mutual sparring was a sufficient basis for a long-lasting relationship remained to be seen.

As if to thumb their noses at the old world crumbling around them, the test pilot and the newly employed office worker continued their Sunday drives in the Austro-Daimler. Harry had now hotted it up to do 80 miles an hour, a considerable speed on the open road, considering a Model T Ford at the time struggled to reach half that pace, even at full throttle.

Muriel admitted to being excited by the opportunities for 'strafing anything willing and able on the roads,' and she poured scorn on those '20-mile-an-hour motorists who love the very centre of the road and hate to move.'[65]

Pedestrians had to keep a lookout for the pair too—according to Muriel, one 'old codger' who chose to amble along the side of the road instead of on the footpath, dropped his hat and stick, and 'remained firmly planted on both feet and stared at us in open-mouthed amazement and disapproval as we whizzed by.' Muriel was having a good time with Harry.

Perhaps it is ironic that Harry's initial phone call to Muriel pretending to be a policemen had a real-life payback when he was

An Austro-Daimler touring car of the period.[66]

booked for 'failing to display an off-side headlight.' With typical ingenuity, Harry had installed just a single headlight on his car. He also failed to produce his driver's licence to the policeman who pulled him over, resulting in a one-pound fine for the first indiscretion and a five-shilling fine for the second. He was probably fortunate not to have also been stopped for speeding on one of his sorties around London in the Austro-Daimler.

It was not the first time in his life he'd tangled with the police, either. Andrew Lang recalled an incident in Harry's younger, wilder days in Melbourne when the future test pilot was driving his boss's new short chassis 40/50-h.p. Rolls Royce:

> There were no numbers fitted to cars in those days, and the chief 'car-catcher', Constable Peverill, had to chase us on an ordinary push bicycle. Hawker at the wheel took the Rolls down to the drive at Albert Park [Melbourne], and off we went, putting her full out separately on each gear to saw what she would do. We were hitting up 57 on third gear—she had four gears—when suddenly a man jumped out into the middle of the road waving his arms. Hawker, not flinching, went straight at him, and the man jumped just in time.
>
> "You silly ass," I yelled, "That's Peverill!"

"I know," said Hawker. "Do you think I was going to stop? He wouldn't know this car again—she's a stranger."'[67]

Typically, back at Caramut Harry managed to coax an extra six mph out of the Rolls in third gear but complained he couldn't get the impressive six-cylinder car past 75mph in top gear. 'His one aim,' Lang said, 'was to get that extra ounce of speed.'[68]

It was an aim that might have been Harry's life-time mantra.

CHAPTER 5

No respecter of fools

Early in 1917, Harry was heading into the Brooklands airstrip in the Austro-Daimler when he took an S-bend a little too fast. The car flipped over and ended up on its back in a ditch.

His passengers, a naval officer from the Admiralty and two other government officials on their way to inspect Sopwith aircraft fresh off the production line, managed to wriggle out unhurt. Harry was trapped underneath, however, his arm pinned by the steering wheel.

When responders lifted the car off, they discovered he'd badly dislocated his shoulder. A doctor put his arm in a sling. Back at the Sopwith works the next afternoon, a well-meaning colleague suggested the famous pilot stay away from testing aircraft at Brooklands until his shoulder had healed. 'That's alright,' Harry said. 'I put three of them through this morning, but this wretched sling is a nuisance [when I'm] flying.'[69] He took the sling off the next day, but the injury was painful and took some time to heal.

Around this time Hawker and the Sopwith team developed a new 50hp runabout for him, to replace the Sparrow. As usual with Sopwith designs, it was a considerable step-up from the earlier model: 'Known as the Sopwith "Bee" it is much more compact than his 1915 50hp SLTBP [Sparrow] runabout which evolved into the "Pup". The short fuselage gives a steep ground attitude which accentuates the broad-chord of the remarkably short wings as do the huge roundels. The low top wing follows current Sopwith design thinking about good all round visibility over the wing. It has a large horn balanced rudder but retains Harry's favourite wing warping, no ailerons.'[70] This appears to be the plane that Harry came to refer to as 'The Swallow'.

One of Harry's old Melbourne mates, Andrew Lang, became a captain in the Royal Flying Corps in Britain. He later recalled that Hawker frequently flew in to the base on the Swallow, 'one of his favourite mounts', always ready for a joke: 'He would swing round on his heel with a grin and say, "The truth about the whole matter is that you army people don't know a [flying] machine from a Chinese kite."'[71]

'All his keenness was for the air, and he hated being away from the [Sopwith] works,' Lang said. Once Harry had checked out a plane, 'with a cheery "So-long!", he would scramble into his machine, pull his cloth cap tight down on to his head back to front, occasionally adjust a pair of goggles—"contact"—and he was gone.'[72]

During his ongoing travels on behalf of Sopwith, in the first half of 1917 Harry visited an airfield at Villacoublay, on the south-western outskirts of Paris. Sopwith used the field as a test-ground for its French-produced planes. On this occasion, there was also a military visitor, a British general, who was strutting around offering his opinion on all things aviation. Harry put up with this for a while, until he heard the general bagging the Sopwith Camel. The single-seat fighter biplane was fitted with two synchronised machine guns mounted just ahead of the pilot's cockpit under a 'hump' that gave the aircraft its name. Although it had a few quirks that could catch out an inexperienced pilot, after its introduction to the RFC and RNAS from mid-1917, the Camel would go on to prove its worth in aerial dogfights. It became one of the most successful fighter planes of the war.

The general claimed to have flown the Camel numerous times, and said it was hard to get it out of a spin. Like its predecessor, the Camel had a rotary engine, and novice pilots sometimes found the gyroscopic forces difficult to handle during take-off. Several had died in crashes. One commentator said that 'in the wrong hands a Camel would eat its pilot for breakfast; it was no respecter of fools.'[73]

But Harry had tested the prototype of the Camel and wasn't going to let the general get away with his criticism of a plane the Australian had helped design. 'I don't believe he's ever flown one,' he whispered to the Paris Works Manager, Monty Fenn. He followed that up by inviting the red-tabbed officer to join him on a short flight. Word quickly spread, and a crowd gathered to watch the show. The staff at Villacoublay were always keen to see Harry in the air.

Hawker contributed significantly to the design and testing of the Sopwith Camel, one of the most successful Allied fighter planes of World War I.[74]

With his passenger strapped in, Harry took the Camel up to around 2000 feet, and immediately put it into a right-hand spin. It was a relatively low point to start from, and the earth came up to meet them very rapidly. But the pilot was a man without fear in this particular manoeuvre. Just a few hundred feet from disaster, he expertly pulled out of the dive and took the biplane back up to the same altitude.

Without a glance at his high-ranking passenger, this time Harry varied the manoeuvre by putting the Sopwith into a left-hand spin. Down, down the spinning plane plunged, until once again not far above the ground the Australian lifted the nose into the sky and levelled the Camel out.

In very quick time, the general had been rescued from two spectacular spinning dives by the master of the spinning dive.

As the renowned pilot brought the Sopwith back to earth, the spectators on the ground watching this joust between the civilian and the general had received their money's worth. When the pair alighted from the plane, Harry didn't say a word but looked straight at the general, as if to say, 'What do you mean, it's hard to get a Camel out of a spin?'

The general, by now no doubt looking very pale, glared at Harry. Then he turned and stalked off. Harry, having proved his point, headed back to England.

Next morning Monty Fenn was obliged to front the airport authorities at Villacoublay. Mr Hawker was stunting too near the ground, they told him. They demanded that Harry write a letter of apology stating that he wouldn't do that sort of thing again.[76]

The general, it seems, was not impressed by Harry's mastery of the spinning dive.

In April 1917 America joined the war, finally goaded into the fray by Germany's aggressive U-boat Atlantic policy of sinking ships of any flag. President Woodrow Wilson called it 'warfare against mankind.' The United States eventually committed more than two million troops to the Allied cause. There was also a spin-off in US aeroplane design that would eventually impact Harry Hawker's post-war flying ambitions.

On the Western Front, troops were battling the elements as much as they were fighting the enemy. Since the war began, they'd dug themselves hundreds of miles of trenches through Belgium and France. From above it might have looked as if an earthquake had zig-zagged its way across the landscape. In 1917 soldiers on both sides found their dugouts filling with water from rain that never seemed to stop. Ground that had erupted under the 'crump' of artillery fire, and felt the indentations of charging boots and the grim thud of falling bodies, now turned to mush. It became a grey morass that sucked in men, horses and equipment the way the war itself swallowed armies and generals' reputations.

In these conditions, the Allies' new-fangled steel monsters, known as 'tanks', initially proved useless in the quagmire, not only cumbersome but claustrophobic.

By this time Zeppelin airships were no longer a major threat to Britain, thanks to incendiary bullets and Allied planes that flew faster and higher. The Germans increasingly resorted to mass bombing raids in daylight, bringing pinpoint destruction. In the early days, Londoners tumbled on to the streets to watch the big Gotha bombers rumbling overhead, as if it was some sort of public entertainment. But soon the sight of the lumbering twin-engine biplanes had them rushing for the shelters before the bombs started to fall.

No one was prepared to predict how long the war would go on. Elements of the French Army believed their cause so hopeless that they mutinied against their officers.

Huddled together under the grey canopy of this gloomy world, Harry and Muriel lit another little flame of hope for themselves: they decided to get married.

It was clearly not optimism about the outcomes of the conflict that triggered Muriel's decision to agree to convert their engagement into a more permanent relationship. Perhaps it was just the opposite: the need for some certainty and happiness in a world that seemed to be shaking itself apart, like the velodrome in Melbourne where Harry had once ridden his motor bike. Harry's flying mates were gobsmacked—surely flying was the only love of his life. When had there been enough time for him to get to know a girl well enough to marry her?

The wedding was scheduled for the afternoon of 17 November 1917,[77] at St Peter's Church, Ealing, not far from the Peaty family home. Muriel was just 21; Harry would soon be 29.

A week beforehand, Harry was making a daytime flight from England to Villacoublay when a minor fault forced him to land his plane in a field in the snow-covered French countryside. The area was well away from the Western Front but, in his civilian clothes, the locals thought Harry might be a spy. So the gendarmes took him into custody until they could confirm his identity.

Harry was not the sort of person who was prepared to sit around waiting for something to happen, however. Knowing he was expected at Villacoublay, the Sopwith test pilot, like his slippery aviation hero, Houdini, somehow managed to extricate himself from the guard room and hitched a lift on a passing British Army truck.

Returning to the Sopwith, which was sitting in the snow in a nearby field, he fixed the fault. Then, with local help and lots of pulling and shoving and perhaps a little swearing, he managed to move the machine into position for a take-off. He arrived at Villacoublay before the sun had set. The downside was that, while dragging the plane through the snow, Harry strained his back. It was yet another contribution to a string of injuries that would come to have a major impact on his body and his life.

When the wedding day arrived, Muriel knew how preoccupied Harry could become with his other passion—flying. So before she left home for the afternoon ceremony, she sent a message to the church to make sure her husband-to-be was there before she arrived. It seemed that Harry's best man, his brother Bert, now an Army captain and on special leave from France, also knew his brother: late in the morning, he headed out to Brooklands, where Harry was putting yet another Sopwith through its paces, and retrieved him in time for the groom to say, 'I do.'

The couple's wedding photo in the Kingston magazine The Sketch a week after the ceremony shows Muriel on the church steps in an ankle-length white dress that drops straight down in a style that would later become popular in the 1920s 'flapper' era.[78] A long lace veil reveals a narrow fringe of curly brown hair above a pretty, rounded face. In one hand she holds the gown's long white train, in the other a bouquet of white lilies.

Harry Hawker & Muriel Peaty's wedding, St Peter's Church, Ealing, London, 17 November 1917.[79]

The former Miss Peaty has a half smile on her lips as if she's ready for anything. Or perhaps she's a little unsure of what she's getting herself into with this diminutive self-confident Australian who, in just five years, had gone from self-taught motor mechanic to aviation record-breaker, aeroplane designer and chief test pilot.

Was she still worried she wasn't Harry's intellectual equal, as she had been early in their engagement, or that he might want 'a different sort of girl altogether'? Would she be able to cope with the fierce temper he'd warned her about when they first became engaged, and which she'd seen flashes of in the disagreements they'd had in the meantime? Did she worry that her husband was a death-defying pilot, who emerged from a crash that might have killed him with just one thought in mind—how to beat the spin that brought him down? Was she concerned at the way he'd stand behind a plane he helped design by taking a general for a stomach-churning demonstration flight?

She knew of course he was the record-breaking loop-the-looper who had no hesitation in pretending to be a policeman on the phone, or in inventing a story for his future father-in-law to cover up a blooper with dates.

In the same photo, Harry is in a dark suit and a tie, standing slightly apart from his new wife. His hands are behind his back, as if public intimacy was to be avoided. His head is bare, revealing his receding hairline, but also showing his disdain for the hat he was obliged to wear for the ceremony. Muriel later discovered it in tatters after he'd kicked it around his changing room.

Harry's smile for the photographer could've been a cheeky one, but it also suggests a certain diffidence that was not part of his Sopwith persona. He might have been one of the nation's top aviators, but did he have the talent and temperament to be a husband? Was he concerned that he was almost eight years older than Muriel? Or that he was a boy from Melbourne who'd spent time in the bush and who was marrying a young woman brought up in suburban London who'd never lived away from home? Or despite the smile and his trademark determination, was he worried about a future that was impossible to predict in a topsy-turvy world, where life couldn't be taken for granted?

There was a wartime ban on using petrol for private touring, but little by little in the months before the wedding Harry had been deviously stockpiling it so that he and Muriel could drive to Cornwall for their honeymoon. The Austro-Daimler was still out of action after the Brooklands rollover. So they took the Gregoire, the car Harry was driving the day he first met Muriel. When they set off from London, the fuel tank was full and there were spare cans in the back.

In order to throw the police off the scent, however, Harry had resorted to the subterfuge of fitting a gasbag to the car, since gas-powered vehicles were permitted. While the gasbag was real, in pre-wedding tests the couple found that the uncompressed coal gas in the mattress-like bag strapped to the Gregoire's roof would take them only about five miles before it ran out. Their honeymoon trip to Cornwall was 500 miles return.

On the trip itself, the only time they used gas was when they passed through larger towns, where the possibility of a petrol licence check was higher. When they stopped for lunch in Launceston in Cornwall, a curious waiter saw the bag on the car and said he'd heard that gas devices were good for only a few miles. With a straight face, Harry blithely assured him that the

Gregoire was using *compressed* gas, which gave the car a range of 80 or 90 miles between refills.

A vehicle powered by gas stored in an overhead bag similar to the one Harry and Muriel Hawker fixed atop their vehicle to bamboozle the police on their Cornwall honeymoon November 1917.[80]

After their return to London, there was hope but still anxiety in the air in Britain as 1918 rolled into view. It was going to be an uncertain year all round, with some unexpected developments—for the warring nations as well as for the newly-wed Mr and Mrs Hawker.

One thing that wasn't in doubt was the viability of Sopwith Aviation Company: 'It seems that 1917 profits could be 25% of income and twice the previous year at around £290,000 [£20 million today] which, even after paying 60% Excess Profits Tax on the majority, should leave more than enough to continue to entirely self-finance the rapid growth of the business and pay dividends on the 32,000 company shares to Thomas Sopwith and three of his sisters.'[81] Harry personally benefitted from the company's success. He was working extraordinary hours and making an extraordinary intellectual and physical contribution to Sopwith and the war effort. In grateful recognition, at the end of 1917 the company rewarded him with a significant bonus and also awarded him back-paid commission of 1.5% of the 1916/17 profits.

CHAPTER 6

A post-war proposition

Over the winter of 1917–18, Harry continued his frenetic work for Sopwith Aviation. He and Muriel had settled into a new home, 'Ennadale', an attractive double-storey brick house on a park-like corner block in the hamlet of Hook, Surrey. It was a short drive from both London and Brooklands.

In the evenings, Muriel read to her husband, because, she said, 'He could never read or write himself for any time, since he performed both in such a slow and laborious manner it was obviously no enjoyment to him.'[82] She didn't think much of his 'schoolboy' taste in literature, such as Bram Stoker's *Dracula*, but they did get through a lot of books.

Harry liked her to start off with an article about planes or cars, and *The Automobile Engineer*[83] was his favourite magazine. Muriel's opinion? 'Generally unintelligible,' she said.[84]

As the early months of 1918 passed, there were still few willing to predict the outcome of the war. Successive German offensives were met by determined Allied counter-offensives, battles raged across

Serbia, Italy and the Middle East. Revolution in Russia resulted in a change of government and that country's withdrawal from the war. It was a tense time all round. In May, Harry encouraged the people of Kingston-upon-Thames to contribute to the war effort by flying overhead and dropping a packet from the Sopwith Aviation Co with an application for £30,000 of War Bonds into the crowded market place.

Around mid-year, fortunes began to change. By now American troops were on the ground in Europe in large numbers, and the Allies began inexorably to push the German Army back. Turkish and Bulgarian forces and the remnants of the Austro-Hungarian army were in retreat, and for the first time an Allied victory was on the cards. In England, the tabloid *Daily Mail* was so confident of the outcome that, in July, it announced the reinstatement of its prize for the first person to fly the Atlantic Ocean.

The official organiser of that event, the Royal Aero Club, immediately slapped the paper down and told it to wait until the war was over. Nevertheless, in aviation circles, potential contestants were already sniffing the air.

One of these was Harry Hawker. In June 1918 he had been made a Member of the Most Excellent Order of the British Empire (MBE). King George V created the MBE award 12 months earlier to recognise wartime achievements in non-combatant roles. In the citation, Harry is matter-of-factly described as 'Trade Pilot, Sopwith Aviation Co Ltd', which doesn't do justice to the Australian's significant contribution to the Allied cause as a test pilot and aircraft designer. Thomas Sopwith's biographer, Alan Bramson, said that the company's CEO 'regarded his prodigy as a genius, and many of the outstanding flying qualities of Sopwith aircraft have rightly been attributed to [Hawker].'[85]

Hawker's Sopwith Scooter, a parasol-wing monoplane he used for aerial displays and as a runabout.[87]

Harry was pleased with the handling a new runabout Sopwith had developed, 'Monoplane No.1', which was described as 'a Camel fuselage without the guns' but also for Sopwith a radical 'wire-braced swept-back monoplane parasol wing at pilot's eye level.'[86] Renamed 'The Scooter', it had a 130hp Clerget engine, somewhat more powerful that the 50hp varieties Harry had been obliged to put up with on his wartime runabouts.

Sopwith Aviation was doing well from the government aircraft contracts it had scored since 1914 and, as part of the design and testing team, Harry was entitled to a percentage of the profits. The company's Camels, one-and-a-half Strutters, Pups, Snipes, and Schneiders were in demand, and the Sopwith Experimental Group was hard at work devising new models and modifications to meet the rapidly changing demands of war in the air.

'One is safe in saying that the pilots who flew Sopwith machines during the war, and came through successfully,' his long-time friend and aviator Andrew Lang said, 'owe a very great deal to the skill and knowledge of Harry Hawker.'[88]

In one wartime year alone Harry test-flew some 300 Sopwith planes, and Muriel had no doubt about her husband's value to the war effort: 'There was no measuring a man's actual worth, but had Fate not kept Harry here [in England],' she said, 'we should have been several iotas deficient in our air supremacy in those dark days ... when iotas were of incalculable worth.'[89]

Later in the year, as Sopwith's profits continued to rise, Harry was rewarded with another jump in the already generous commissions he received. Flush with funds, and perhaps to celebrate his MBE, he bought two Sunbeam aeroplane engines (one for spares) along with a 35 h.p. Mercedes car chassis, and set about building a high-powered super-car. He recruited Muriel to help rivet the sheets of aluminium that made up the seven-foot-long bonnet and, although the large expanses of metal were awkward to handle, she revelled in her newly learned skill.

The couple referred to their home-built car as a Sunbeam, in recognition of the 225 h.p. engine that pushed it along the roads around Hook. Muriel was excited that it 'exceeded all expectations both to speed, flexibility, and especially acceleration.'[90]

One day while out in the Sunbeam they saw a big American Packard up ahead, and Harry quickly caught up and effortlessly overtook it as the two cars headed up Kingston Hill. He waited at the top, and the other car pulled alongside. The driver was an American, and good-naturedly called across to ask where the Sunbeam's power came from.

'Same as yours,' Harry said. 'Twelve cylinders. Only better ones.'[91]

Muriel was continually on the lookout for her husband's temper tantrums, but the most she saw was what she called his 'irritability' when he was under pressure to finish a job. Once the work was done, she saw his mood quickly change back to the more affable Harry. In his home workshop, he sang or whistled while he worked, unless something went very wrong, and then she knew not to try to talk to him until he'd sorted out the problem.

It seems Harry's singlemindedness extended into all facets of his life.

Hawker outside the Sopwith plant with the car he created by wrestling a 225hp Sunbeam engine into a Mercedes chassis in his home workshop. Muriel helped rivet the bonnet.[92]

Strategy, technology, and the increasing weakening of the enemy forces finally began to tilt the war in the Allies' favour. In August 1918, more than 450 British tanks spearheaded a successful British offensive against German troops on the Western Front. A month later an unprecedented 1500 Allied aircraft combined as part of a coordinated air-ground attack. After four years of conflict, the aeroplane was finally coming into its own as a weapon of war. It was a development that Sopwith and Harry Hawker had been an important part of.

The stagnation of the Western Front was over, and armies were on the move—the Allies advancing, their enemies retreating. Gains were finally measured in miles instead of yards; the German's Hindenburg Line bent, then yielded, irreparably broken; battles were no longer extended, but became quick and decisive. The German Army was exhausted from the constant fighting, and weakened by lack of food and low morale.

One by one Germany's wartime partners dropped out; in early October the country's military leaders convinced Kaiser Wilhelm II that the only option was to petition the Allies for peace. After some political to-ing and fro-ing in the weeks that followed, the Armistice document was signed in a railway carriage in France. On 11 November 1918, after more than four years of conflict, the drums of war finally stop beating.

In the ensuing silence, the victors prepared to sit down with the vanquished in the French city of Versailles to decide on retribution, restitution and atonement.

For Harry Hawker and hundreds of thousands of others in nations across the globe who had known nothing but war for the past four years, the question was: what would they do now? The world was not the way it had been: political affiliations had shifted, governments had been ousted, millions lay dead, and national economies had been skewed towards war production.

For those who'd been in uniform, what might civilian life hold? Would their previous jobs be open to them, and would they want to go back to them anyway? As an American popular song of the times asked: 'How ya gonna keep 'em down on the farm after they've seen Paree?'

Harry's employer, Sopwith Aviation, had been geared towards fighter and bomber manufacture. What would be its future now that the demand was no longer there? Would there be a market for peacetime aircraft which might sustain the company? The question of 'What next?' was of added significance for Harry because he now had another member of the family to consider: baby Pamela Muriel Hawker was born in October 1918.

Harry and Muriel Hawker with their first child, Pamela, in the garden of their Surrey home.[93]

The new baby came into a world that was already quite different from the one her mother had been born into in the last decade of the previous century. The technology that had begun to transform the way wars were fought would help bring about major developments in the home and in industry. Car travel would become commonplace, and Pamela would be able to fly in airliners whose development had been fast-tracked by the urgent needs of the war her father had been part of. A recent invention called 'radio' would expand her links with the world.

In Britain she was unlikely to receive equal pay with men in her lifetime, or even be allowed to do certain jobs, but at least by the time she was an adult, women in Britain would have won the right to vote in national elections and even to stand for parliament. What no one could possibly forecast was that in 1939, the year Pamela would turn 21—the age at which her mother married—the world would once again be at war.

With his daughter just two months old, in December 1918 Harry thought he might've found his answer to 'What next?' The *Daily Mail* had duly reinstated its prize for being first to fly the Atlantic Ocean, and Tommy Sopwith had asked his genius of a test pilot if he'd like to have a crack at it.

CHAPTER 7
Waiting for the future to unfold itself

A couple of years earlier, Harry Hawker would have jumped at the chance to be first to fly the Atlantic, without a second's thought. But he was a husband and father now, so he felt constrained to seek his wife's blessing. 'You know I'd like to go,' he told her, 'but the decision is entirely up to you.'

It seemed like a generous gesture on his part, but it put all the pressure on Muriel. The 22-year-old found herself 'torn between my duty to Pam to ask him to stay and my duty to him to let him go.'[94] If she said 'no', she wondered if she'd be able to face her husband when another pilot inevitably eventually won the glory.

The *Daily Mail* prize was the brainchild of the newspaper's owner, Alfred Harmsworth, better known as Lord Northcliffe  (see photo[95]), an early 'press baron'. Northcliffe had taken over the London-based *Daily Mail* in 1896 and transformed it into a tabloid news-sheet, aimed at the mass market. The paper not only reported the news but controversially led crusades for social and political change. One of Northcliffe's passions was the development of aviation. From 1906 a series of aerial competitions sponsored by the *Daily Mail* achieved their aims of stirring popular interest in aviation and stimulating aircraft manufacturers as well as trailblazing pilots to push the limits—not to mention sending newspaper sales soaring. Early winners were Louis Bleriot, awarded £1000 for his flight across the English Channel in 1909 and, the following year, another Frenchman, Louis Paulhan, who collected £10,000 for the first flight from London to Manchester within a 24-hour period.

To counter these wins from 'foreign' fliers and encourage local development, between 1911 and 1914 the *Daily Mail*

Hawker and Kauper in their Sopwith were the only entrants in the 'Race around Britain' in 1913 in which contestants could land only on water.[96]
They crashed into the sea near Dublin on their second attempt at the race.

sponsored 'round-Britain' races in British-made machines. In 1913, there was one especially for 'waterplanes', following a 1600-mile route around Great Britain within 72 hours, landing only on water. There was only one entry for the £5000 prize—a Sopwith fitted with wooden floats. The nominated pilot was Harry Hawker, with Harry Kauper as mechanic.

At that time, Harry had held his pilot's licence for just over 12 months. However, in that period he'd set the height, speed and distance records that had already gained him public attention. As a result, in August 1913 thousands of excited spectators watched from yachts, motor boats and the shore as the two Australians took off from sunlit Southampton Water in southern England. But when they landed on the water at Yarmouth on the Isle of Wight that same morning, Harry collapsed as he was being ferried ashore. A doctor diagnosed sunstroke and possibly the effect of the plane's exhaust gases. Harry was forced to retire from the race. Another Australian pilot, Sidney Pickles, was drafted in at short notice to take his place. But the seas at Yarmouth proved too rough for a take-off, and one of the plane's floats was damaged. For the time being, the round-Britain attempt was abandoned.

Almost two weeks later, the indefatigable Hawker tried once more, again with Kauper in the passenger seat. This time they completed the run up the east coast of England with only a minor stop for repairs. On their way across Scotland to Oban on the west coast, they had to battle a fierce head wind, but were still on track to meet the time limit. There was a slight oil leak in the cockpit and, throughout the flight, oil continued to drip onto Harry's boots, but they didn't regard it as a major problem.

Heading to Ireland the next day, the pair were confident of finishing the circuit within the 72-hour time limit. However, they were concerned about a persistent engine rattle. They decided to land the amphibian on the Irish Sea near Dublin to check it out. As they were coming in to touch down on the water, one of Harry's boots, greasy from the oil leak, slipped on the rudder-bar, and he lost control. The plane immediately plunged sideways into the ocean, a stone's throw from the Irish coast. Fortunately the water was shallow and the two men scrambled out. Harry was unhurt, but mechanic Kauper ended up with a broken arm and cuts to his head.[97]

The seaplane was a write-off, but Harry saw to its retrieval before heading home to Muriel. He dismissed the accident as 'just a piece of ghastly bad luck.' However, the consequences for his body might ultimately have been more serious than he thought at the time. Nevertheless, two days later he was in the air again, testing more planes.

Five years later, in November 1918, it was the *Daily Mail's* latest offer that had Harry's attention. For her part, Muriel was not surprised her husband of 12 months wanted to be first to fly the Atlantic. In fact, she'd been expecting it. She knew Harry and the design team at Sopwith had already been considering adapting their wartime 'B1' bomber prototype for a transatlantic role. All they needed was a reliable and more powerful engine.

The rules said the *Daily Mail* prize would be awarded to the aviator 'who shall first cross the Atlantic in an aeroplane in flight from any point in the United States, Canada or Newfoundland to any point in Great Britain or Ireland.' This feat had to be completed within 72 consecutive hours, could be attempted in either direction, and each aircraft had to carry at least a pilot and a navigator. The rules were almost identical to those promulgated by the Royal Aero Club five years earlier, except for one additional proviso: 'No aeroplane of enemy origin or manufacture may be used.'

As Muriel thought about her response to Harry, did she see in her mind's eye the choppy green expanse he wanted to fly across? She knew the Atlantic separated North America from Europe and, if she agreed, for a short time would keep her apart from her husband. If he didn't make it across, it could separate them forever.

Finally she gave him her answer: 'Why should you think I want you to stay?' she said. 'I want to be proud of you.'

One of the paradoxes of war is that it speeds up the development of weapons and machines to ensure more effective killing and maiming, while at the same time often leading to significant post-war benefits for humankind.

During World War I, planes on both sides rapidly developed the capacity to fly faster, higher and for longer, partly through the efforts of pilots and designers like Harry Hawker. Lightweight biplanes were transformed into fast-diving shoot-through-the propeller fighters, while recognition of the destructive potential of bombers led to the development of larger planes and more powerful engines. Nevertheless, the exploitation of aircraft for purely military purposes also meant that long-distance flying was largely neglected, except for bomber raids across Europe.

At the time, the only way to cross the Atlantic was by ship. In 1907 the Cunard liner, *Mauretania*, had set the record of four and a half days, from Southampton to New York, a time that would not be eclipsed by a ship for another 30 years.

In 1910, there'd been a half-hearted attempt to fly across. An American reporter and explorer, Walter Wellman, had set off for England from Atlantic City, New Jersey, with five others, in a lifeboat suspended below an air balloon powered by two 80 hp motors. Not long after take-off, the balloon developed a leak, however, and the craft folded itself down into the ocean. The crew was later picked up by a British steamer 250 miles north-west of Bermuda. An attempt the following year by the airship's designer, Melvin Yaniman, in a new and larger dirigible, *Akron*, ended in disaster when the craft exploded half an hour after take-off from Atlantic City, killing Yaniman and his four-man crew.

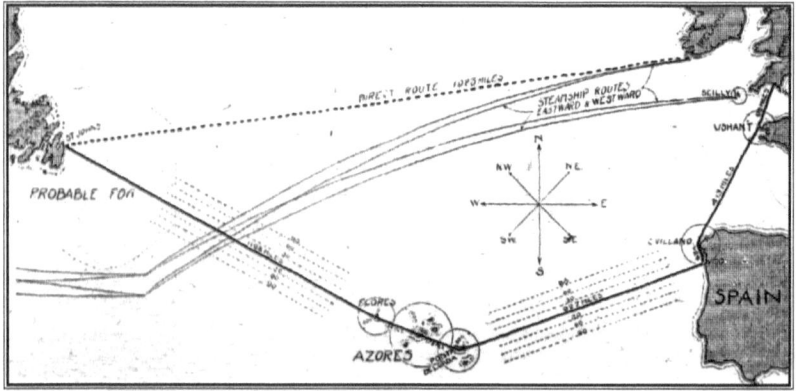

A rough sketch in Flight magazine in July 1918 of possible transatlantic routes from Newfoundland. In the event, British teams took the direct route, heading for Ireland; a US Navy team went via the Azores, but their final destination was Portugal, not Spain. Note the warning of 'probable fog' off Newfoundland.[98]

For the post-war attempt, one important matter each team had to decide was their starting point. The smart money said Newfoundland was the place—it was a British colony, the flight from there to Ireland was the shortest distance as the crow flies (just under 1900 nautical miles), and there was every likelihood of a tailwind, which would save fuel and get you there quicker. An added advantage was that, if you timed it right, you'd arrive in daylight to a heroes' welcome in Ireland, if not England.

The downside was that first you had to ship yourselves and your aeroplane (in crates) to Newfoundland and find a piece of land that was flat enough and long enough to be developed into an airstrip, since there was no airfield there. Then you had to wait until the island's foggy and unpredictable weather opened up long enough to give you time to take off in your now reassembled machine.

On the other hand, the disadvantages of taking off from the opposite direction and heading east to west—most likely flying into a headwind, hence suffering additional fuel usage and risking running out of petrol, taking longer, and landing among strangers—might be countered by being able to prepare your aircraft for an earlier start and a take-off from a familiar airfield in Britain or Ireland and perhaps in more benign weather.

Whichever end you started, there was one shared unknown: the weather mid-Atlantic. By this time, government meteorological offices on both sides of the ocean were constantly collecting and analysing reports from transatlantic shipping. However, in 1919 long-range weather forecasting was in its infancy. There was no guarantee you wouldn't be caught in a fast-developing mid-ocean storm no one knew about.

So Harry was aware he needed to find himself a very special navigator, someone with the skills to plot a course that would guide them to their destination in the shortest possible time. The Australian's mind went back to Lieutenant-Commander Mackenzie Grieve, a Scottish-born Royal Navy navigation officer he'd met in 1915 during aircraft carrier trials at Scapa Flow, the Orkney Islands harbour that housed the British Grand Fleet. At that time, purpose-built aircraft carriers were a novel idea, and the Navy was experimenting with converting other types of ships into vessels from which seaplanes could be launched.

Nine years older, and taller than Harry, with the sharp profile of an Easter Island statue, Mackenzie Grieve (see photo[99]) was also quieter than the ebullient Australian. He'd joined the Navy at age 14, and his postings had taken him to various parts of the British Empire, including China, Australia, and the Mediterranean. He'd had a couple of run-ins with the Navy's top brass over the years, but had managed to redeem himself. While based at Scapa Flow the 25-year naval veteran had been praised for his excellent wayfinding skills and 'good proficiency in chronometrical and astronomical observation' along with his ability to navigate among the currents off the north-west coast of Scotland.

Having seen the Scot's navigational skills in action and his calm demeanour in a challenging environment, and perhaps attracted by an underlying feistiness, Harry invited the Navy veteran to join him in his Atlantic attempt. Mackenzie Grieve jumped at the chance, and the Navy agreed to release the Lieutenant-Commander for the task. To better prepare himself, Grieve put himself through an air pilot's course at Royal Air Force Station Eastchurch, which he completed in six days, although he never claimed to be a crack pilot. Nor did he need to be when Harry was in the cockpit, but at least he was a back-up if something went wrong.

Both men knew they needed to move fast—the first entry for the transatlantic attempt reached the Royal Aero Club on 15 November 1918, just one day after the official announcement of the reinstatement of the prize, and it was not the one from Sopwith.

As 1918 slipped into 1919, the protagonists from the Great War began to gather in Versailles to argue over the spoils. In the aviation world, meanwhile, the tension started to mount as the transatlantic contenders rushed to prepare their flying steeds. The rules didn't specify a take-off deadline, so it would be down to which crew was first out of the starting gate.

Sopwith were among the frontrunners for the transatlantic venture with their modified B1 bomber, which they designated '*Atlantic*'. From tip to tail the plane was some 10 metres in length, slightly longer than a high telegraph pole. The wings stretched 15 metres, around 20% wider than those of a modern Boeing 747.

Tommy Sopwith had no doubt a plane could fly the Atlantic, even though none had ever bridged that distance before. 'Crossing from America to England by air is not the problem it was a few years ago,' he said. 'Undoubtedly the flight is possible. A dozen machines of today could do it at once if aeroplane makers and pilots were not all so busy with war demands.'[100] All the B1 needed was a more powerful engine. They found that in a 360hp V12 Rolls-Royce Eagle.

Harry was heavily involved in the design, of course, and his ever-active brain came up with two innovations. The first was a detachable undercarriage they could drop soon after take-off, thereby getting rid of unnecessary drag and hence improving both speed and fuel consumption. Of course the downside of this was that they had no landing gear when they wanted to come down again, but Harry hoped that sacrificing the undercarriage would be offset by getting to the finishing point sooner. To compensate for the lack of wheels, one of the other modifications to the *Atlantic* was extra reinforcement in the shape of skids on the underside of the fuselage to assist with the likely rough landing.

The Sopwith Atlantic, *in which Hawker and Grieve hoped to win the transatlantic prize.*[101]

'The old Wright pilots always used to prefer to land on their skids rather than on wheels,' Harry said, 'and the bottom part of our fuselage was much the same shape as the old Wright skids.'

The other advantage of dropping off the undercarriage on the flight was that, if the worst happened and they had to ditch in the sea, the skids should mean a smoother landing on the water.

This might then give them a few life-saving minutes to launch Harry's other invention: a wooden lifeboat moulded to fit upside down behind the cockpit as part of the plane's fuselage, and held in place by quick-release catches. It was shaped like a Dutch shoe, and gave them a little bit of insurance, just in case.

The two cockpits in the Sopwith *Atlantic* were side by side, with the pilot's slightly ahead of the navigator's, but both were open to the elements. So Harry and Grieve would need their best thermal underwear and waterproof outerwear to keep out the cold at their intended altitude of 12,000 feet. It was estimated that the 330-gallon (1500-litre) fuel tank would keep them in the air for around 22 hours, a fact that Muriel took particular note of.

The earliest entry for the prize, from Whitehead Aviation, turned out to be more talk than action when the self-promoting owner pulled out after failing to convince backers that his proposed four-engine leviathan was a goer. On both sides of the Atlantic, however, more serious contenders were rushing to put together an aircraft and a crew capable of bridging a distance that, just five years before, had been regarded as almost impossible.

Only one team planned to leave from Ireland: flying a Short Brothers single-engine biplane, appropriately called *Shamrock*. The aircraft would be prepared in England and take off from the Emerald Isle, braving the likely headwinds. All the other contestants opted for the west-east route, with a take-off from distant Newfoundland.

Ranged alongside the Sopwith team were a single-engine biplane, the *Raymor,* a portmanteau of the names of the pilot, Fred Raynham, a long-time friend of Harry, and the navigator, Fairfax (Fax) Morgan; a Fairey Aviation seaplane, with Sidney Pickles at the controls; and an American entry—former Swedish naval officer Hugo Sunstedt's purpose-built twin-engine amphibian,

Sunrise. A U.S aviation company, Handley-Page, put forward a crew of four led by retired British Vice-Admiral Mark Kerr to fly its modified four-engine bomber.

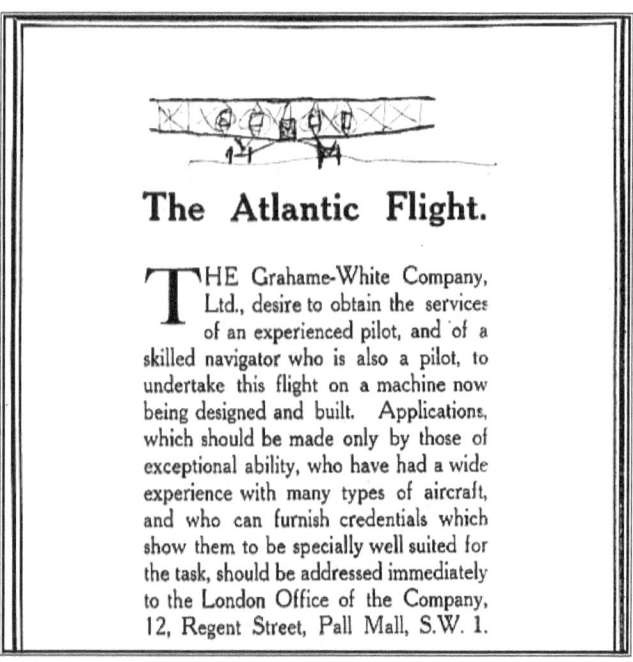

Potential contestants came from all corners of Britain when the transatlantic prize was announced in mid-November 1918.[102]

There was also a late entry from England in the form of a twin-engine Vickers-Vimy ex-bomber, with John Alcock as pilot and Arthur Whitten-Brown as navigator, but they were believed unlikely to be ready until mid-year. From across the Atlantic the U.S. Navy was rumoured to be preparing for a crack at being first across, but not as an official entrant in the *Daily Mail* competition.

Earlier in the year, the Sopwith Board had recognised the transition from war to peace and the subsequent downturn in aircraft manufacture by formally agreeing 'to manufacture, sell and repair motor cars, motor cycles, motor vehicles and conveyances of all kinds.'[103] Tommy Sopwith had already predicted the rise of a civil aviation market, but he knew that would be some time in coming. He needed products that would sustain the company in the meantime. The CEO hoped a partnership with an old friend, Granville Bradshaw at ABC Motors, to produce 400cc horizontally-opposed twin-cylinder ABC motorcycles, would fill the bill. At the same time the company changed its name to Sopwith Aviation and Engineering Co. Ltd. Harry Hawker became entitled to 1.5% commission on sales income from fully built aeroplanes, 'a big incentive to focus on developing successful post-war designs',[104] as one observer commented.

In January 1919 Sopwith announced its transition to a post-war motorcycle manufacturer.[105]

As the Sopwith *Atlantic* went through its final trials in February 1919, Muriel Hawker might well have wondered if she'd done the right thing in letting Harry go. But she'd lived with the possibility of losing him in the air since they'd met in 1915, and he'd had some close shaves and escaped mostly unscathed. So she could only hope that his luck continued. She'd constantly seen 'that intense fire of enthusiasm' burning in her husband and knew he couldn't be stayed.

It might also have been that, deep inside, she understood that the flickering flame that drove Harry Hawker was the special quality that attracted her to him in the first place. When he and Grieve completed their longest practice loop from Brooklands, 900 miles, she was ecstatic: 'Not a hitch! Not even in the sandwiches I cut for them!'[106]

Everything was ready, it seemed, for a British assault on the Atlantic, and Sopwith booked passages for Harry and Grieve on the SS *Digby*, leaving Liverpool on 20 March 1919 for the nine-day voyage to St John's, Newfoundland. The Sopwith *Atlantic* would travel in several crates in the hold, to be re-assembled on arrival like a giant Lego® model. Also on board would be Rolls Royce engineer Eric Platford, Sopwith mechanics, and a movie cameraman, who already had film 'in the can' from the team's Brooklands preparations.

The day before the ship was due to depart, Harry began packing his suitcase in their bedroom at 'Ellendale' while Muriel was busy elsewhere in the house. Soon the two of them would drove to Euston Station in central London so he could catch the train to Liverpool. It was four months since the Armistice and the end of more than four years of intense wartime pressure on Harry.

Now he was about to set out on a new adventure, with different challenges—a long-distance flight across uncharted skies, with other experienced and well-supported teams hot on his heels. The media was reporting every move for a hungry readership, knowing that the transatlantic crossing brought a glimmer of hope after the dark days of the war. The public needed heroes like Harry Hawker, symbols of a brighter, more exciting world that was emerging from the ashes of a long and bitter conflagration.

Hawker and Mackenzie Grieve took the Sopwith Atlantic *for a round trip 900-mile trial flight from Brooklands, February 1919.*[107] *'Not a hitch! Not even in the sandwiches I cut for them!' Muriel reported.*

Perhaps it was because he'd been so preoccupied with preparing for the flight that Harry hadn't had time to think about what this venture meant for him and his family. He and Muriel had known each other for four years, had been married for 16 months and now had a four-month-old daughter. He didn't need to be a mathematician to add up the time they'd be away: a nine-day voyage to Newfoundland, around two weeks to reassemble and test the plane, a mid-April departure under a full moon, and a glorious landing at Brooklands less than 24 hours later. Altogether they'd be away close to four weeks.

Not long, but it seemed that the famous pilot suddenly realised the enormity of what he was about to take on, the uncertainty of what was to come. The space between him and his family would be more than simply a matter of time and geographical distance. Suddenly, unexpectedly, Harry Hawker was crying.

This wasn't the way it was supposed to be, at the beginning of a journey so full of promise. A tough boy from the suburbs of Melbourne didn't cry, especially one who'd achieved so much since he'd arrived in England. But the war had changed all that. So much to weep about. Now Harry was struggling with the thought of leaving his wife and daughter behind while he went off to tame yet another beast.

Muriel came in to see how his packing was going. Ever since she'd given him her blessing, she'd been determined to hold it together, even though underneath she'd been tense with worry, trying not to think about what could happen if the flight didn't go according to plan. Despite all Harry's assurances, in the time she'd known him she'd seen enough of the realities of flying to know there were no guarantees.

Now, when she saw the tears running down her husband's cheeks, all the anxiety she'd held in for the past couple of months burst out. The 23-year-old rushed to hug him, her own eyes now brimming. They clung to each other, sobbing into each other's shoulders, trying to reassure the other that everything would be okay.

Outside, the weather matched their mood as they set off—sombre, dark and cold. The wind was whipping the trees around their house, and the rain danced in the headlights as they headed to Euston Station. For some reason, despite the almost cyclonic conditions, Harry opted to take the Sunbeam. The big car might well have had a neatly riveted bonnet, but it also had no hood over the passenger compartment. So, as they roared through deserted London streets in drenching rain slashed by an occasional knife edge of sleet, Harry crouched behind the whisper of a windscreen.

Muriel hunched in the well on the passenger side, her head resting against her husband's knee. She quietly wished that she'd married someone without ambition, like a farmer's son. Someone who didn't feel the need to go where no man had ever gone before. If only I could sleep away the time ahead, she thought.

When they reached Euston station, they had one final hug, said one final goodbye. As Harry disappeared into the carriage, Muriel was inconsolable. She couldn't wait for the train to pull out.

Heading disconsolately back to the car, all she could think was that Harry had gone from her. The only thing she could do was wait for the future to unfold itself.

CHAPTER 8

'Mildly surprising to downright unpredictable'

Codfish and newsprint. British, not Canadian. The first transatlantic wireless message flashed there from Cornwall in 1901. That's probably about the extent of a Brit's knowledge of Newfoundland when Harry Hawker and McKenzie Grieve arrived there on 29 March, 1919.

It was not a promising start: in what should've been the spring thaw, the harbour at St John's, the main town in the dominion, was still thick with ragged ice floes, jostling like ice cubes in a whisky glass. It seems the late ravages of winter that were plaguing Britain that month were also being felt on the other side of the Atlantic.

When the Sopwith team arrived in Newfoundland by ship from England in the spring of 1919, St John's harbour was partly frozen. They and their heavy crates had to be unloaded elsewhere on the island and railed across country.[108]

What might have gone through Harry's mind during the nine-day voyage from Liverpool? Did he think about how he might slash the Atlantic crossing time to less than a day, becoming a Pied Piper of long-distance aviation and helping transform international travel? Or did he look up at the heavens from the deck at night and imagine himself piloting the *Atlantic* through the clouds and the darkness and wonder what sort of weather they might face on the way?

What were his thoughts about Muriel during those days at sea, and their tearful goodbye at the railway station the day he left London? Did he ever consider he might never return to his wife and his daughter?

With St John's harbour otherwise occupied, the captain of the SS *Digby* was forced to unload the Sopwith party and their crates at Placentia Bay, on the south-west coast of the island, where they were transferred by small boat to a nearby town. They then transferred themselves and their chattels to a clattering steam train that bore them 60 miles north-east across country to the town of St John's. The train chuffed along what the private owner called the finest freight line between Canada and Newfoundland; his critics derided it as two streaks of the finest rust.

Newfoundland is a massive slab of an island that looks as if it's been chainsawed from the mainland. Over the centuries the North Atlantic has etched rocky bays and inlets along its shoreline which echo with the cries of orange-billed Atlantic puffins, razorbill auks and black-legged kittiwakes. The landscape is almost as rugged as the coastline, the corrugated surface of the island's central plateau dotted with boulders discarded by long-gone glaciers and peppered with the irregular shapes of lakes and ponds, like dark pools of spilt ink. At the time of Harry and Grieve's visit, along with black spruce, thickets of mainly blue-green balsam fir forests provided the raw material for the local newsprint factories (one of which Lord Northcliffe happened to own).

No part of the island is more than 100 miles from the sea, so it's continually at the mercy of Atlantic gales. In winter it is sometimes knee-deep in snow. Otherwise it's often part-covered by cotton-wool fog that rolls in from the Grand Banks to the east, where the cold Labrador Current and the warm waters of the Gulf Stream intersect to create a fish-food banquet for Atlantic cod, swordfish and haddock. Occasionally an iceberg breaks away from the polar regions to the north and slides menacingly down the east coast of Newfoundland into the Atlantic shipping lanes. Even today local tourist websites warn visitors to Newfoundland to expect weather ranging from 'mildly surprising to downright unpredictable.'[109]

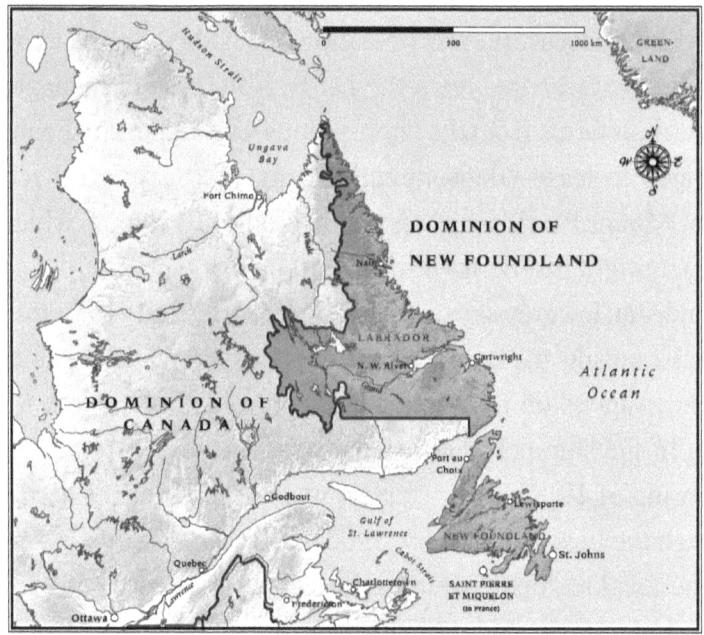

The British Dominion of Newfoundland as it was at the time of the 1919 transatlantic attempts. All of the teams were based on the Avalon Peninsula in the south-east, where the only city at the time, St John's, is located.[110]

So, as their train rumbled across the island's undulating central plateau through patches of stubborn snow, on the first day of their big adventure Harry and Grieve no doubt learned what any of the local 'Newfies' would've told them for free: if you're looking for an ideal take-off point to bridge the Atlantic in a World War I-era plane and want an area big and flat enough for an airstrip and weather conditions consistently favourable for flying, Newfoundland wouldn't even be on your list. It was only its relative proximity to Europe as the crow flies that made the island a preferred jumping-off point for a transatlantic flight.

Nevertheless, the Sopwith team was the first of the contenders to arrive, so if they could maintain that edge, they were in with a chance.

When the newcomers arrived at St John's station, a surprisingly elegant chateau-like structure for a frontier town of 30,000, there to meet them was Monty Fenn, former manager of Sopwith's successful Paris operation. He had come ahead of the main party. Over the years the hardy Newfies had managed to wrest small farms from the unpropitious landscape, and Fenn had managed to lease Glendenning's Farm, a 40-acre (16-hectare) site at Mount Pearl, six miles south-west of St John's, which he thought might just do for a makeshift airstrip.

Under an icy grey sky on that late March day in 1919, primitive derricks swung the cumbersome wooden Sopwith crates from the rail wagons on to low horse-drawn sleds for the trek to the farm. In the summer, these sleds would be rubber-tyred, but in the spring of 1919, heavy runners were needed for the hard slog through the unseasonal snow, mud and slush.

The local residents were excited about the arrival of the first transatlantic crew and a bevy of reporters. Most workers were employed in the timber or fishing industries. They came from mainly Irish and English stock, with a small number of Scots. 60 years earlier the little self-governing British dominion had refused an invitation to join the confederation of Canada and had been fiercely independent ever since.

During World War I, it sent more than 6000 of its men to fight for the Allied cause on the Western Front. Some 1200 of them never returned. With the end of the war and brighter prospects for the struggling fishing industry, however, hope was in the air in this distant outpost of empire. The promise of the first Atlantic flight was a bonus. 'St John's is now the starting point of the greatest air flight ever undertaken,' the local *Daily Star* proudly proclaimed.[111]

BRITISH FLYER TO MAKE OCEAN FLIGHT

LONDON, March 18.—British aviators are to try for a flight across the Atlantic. A secretly built airplane, accompanied by Harry Hawker as pilot and Commander MacKenzie Grieve, Royal navy, as navigator, was shipped from England yesterday for St. Johns, N. F., from which it will start soon in an attempt to win the Daily Mail prize of £10,000 for the first machine to fly across the Atlantic.

The machine is a Sopwith two-seater biplane, with a 375 horse-power engine. The fusilage is boat shaped, and will support the machine in the water.

Pilot Hawker said he believed that the flight would occupy about 19½ hours. The machine, he said, had flown 900 miles in nine hours and five minutes on one-third of its petrol capacity, and is capable of maintaining a speed of 100 miles an hour for 25 hours.

Worldwide the media were interested in the race to be first across the Atlantic. Hawker would have laughed, however, to see his and Grieve's Sopwith described as 'secretly built'.[112]

As with Newfoundland itself, however, the city was hardly 'fit for purpose' for a transatlantic flight. It's at roughly the same latitude as Paris, France, but that's where the comparison with the City of Love ends, because St John's proximity to the sea and to the Arctic and its position on the coast of Newfoundland even today makes life challenging for its residents. Nationally, it's officially the foggiest, snowiest, wettest, windiest and cloudiest of all the major Canadian cities.

When they finally reached the farm, tired, cold and perhaps wondering if starting from England mightn't have been such a bad idea after all, the two fliers received another surprise. As Harry reported: 'The aerodrome was an L-shaped piece of ground about 400 yards on its longest limb, and about 200 yards along the shorter... The L shape was due to the fact that the ground skirted a hill about 200 feet high with pretty steep sides... The short limb was strongly uphill from the south, at which end it had high trees, and there were low trees at each end of the long limb.'[113]

In other words, like no airfield Harry had ever seen.

What's more, at 450 feet above sea level the airstrip seemed to catch winds from all directions, promising to make take-offs even more tricky. The ground was patchy with slow-melting snow, like frosting on top of a badly iced cake, and there were occasional soft patches that might slow or even bog a heavily laden plane. Under the snow, the ground was rough and flinty, as if it was the very core of Newfoundland. With the shape of the field, the condition of the ground, and the trees at each end, the pilot of the *Atlantic* was going to have his work cut out to lift the big plane into the air.

Before he'd left England, Harry had set Wednesday 16 April, the second night of the full moon, as the target date for departure. He was planning for an afternoon take-off and hopeful of a moonlit flight across the heavens, if they could stay above the clouds. Now the wintry weather and the state of the strip of dirt at Glendenning's Farm threatened to thwart those plans.

Thanks to Fenn there was already a high, rough rectangular lumber shed erected on the site, braced at the ends against the wind. This huge barn had a very wide and almost full-height sliding timber door across one of its long sides, and was topped by a gabled timber roof. It was a welcome alternative to the tent the advance party had optimistically brought with it. So at least the Sopwith team would be under cover as they began to unpack the crates and to reassemble the *Atlantic*. The Rolls Royce engineer would help make sure the engine was fine-tuned for the flight.

The shed at Glendenning's Farm, Newfoundland where the Sopwith Atlantic *was assembled. In the foreground is one of the wooden crates the plane had been shipped in from England. The rough textured ground and constant snow were an ongoing challenge to Hawker and his team.*[114]

In the preceding days Fenn had employed a gang of 60 local men to help clear and stabilise the ground, some of them no doubt not long back from the Western Front. But this was a frozen farm paddock, and they hadn't made much progress. When the surface would be stable enough to support a take-off and the weather clear enough for a trial flight, let alone for Harry and Grieve to head off across 1900 miles of ocean, was anybody's guess.

If they listened very carefully, the new arrivals might've heard other, distant sounds above the grind of men levelling the field and the buzz of mechanics re-assembling the Sopwith. These were noises from the other side of the Atlantic—the hum of cranes loading the *Raymor* aboard ship in England as Raynham and Morgan prepared to leave for Newfoundland, or the roar as the Short Brothers tested the engine of the *Shamrock* in readiness for its departure from England and Ireland. From the United States, there was word that the Sunrise trials were going well over Newark Bay in New Jersey. And the rumours about a U.S. Navy bid grew louder.

With no easy communication across the Atlantic, Muriel waited uneasily at home in Hook. After the miserable drive to Euston Station and forlorn farewell the day Harry left, she went home 'oppressed by a feeling of great desolation.'[115] After ten days, apart from a brief message to tell her he'd arrived, she knew nothing of Harry's progress in Newfoundland. Pamela was now four months old and they were fortunate to be able to afford a nanny, but Muriel found herself staying close to 'Ennadale', never venturing out for more than a couple of hours, in case a message might come through about Harry while she was away.

Marconi's invention and the demands of war had pushed the development of wireless communication, but it was still relatively primitive. It was mainly the media and big business that sent 'cables' via the wire services. Ordinary citizens like Muriel still relied on the daily papers for their news, and she subscribed not only to that of the race sponsor, the *Daily Mail*, but also to other major newspapers of the day.

With no direct contact, Muriel Hawker was forced to become a spectator to the distant drama of her husband's attempt to cross the Atlantic. She could only watch the story unfold day by day in the local newspapers, like a serialised 19th century novel, and keep an eye out for street-corner posters that might alert her to what was happening 10,000 miles away.

As March edged into April, spring still had not sprung, and Newfoundland seemed to be trapped in a snow dome. There was a meringue-like crust of white across the land, and when the air was not filled with fluttering snowflakes, heavy rain swept across to transform the snow into a coffee-coloured slush. On the few occasions the sky threatened to clear, easterly winds quickly herded in dense silver-grey fogs from the fishing banks.

Of course, immigrant Newfoundlanders and their descendants had survived in these sorts of conditions for several hundred years, eking a living from fishing and logging. No wonder they were proud of their independent status and spirit.

Harry and Grieve respected the locals, but they didn't want to join them. The two fliers were transients, passing celebrities, thankful for the local support and infrastructure, such as it was. However, for them Newfoundland was but a launching point for a destination elsewhere.

A summertime streetscape, St John's Newfoundland, c 1920.[116]

The pair were booked into the *Cochrane Hotel* in St John's, which Harry jokingly referred to as the 'Cockroach'. But it was a fashionable hotel, run by three unmarried sisters, Kitty, Minnie and Agnes Dooley; a fourth sister, Lizzie, was married to the hotel's owner. Among the *Cochrane's* former guests were the wireless wizard, Guglielmo Marconi, and allegedly, in 1917 a ship-wrecked Leon Trotsky, on his way home to a revolution in Russia. A local supporter lent Harry and Grieve a Ford car, and they drove the six miles out to the site each day, often having to stop on the way to dig the vehicle out of snowdrifts.

Protected by their big barn, the Sopwith team painstakingly fitted the plane's parts back together, re-installed the engine and generally made the aircraft what Grieve might have called 'shipshape'. Unlike his Royal Navy navigator, Harry wasn't used to a life where the weather was such a dominant player. Nor was it in his nature to hang around waiting for the stars to align. Although he preferred to make a test flight, with other teams breathing down their necks he hadn't ruled out taking the big plunge if the opportunity arose. Two hours would be sufficient, Harry said: 'Just time enough to get the tanks filled up, the mail aboard, the thermos flasks filled, and the engine nicely warmed up.'[117]

Even in the depressing weather, whenever there was a break Monty Fenn's work gangs rushed out to dig drains to channel water from the take-off strip and stabilise the softer parts with layers of small stones, flinty offerings to the weather gods. At the *Cochrane*, Agnes Dooley entered into the spirit of readiness by preparing a packet of sandwiches for the two fliers every day after breakfast, and filling their thermos flasks with hot water.

Frustratingly, even when the local sky gave them a pearly glimmer of hope, the weather men shook their heads about the diabolical conditions over the Atlantic. Although all the entries

Mechanics working on the Sopwith Atlantic *at the Newfoundland field while Hawker and Mackenzie Grieve waited for the weather mid-Atlantic to clear.*[118]

for the *Daily Mail* prize came from private aviation companies, national pride was at stake, so the Air Ministry, the Admiralty and the Meteorological Office were all providing support for British entrants. The British Government had set up a network of observers for the transatlantic efforts, with meteorologists posted to Lisbon and the Portuguese-owned Azores, as well as St John's. There were also regular weather bulletins from Carnarvon in Wales and the United States and, by wireless, from ships at sea fortunate enough to be fitted with this newfangled apparatus.

The degree of support sounds impressive, and might have worked at sea level, but predicting how weather patterns intersect with aircraft and flight paths was still an emerging science in 1919. It had mostly been learnt in the past few years under the extraordinary circumstances of war, and mainly over land. No one had ever crossed the Atlantic at 12,000 feet. It literally was uncharted territory.

CHAPTER 9

'Possess our souls in patience'

Muriel was following the newspaper reports about the foul weather in Newfoundland from 2000 miles away. She was still confident Harry would head off in mid-April, because she knew he wanted the full moon to light his path home. 'Never before had I taken such an interest in the moon as during these few weeks,' she said later. 'I knew every phase.'[119]

The Admiralty was trying to keep her up to date with Harry's movements, but they too struggled for information, frequently resulting in initial hope and subsequent letdown: 'Often I would have news about seven in the evening to the effect that Harry was about to start,' she said. 'I sat up until the news was contradicted.'

It was a frustrating time for her husband too, as he waited anxiously for a break in the weather. All the time he was watching over his shoulder for Raynham and Morgan to arrive, wondering when Hugo Sunstedt might turn up from New York with his amphibian, and knowing that every passing day increased the likelihood the US Navy would enter the race.

No doubt against all his inclinations, Harry said there was only one thing to do: 'Possess our souls in patience and simply wait.'[120]

While they waited, a nearby lake in a lightly wooded area overlaid with snow gave them a chance to try out their survival gear. The 30-year-old Australian and the 39-year-old Scot (see

photo[121]) frolicked clumsily in the icy water like a couple of playful walruses, decked out in specially designed inflatable waterproofed suits that fitted over their standard travel outfits.

Satisfied that the wetsuits would keep them dry and warm, the pair struggled back to the bank and prepared for their next task—testing the boat. Harry's brainchild had been unclipped from its upside-down position on the plane's upper fuselage for the occasion. Grieve knelt upfront and sturdily rowed the stubby boat in a sweeping circle, a horizontal loop-the-loop, using a paddle shaped like a short cricket bat with a long handle. Harry sat grinning in the rear.

The punt-like shape made the boat difficult to steer and they were laughing again, enjoying the moment. Nevertheless, they were also well aware that if it came to this over the Atlantic, their chances of survival would be very slim. The Atlantic was an unpredictable beast, and could morph from playful kitten to roaring dragon within minutes. Nevertheless, Harry had told a reporter he had every confidence in the Sopwith and wasn't concerned about it having only a single engine. 'If the plane did come down,' he said, 'I'd prefer to smash into the water than smash into the ground.'

On Thursday 10 April, six days before Harry's planned take-off date, Raynham and Morgan arrived in St John's by ship with their Martinsyde, also a single-engine biplane.

The tension immediately ratcheted up. Harry knew Fred Raynham well and respected him as a pilot. On paper the *Raymor's* capacity for the flight matched the *Atlantic's*. In fact, Raynham thought his plane was faster because it was lighter. The question was: could they get it off the ground before the Sopwith?

The two pilots first met when Raynham was manager of the Sopwith aviation school at Brooklands in 1912. Shortly afterwards, the newly qualified Harry outlasted Raynham to win the trophy for a British pilot in a British-built plane who stayed in the air longest in one continuous flight (almost eight-and-a-half hours). When Harry was in Australia with the *Tabloid* in 1914, Raynham took the opportunity to snatch the British altitude record back, and he and Harry had remained friendly rivals.

Hawker and Grieve took turns paddling the little lifeboat during practice on a nearby lake in Newfoundland.[122]

Raynham's navigator for the transatlantic flight, Fax Morgan, was an experienced wartime pilot and a flamboyant character. Awarded the Croix de Guerre by the French Government and the Distinguished Service Order by the British, he had an artificial limb as a legacy of his wartime activities. On a visit to Newfoundland two months earlier, with the help of a local reporter, Morgan had located a stretch of land to lease at Pleasantville, alongside Lake Quidi Vidi, on the eastern flank of St John's. Harry had already taken a look at the site and reckoned it was too narrow and didn't have enough wind assistance for a take-off. He much preferred his farm at Mount Pearl, whatever its faults.

The *Raymor's* arrival coincided with an improvement that day in the weather from downpours to overcast. Harry immediately told his team to prepare the *Atlantic* for a test flight that afternoon. After almost a fortnight of inaction, it seemed the appearance of another team had spurred Harry and Grieve into making a move, lest these newcomers get the jump on them.

Under a leaden sky a small band of helpers trundled the Sopwith across the big wooden-slatted barn doors (which, when flattened, doubled as wooden decking over the soggy patches) and up to the start point. Ironically, it was a lacy membrane of frost over the still-sodden ground that provided sufficient hardness for a take-off.

As the word spread, a sizeable crowd of excited spectators gathered mid-afternoon. They clapped and cheered when Harry and Grieve clambered into their cockpits and went through the pre-take-off checks. The pair buttoned dark woollen overcoats over their suits. They'd done this before, at Brooklands, but no doubt their hearts were buzzing as they prepared for the first trial of the machine over Newfoundland.

Harry decided against a full tank of fuel for the trial flight, but made the load heavy enough to test the plane's ability to handle the sticky airstrip and clear the trees.

The Rolls Royce engineer, Eric Platford, looked on as the 375hp Eagle engine roared into life. Harry let the engine rumble for a while, warming it up before he brought it up to full revs, its wooden propeller spinning hypnotically against the grey sky. Already he'd swapped the four-bladed propeller they used at Brooklands for a two-bladed one that would give them more lift at take-off.

Then it was 'chocks away!' and the big plane lurched forward and began to pick up speed as it trundled over the hard surface. Harry could doubtless feel the vibrations through his seat, but was on the lookout for soft patches that might take away the momentum. He also needed to keep an eye on the hillock that threatened to brush his port wing.

Hawker was always optimistic about his chances, whether in the air, on the racing track or on water.[123]

A Royal Flying Corps officer once said disparagingly that Harry flew a plane as if he was throwing a cricket ball about in the air. But on this occasion it was more like a slow lob from the outfield as the Sopwith shook free of the dark earth at the end of the strip and began to rise, the engine throbbing with intent. The trees were directly below the machine now and it seemed as if it was clear, when suddenly it hit an air pocket and dropped sharply. There was an involuntary gasp from the crowd, which turned into cheers and applause as Harry's experience triumphed and the *Atlantic* lifted into a sullen but rainless Newfoundland sky.

By now it seemed that every resident of St John's had heard about the test flight. Thousands thronged the streets to watch the big bird overhead. For most of them it was the first time they'd seen an aeroplane. Even the Newfoundland Senate, which happened to be meeting at the time, on hearing the sound of a plane in the air, immediately suspended business, and members rushed outside to gaze skywards. Harry rewarded the Newfies with a 45-minute flight at 3000 feet. He weaved the transatlantic contender through a series of speed tests over the town and the nearby scoop of water known as Conception Bay. There was great excitement in the streets as the locals got their first look at the plane that was likely to make the first attempt at crossing the Atlantic, starting from *their* island.

Also looking upwards, no doubt, were Freddy Raynham and Fairfax Morgan, busy unpacking their Martinsyde aircraft at their lakeside airstrip at Pleasantville.

Harry was happy enough with the trial flight but, as he came in to land, the wheels caught for a moment in the chocolate mud, an ominous sign for a take-off with a full fuel load if the rain persisted. The only glitch during the flight was when the wireless was put out of action because the little fan spun so fast in the propeller's slipstream that it burnt out the generator. Harry cabled to England for an improved model, but neither flier put much store in the primitive device to keep them in touch with would-be rescuers once they were airborne. They'd already dismissed it as a navigation aid.

While contenders for the transatlantic crown were posturing, preparing, or possessing their souls in patience that month in 1919, the fates of nations were still being decided at the Paris Peace Conference. Although the talks had begun in January, it would be June before the Treaty of Versailles was formally signed, amidst much kicking and screaming from the Germans, who protested it was too one-sided.

10,000 miles away in Newfoundland, Hawker and Grieve decided they were satisfied with their trial flight, and that they'd head off as soon as the weather looked even mildly forgiving.

The next day, Friday 11 April, the winds were so strong, however, the *Raymor* team couldn't erect the tent they'd brought with them. But Saturday was milder—the wind ragged but bearable, the sky glowering darkly but without rain, and the fogs keeping to themselves on the fishing banks. Harry made a decision: the *Atlantic* would take-off on its transatlantic mission at two o'clock that afternoon.

A local newspaper reporter had no doubt that the reason for the Saturday start was the 'great progress' Raynham and Morgan were making.[124] The *New York Times* correspondent agreed: 'Hawker had no intention of starting before Sunday till he heard reports of the good progress the Martinsyde people were making.'[125]

The Sopwith team swung into action: They strained the 330 gallons of petrol and 24 gallons of oil six times before filling the tanks, and funnelled 17 gallons from the St John's water supply into the radiator. A bag of specially post-marked mail was loaded aboard. Emergency rations, a torch and a collapsible bucket were packed into the lifeboat before the little craft was upended and locked into place on the fuselage.

The *St John's Daily Star* breathlessly reported: 'At noon the machine was practically ready and Messrs Hawker and Mackenzie-Grieve were only waiting a slight change in the wind when they would jump on board and begin their memorable journey.'[126]

The two fliers had now been on Newfoundland for just over a fortnight. Harry was quoted as saying that the flight would take 19½ hours; Muriel was allowing 22.

As the proposed take-off time loomed, the St John's weather was still holding. The weather elsewhere was not—there were reports of wild winds along most of their planned route. If you head off now, the local RAF Met. Officer, Lieutenant L. J. Clements, told them, you'll fly into disaster. Harry decided

The Sopwith Atlantic *prepares for take-off from Glendenning's Farm, Mount Pearl, May 1919.*[127] *The rough earth airstrip would turn to quagmire in snow and rain.*

to postpone the take-off until 5 pm and see what the forecast was then. Monty Fenn immediately called on his small gang of workers to rush out with dump carts and hand-pulled heavy rollers for a last-minute touch-up of the rough airstrip.

While the Sopwith team prepared, news came through that the US Navy had formally announced its intention to make a transatlantic attempt, using a flotilla of seaplanes. It planned to head off from Newfoundland in early May, just over two weeks away.

Now that a departure for the first-arrived British team was imminent, pilot and navigator dealt with the delay in different ways. Grieve busied himself adjusting the compass and following the weather reports. Harry checked and re-checked the plane, but couldn't settle down to any one task. He wandered around the site, looking up at the sky, while around him men rugged up in all manner of coats, gloves and hats, were beavering away to smooth the *Atlantic*'s path. There were many uncertainties with this flight, beginning with the take-off, and no doubt his head was full of them. Was he also thinking of Muriel and Pamela, and imagining being soon reunited with them on English soil?

Fred Raynham dropped in to say goodbye. He said preparing the *Raymor* had taken longer than expected, but he hoped to be in the air on Monday, without a trial flight. Harry told his friend he thought the Pleasantville airstrip was too narrow, and the wind direction was wrong, but his fellow pilot seemed untroubled by the prospect.

Raynham didn't stay long, but before he took his leave he put out his hand. 'Good luck,' he said to Harry. 'See you again.'

Both men knew that if something went wrong for either of them, this could be the last time they met.

It was still more than an hour to the new take-off time, and the wind was building up. Around 4pm there was a smattering of rain, threatening to undo the recent good work on the runway. As the clock ticked onward, the anemometer, which recorded wind speed, jumped towards gale force. Ominously, heavy clouds began to crown the surrounding hills.

Let's make it 6pm, Harry said, and see what the weather's like then. The reporters, who'd been hanging around waiting for a take-off, reluctantly retreated to the farm's cow-shed to begin writing their despatches. Even as they wrote, a new report came in from the Met. Office: a violent storm was raging mid-Atlantic.

Harry and Grieve had an urgent confab with Monty Fenn, Lieutenant Clements, and Eric Platford. They agreed a departure now would not only be risky on the deteriorating airstrip, but would mean burning excessive fuel and losing time battling a notorious Atlantic tempest. They'd also risk arriving in Ireland or England in darkness, not a good idea in an aircraft without an undercarriage. (The *New York Times* correspondent had already declared such a landing 'practically suicide'.[128])

They decided to postpone the flight. Noon next day, Sunday 13 April, became their new target.

CHAPTER 10

A game of cat and mouse

The following morning, Newfoundland struggled to open its eyes, and not just because it was Sunday. The sky was darkly brooding, and there'd been rain overnight. Harry wanted an afternoon take-off, but already the airstrip would have been described by a horse race-caller as 'slow'.

Within hours there was more rain, and the track became 'heavy'. Just when the weather seemed to be changing in their favour, it had gone back to its old bad habits. Harry's usual optimism was overshadowed by his concern for the chances of getting the 6000-pound *Atlantic* off the ground.

Shortly afterwards, the decision became a no-brainer. The wind changed to the south-east, and a classic Newfoundland fog, as thick and creamy as fish chowder, moved across the island and sat there, as if to say, 'Sunday is a day of rest.' Harry had no choice but to take its advice.

He cabled Sopwith: 'Bad weather.' After two weeks of postponements, Tommy Sopwith and Fred Sigrist knew what that meant. So did Muriel Hawker. No doubt frustrated and anxious, and not in direct contact with her husband, she knew she would have to possess *her* soul in patience a little longer.

This had been the Sopwith crew's big chance—close to their planned take-off date, and ahead of the *Raymor*. Now they were level pegging again. And 100 miles to the south, the US Navy was readying its seaplanes.

On Wednesday 16 April, the day Harry and Grieve had originally intended to start, both teams remained trapped in their icy cocoon. The full moon, which was supposed to guide them home, had remained stubbornly hidden the whole time they'd been there. Ironically and frustratingly, the moon in its golden prime was very visible to Muriel every night through her windows at 'Ennadale'.

Heavy snowfalls in St John's not only frustrated Hawker and Grieve's take-off efforts, but they often had to dig their borrowed Ford sedan out of snowdrifts on their way from their city hotel to the farm site.[129]

While they waited for Harry to take off, the American press in particular commented on his financial situation. One report suggested he was the highest paid pilot in the world, with an annual income of more than £100,000.[130] Unlike many ex-World war I pilots, Harry did have a steady and apparently substantial income from his employment with Sopwith. Nevertheless, he was hardly the epitome of the smart man about town in St John's:

He has given no evidence of great income. He dresses almost indifferently, sometimes wearing a lounge suit, whose most striking detail is trousers with extreme peg-tops, sometimes wearing khaki riding breeches, with gray [sic] golf stockings. He seldom appears without a cap whose vizor is drawn far forward and makes him still more boyish in appearance.[131]

Next day, Thursday 17 April, there was finally a slight break in St John's weather. Raynham decided to take up the red and yellow Martinsyde for an afternoon test flight. Once more the residents were excited by the prospect and trooped out to the Pleasantville site in horse-drawn carriages and cars and on foot, forcing the local police into the unexpected task of crowd control. Harry and Grieve also turned up for the occasion, and the *Daily Star* reported that both teams seem 'very chummy'. It was a surface bonhomie, however. The *Raymor's* flight went well, and Harry immediately started looking for a less sodden piece of ground at Mount Pearl. One that might help the Sopwith get away sooner. A local reporter described the Australian as 'restive'.[132]

He was even more restive the next day, when local and distant weather reports were so promising that both crews decided it was time to go. The two teams set midday as the flight time, but each was watching the other team's mechanics for indications of an earlier start.

Raynham announced he'd laid a bet that he'd be in England by Easter Monday, 21 April. Tongue-in-cheek, he told a reporter that this information was intended as an aside and 'not for his rival's ear.'[133]

Once again the weather intervened in this psychological stand-off: a driving mid-morning snowstorm dumped six inches of white frosting across the ground and a half-gale blustered its way across the airstrips. Both teams had no option but to cancel.

Workmen prepare Raynham and Morgan's Raymor for a flight from its Quidi Vidi airstrip, Newfoundland. As with Hawker and Grieve, the rough ground, tight airfield and late snow were constant impediments.[134]

While the four fliers were preoccupied in Newfoundland, out of the blue came word that Major J. C. P. Wood and Captain C. C. Wylie had taken off on Friday 18 April. Their dual-control *Shamrock* left Eastchurch RAF base in Kent in bright sunlight, on their way to a transatlantic take-off from Ireland. Residents along the east coast of the Emerald Isle had been encouraged to keep a lookout for the plane, and reporters gathered excitedly at the final take-off point.

Muriel likely heard of the *Shamrock* take-off before her husband did, and her heart surely missed a beat. Harry and Grieve were trapped in Newfoundland by the weather, their ideal departure date already past. They'd been waiting their chance for more than two weeks, and now it seemed they could be pipped by a contender from the British end.

It was not to be, however. Four hours into the flight, just as the plane headed out across the Irish Sea, the *Shamrock's* engine cut out. Wood managed to turn the plane around, back towards the coast of Wales, and glided in for an emergency landing on the water. Picnickers on the nearby island of Anglesey dashed out in a launch to rescue the two men, who were uninjured. The plane was later towed ashore, but that was the end of the *Shamrock's* transatlantic attempt.

No doubt the Newfoundland contenders had mixed feelings about this outcome: glad that the two fliers escaped unhurt, but also relieved that the first serious attempt at a transatlantic crossing had failed. It was a reminder, however, that there were strong rivals out there who could take the initiative at any moment, and also of course, that despite all the planning and testing, things could go horribly wrong very quickly.

One of those entrants snapping at Harry and Grieve's heels was Hugo Sunstedt, the only official US entrant for the *Daily Mail* prize. Already in his former career in the Swedish navy Sunstedt had made eight flights of over 1000 miles each, and he aimed to bridge the Atlantic Ocean from Newfoundland in 16 hours.

But his radical-design *Sunrise*, a huge twin-engine amphibian biplane with an upper wing span more than twice that of the *Atlantic's*, required extensive trials in the US. 'I am in no hurry to get started, except that I must start before anyone else does,' Sunstedt had said in February. 'Before I go the seaplane will be tried on the water, and in the air empty, with half her load of gasoline and oil, and then with the full burden. But when we do go we will go fast.'[136]

Wood and Wylie's Shamrock, *from Short Brothers, the only transatlantic contender to attempt the east-west route.*[135]

As April petered out, the two British teams in Newfoundland played tag with the weather. Even if the classic Grand Banks fog and heavy local rain held off, the moody storm gods in the mid-Atlantic conspired to continue to thwart their plans.

Harry sometimes felt like having a go in spite of not being able to see a foot in front of him. But this was thick Newfoundland house-specialty fog, and he decided that their makeshift airstrip wasn't 'the sort of ground one could negotiate blindfold.'[137] Earlier, he had found an alternative take-off site, but decided Glendenning's Farm was a better option, with all its limitations.

Raynham however decided he'd had enough—he declared his next take-off, whenever it was, would be for Ireland. Curiously, however, two days later, he announced his intention to make another trial flight. Harry was suspicious, especially when he learned that the *Raymor's* fuel tank was full. He instructed the Sopwith team to roll the *Atlantic* out of its shed, and make sure it was ready for a quick departure, just in case. Once again the fog defeated both of them.

To add to their misery, a message from the Air Ministry arrived on 23 April, asking the reasons for Harry's and Raynham's failure

Aviators weren't the only ones frustrated by fog. This photo shows schooners in full sail in St John's harbour waiting for the fog to lift.[138]

to start, given the favourable weather conditions reported mid-Atlantic.[139] Puzzled by the implied criticism, the two teams discovered that some of the earlier weather reports purporting to be from Canadian and American meteorological sources were fake, sent by persons unknown. Newspapers claimed that on one occasion, when British meteorologists had advised of clear weather across the Atlantic for a 24-hour period, North American reports were 'contradictory' and had deterred the fliers from taking off.[140] It was alleged that during that time 'the conditions were ideal and almost unprecedented for the time of year, the anti-cyclone area extending all over the route; and had the airmen started through the coastal fog they would had soon flown into bright skies and light winds.'[141] In other words, if they'd taken that chance, they could well have been home by now.

There were dark hints that all of this confusion emanated from American 'interference', intended to delay the British efforts. The Air Ministry denied sending the 'please explain' message to the British fliers, and promised that future reports from its Meteorological Bureau would be in code.

The strain on the two teams was beginning to tell. Day after day, they continued tinkering with their machines, but there was a limit to that. Moreover, the out-of-the-way town itself was hardly geared for tourism. Harry said that even if was the most entertaining place in the world, they'd still find it 'irksome', because all he wanted to do was 'get the thing over and done with as soon as possible.'[142] He admitted that the enforced idleness of all four British fliers sometimes led to a bit of anger among them.

To ease the tension, the four British entrants eventually agreed on a simple strategy: each team would give the other two hours' notice of their intention to take off for THE flight, and at the same time would arrange for a message to be sent to ships on the projected route. Harry said the agreement made the atmosphere 'a little less electrical.'[143] They also decided they'd split the mailbag to be carried for the Newfoundland Post Office. The four now began to spend more time together, jointly checking the weather reports at the meteorological station, and playing practical jokes on each other.

In the tradition of sailors across the ages, Lieutenant Commander Grieve RN carried two good luck charms: a piece of white heather from his home country, and a lady's white handkerchief (origin unknown). Reporters asked Harry if he was also carrying a good luck charm. 'I only believe in one mascot,' he said, 'and that is Grieve.'

The weather continued to be what Harry called 'uniformly rotten',[145] and suddenly it was the merry, merry month of May. At least, it was merry back in England, where there'd been an extended spell of fine spring weather. After getting over the surprise, the British public were becoming impatient about the delayed take-offs in Newfoundland. The papers had been full of

Hawker and Grieve hoped to spend only two weeks in St John's, Newfoundland, but weather conditions trapped them there for seven. Harry said that even if the city was the most entertaining place in the world, they'd still find it 'irksome.'[144]

the transatlantic attempt for months. Surely the weather on the other side of the Atlantic couldn't be so consistently bad that these expert pilots weren't able to take off? Harry Hawker had a stack of flying records and an MBE, for goodness sake!

Dozens of letters and postcards arrived at St John's urging the teams to get on with it. Two women working in the British War Mission in New York sent a cable to the unmarried Grieve: 'Sir, do buck up and start. We cannot stand the suspense much longer.'

Muriel Hawker might well have felt like sending the same message to her husband. In early May she'd told a reporter: 'I received a cable telling me of his safe arrival, and I have heard nothing since.' They'd now been separated for six anxious weeks instead of the four he'd predicted. When would she see him again? Would she see him again?

Meanwhile, 1200 miles to the south, Hugo Sunstedt was confident the *Sunrise* would soon be on its way. In sunshine Harry could only dream about, Russian Lieutenant Procofieff Seversky took the big amphibian up for another test flight over Newark Bay, New Jersey. All went well until he was coming in to land on the tranquil blue waters, when the biplane for some reason sideslipped at low level and crashed heavily into the sea. The pilot and co-pilot escaped unhurt, but the specially made balsa floats were badly damaged.

So badly damaged, in fact, that even the super-optimistic Sunstedt didn't think the aircraft could be repaired in time to be a serious challenger for first across. So, after a long build-up and one short-lived incident, the first purpose-built and only official fully US entry for the *Daily Mail* prize withdrew from the competition.

About the same time that Sunstedt declared himself out of the transatlantic race, the US Navy was declaring itself in, with a vengeance. The converted US minelayer *Aroostook* nosed into the harbour at the tiny fishing settlement of Trepassey, 100 miles south of St John's, to establish a supply base for the Navy's attempt to cross the Atlantic by flying boat.

CHAPTER 11

Not without a struggle

The US Navy's interest in flying the Atlantic had its roots in the nation's entry into World War 1 in April 1917, when German U-boat attacks were at their peak. The US Navy commissioned aircraft designer Glenn Curtiss to develop an amphibian that could be used in European waters as a sub-spotter, one they could first fly across the Atlantic to avoid the risk of losing the new aircraft to U-boats. With a shape reminiscent of a Dutch shoe, the Navy-Curtiss, or NC, emerged from production just a month before the Armistice, so it never did have a chance to show what it could do.

The Navy ordered four of the planes post-war, however. It was sure they could fly the Atlantic, although as a government agency, it wouldn't enter the Daily Mail competition. The big Navy-Curtiss biplanes, which each had three tractor engines and an added pusher engine, were designated *NC-1, 2, 3* and *4*. It didn't take long for the American sailors to transform 'NC' into '*Nancy*', and the amphibians became the four *Nancies*.

With the Sopwith and Martinsyde teams already in Newfoundland, a reporter asked Navy Secretary Josephus Daniels if the US hoped to beat the British to the punch in being first across. 'We hope to beat the world!' Daniels replied.[146]

To show they meant business, 36 hours behind the Aroostook two small cruisers slid into Trepassey. They were followed next day by five destroyers, and then there was a daily procession of warships. Officially the US Navy had been at pains to play down any suggestion that this was a race with the British, and described it as a 'scientific experiment'. No one believed them, least of all the press.

The plan was that the Navy amphibians wouldn't follow the direct northern route the British fliers were taking, but would make two hops via a southern arc that would bring them first to the Portuguese-held Azores for refuelling, and then on to Lisbon. Although longer, it was a route considered to have better weather than the northern one. What's more, to bolster their chances, the Americans proposed to string warships across the Atlantic, roughly 50 miles apart, to support the efforts of the *Nancies'* crews.

The British press promptly give the thumbs-down to the American plan, complaining that even if the US Navy was not officially competing for the *Daily Mail* prize, not only were the Nancies taking the easier route, they were doing it in two hops. *And* the aircraft were being mollycoddled every nautical mile of

NC-4 and the other two US Navy amphibians under preparation at Rockaway base, New York, for their tilt at being first across the Atlantic in May 1919.[148]

the way by a chain of warships to make sure they stayed on track and to catch them if they fell.

'Might as well fly the English Channel fifty times,' Fax Morgan huffed.[147]

Reporters who've been hanging around St John's waiting for some action from the British teams decided more was happening at the temporary US base further south. The scribes hired a railway dining car, equipped it with a stove, table, beds and a cook, and had it hauled down to Trepassey as accommodation. They called it *Nancy-5*.

Still unable to get away from St John's, the Sopwith and Martinsyde crews waited nervously for news of the *Nancies'* arrival at Trepassey, the American take-off point for the Azores and Europe.

To add to the two British teams' anxiety, on 10 May two more contenders arrived by steamship in St John's harbour. The Handley-Page team, led by retired British Vice-Admiral Mark Kerr, brought with them a giant biplane, the V/1500, and a very experienced crew of three. This formidable combination set themselves up near the thriving fishing town of Harbour Grace, 60 miles by rough road north-west of St John's, on the opposite side of Conception Bay, sending uncomfortable ripples across to Harry and Raynham.

Two other British fliers with an eye on the prize also arrived in St John's that day, but didn't have their plane with them. Captain John Alcock and Lieutenant Arthur Whitten-Brown slipped into town on the Mauretania. Their modified Vickers Vimy bomber was still en route by ship, and not due until late May, by which time it seemed likely one of the earlier crews would've made the first non-stop transatlantic crossing.

For the two original British teams, Newfoundland must suddenly have seemed crowded with aviators keen to fly the Atlantic. There were rumours too that other teams back in England were still preparing their entries, including the one from Fairey Aviation, with Sidney Pickles as pilot.

The giant Handley-Page V/1500 biplane arrived in Newfoundland by ship on 10 May 1919, putting more pressure on Hawker and the Sopwith team.[149] *Hawker had been hoping to get away by mid-April.*

In these early weeks of May, the Newfoundland weather mellowed considerably. However, conditions mid-Atlantic continued to be treacherous. Desperate to occupy their time in the spring-like conditions, Harry and Grieve started taking little tours around the countryside in their borrowed Ford. Raynham, whom Harry jokingly referred to as 'Tinsides' because of his Martinsyde plane, ventured out for a few rounds of golf. His navigator, Morgan, resting his prosthetic leg joint, kept in touch with the weather reports on behalf of both teams.

It was a surreal scenario, and one the Americans were about to blow apart.

While Harry and his three colleagues were filling in time in St John's, on Thursday 8 May *Nancies 1, 3* and *4*, under the command of Commander John Towers, took off from their base at Rockaway Naval Air Station, New York, heading for Newfoundland. (The other amphibian, *NC-2* was damaged during trials and subsequently cannibalised for spares for the others.) Each plane carried a captain and pilot, radio operator, a flight engineer and a mechanic.

On the way to Newfoundland, however, all three planes were beset by problems that threatened to derail their Atlantic attempt before they got started—cracked propellers, dropping oil pressure, bumpy landings in 40-knot winds, cranky engine starters, and brass-monkey weather in the cockpits. *NC-1* and *NC-3* eventually made it to Trepassey, but *NC-4* was somewhere behind, having been forced down on the sea off Cape Cod when it lost power in two engines. It wasn't located by any of the minder warships, but the crew managed to taxi it through the night to shore. The Press dubbed it 'the Lame Duck'.

For Harry, word of the first two Nancies' arrival in Trepassey sharpened the tension. 'It made the waiting game still less attractive than ever,' he said.[149]

However, while *NC-4* was undergoing repairs, *NC-1* and *NC-3* were pinned at their take-off point by reports of wild weather on the Newfoundland-Azores route. It was not until Thursday 15 May that the weather at sea cleared enough for them to contemplate a take-off. Towers was anxious to leave, concerned the British fliers might steal a march on them. He was in two minds about waiting for the lagging *NC-4*. But the heavily loaded *NC-1* and *NC-3* had trouble getting off the water in the tricky winds at Trepassey, and *NC-4* eventually caught up with them.

24 hours later, just before 6 p.m. on Friday 16 May, the US *Nancies* lifted off one by one and were finally in the air together, the first aircraft to attempt the transatlantic crossing since the war. Coincidentally, it was exactly a month since the original date Harry and Grieve had set for their take-off.

While all eyes were on Trepassey, there was another America saga happening in St John's, a sideshow to the main event further south. A US Navy blimp, *C-5*, came to town the same day the *Nancies* departed for the Azores. The captain announced that they too were about to attempt a transatlantic crossing. The blimp's support ship, the cruiser USS *Chicago*, arrived in St John's a couple of days earlier, creating yet another stir among the locals when it berthed at the wharf.

The C-5 was the newest of the Navy's non-rigid airships (i.e. with no internal frame), filled with hydrogen, with a submarine-shaped gondola suspended beneath it for the crew of six. Its

The US Navy's C-5 blimp, which was also a contender to be first across the Atlantic. However, US authorities denied this, and publicity for the Nancies' *transatlantic attempt masked news of the blimp's passage to Newfoundland from New York in May 1919.*[150]

twin engines propelled it from its base at Montauk, New York, to Newfoundland at a steady 60 mph. Arrangements had been made to tether it temporarily at a sports field alongside Quidi Vidi Lake in St John's. Once again the Navy tried to play down any suggestion that the appearance of the C-5 had anything to do with the cross-Atlantic race. Before it left New York, however, its captain, Lieutenant-Commander Emory Coil, told reporters, 'We'll beat the seaplanes yet.'[151]

On its way to its mooring point by the lake, Coil and his team lost their way in one of the Newfoundland fogs that Harry Hawker knew so well. After first making contact with the *Chicago* for directions, they began to follow the railway line. Later they were forced to swoop their 192-feet-long, four-storey-high dirigible to within shouting distance of a group of startled locals to seek advice. On arrival at the sports field, under the excited eyes of a large crowd of Newfoundlanders, they tethered the airship by steel mooring cables and ropes tied to a circle of anchors hammered into the ground. Here they planned to replenish its airbag with hydrogen brought over in cylinders from the *Chicago* on the same horse-drawn sleds that had dragged the Sopwith to Mount Pearl. When asked about his plans, Coil wasn't forthcoming, but gave the impression that the *C-5* could be up and away within 24 hours. During the refuelling, he and most of the crew headed off to the *Chicago* for rest and recuperation.

The small team of junior officers and a squad of sailors from the *Chicago* left behind noticed the wind picking up. The airship began tugging on its anchor ropes. Gusts of 30 and 40 knots or more started to toss the blimp around, alarming its keepers. They became even more concerned when the dirigible started to rise, as if attempting to escape. Quickly they began hauling on the ropes, trying to stabilise it. Everyone was shouting now, and spectators rushed in to help. The *C-5* didn't want to be stabilised, however, and swung in an arc then suddenly plunged downwards, like a horse that didn't want to be ridden.

When the bloated craft seemed in danger of tearing itself to pieces, the two duty officers decided the only thing to do was rip out the balloon's emergency panel. This would release the gas and so deflate the cigar-shaped bag. They clambered up the wildly swinging ladder into the gondola and yanked firmly on the emergency ripcord. However the cord snapped, and the emergency panel stayed where it was.

At the same time two of the steel mooring cables came apart, sending the airship into further contortions. Like pirates defending their ship, the two officers whipped out sharp knives, hoping to be able to slash the airbag open. But before they could do so, a huge gust of wind lifted the *C-5* into the air. The remaining cables gave up their hold. As the dirigible launched itself into the afternoon sky, the two officers jumped for their lives.

The rush was on at Quidi Vidi field at St John's on 16 May 1919 to secure the C-5 blimp before it wrenched completely free of its anchor ropes, to no avail.[152]

The assembled crowd, some with minor injuries from whiplashing ropes, watched in astonishment as *C-5* took its farewell. It drifted erratically across the town and out to sea. Soon it was out of sight. Coil was still on his way back after being summoned urgently from the *Chicago*. He never saw the airship again.

Harry Hawker reportedly thought the incident 'damn funny': 'They flew it all the way from New York and now it is on its way to Ireland without a soul on board,' he said.[153]

Assistant Secretary of the Navy, Franklin D Roosevelt, was phlegmatic: 'That ends one of our hopes of crossing the Atlantic,' he said.[154] For the Americans, it was down to the three amphibians now in the air.

As usual, Muriel Hawker had been following the *Nancies'* saga via the press. She continued to dart out for the latest news, to keep in touch with the Admiralty, and worry about Pamela, who now hadn't seen her father for close on two months. Muriel was still on the lookout for newspaper street-corner posters that might alert her to her husband's departure, but she'd become used to disappointment.

On Friday 16 May, all this changed. She was out in the car when she was confronted by a newspaper poster with bold black lettering to the effect: AMERICAN SEAPLANES DEPART TREPASSEY FOR AZORES.[155]

Muriel's heart must surely have been pounding as she rushed to the nearest phone box to ring the Admiralty to check the report, and see if she could get any news of Harry. After all this time, all the anxiety, all the moon-watching, all the false reports of starts, she knew that this time her husband would not be held back.

Muriel might well have known about the US take-off before her husband did, because news of the *Nancies'* Friday evening departure didn't reach St John's until next morning. And Muriel was right: although the weather report for the northern Atlantic was still not brilliant, Harry knew that if the Navy planes reached the Azores, he'd have no option but to start. The support crews began preparing the *Atlantic* and the *Raymor* for the crossing.

All day Saturday, the four British fliers sweated it out, waiting for news of the *Nancies'* progress. It came in the evening: the Americans had reached the Portuguese-owned islands. One more hop and they'd be in Europe.

Harry immediately announced he'd take off next day, Sunday 18 May, regardless of the weather. One American commentator suggested Harry 'panicked';[156] another said the Sopwith crew were 'stampeded' into going.[157] Muriel had a different view: 'I knew he wouldn't let the Americans arrive first without a struggle,' she said.[158]

Raynham too declared he was leaving the same day as Harry. Both teams raced to put the final touches to their aircraft for the 1900-mile flight.

CHAPTER 12

'Many a prayer was breathed for their success'

Next morning, Sunday 18 May, there was a frisson of excitement in the Sopwith camp. After seven long, frustrating, weather-dominated weeks, after all the false starts, all the rumours, all the tension, all the uncertainty, at last the *Atlantic* was going to take off on its ultimate flight, one that could see Harry and Grieve go down in history as pioneers of the transatlantic run.

They were well aware that ranged against them were Raynham and Morgan's Martinsyde, currently under furious last-minute preparation across town, and the US Navy's three *Nancies*, sitting in the Azores, ready for the final leap to Europe.

An American commentator said, 'Hawker's farewell announcement that he was bound to beat the Yankees—some of the newspapers reported that he said "damned Yankees"—had a fine swagger that was appreciated here [the United States] perhaps, more than it was in England and Canada, where boasting was considered too American to be good form.'[159]

Now Harry ran the engine for a while and was confident it was ready to go, while Grieve checked his charts, packed his sextant and tested the wireless. The replacement transmitter had arrived from England and had now been fitted. However they hadn't had a chance to try it in the air. For them it was an untested backup, and Grieve told reporters he and Harry were counting on the machine, not the wireless.[160]

Harry was upbeat. As the plane was being loaded, he playfully hefted Grieve's overnight bag in his hand, and laughingly asked his navigator if he really needed to pack his pyjamas since they'd be back in England before he had time to use them.

Asked by a reporter yet again about their chances, Harry said, 'I have a perfect machine for the trip, and the engine is the best in the world. I am confident we'll get across.'[161] Grieve was also relaxed. He reckoned they'd be okay as long as they could find Ireland.

The two men were aiming for a late afternoon start. Ideally that meant a few extra hours sunshine and an extended twilight as they settled into the rhythm of the flight. This would be followed by some eight hours of night flying, when navigation was trickier, and then a daytime flight the rest of the way, towards a jubilant touchdown in Ireland or England. Once again Harry was asked about coming in to land without an undercarriage. Echoing an American counterpart, an English reporter had described the Sopwith bid as 'elaborate preparations for a double suicide.'[162]

'I expect to make a perfectly good landing, and have no fear of badly crashing the machine,' Harry said calmly.[163]

First the famous pilot had to lift the plane off the ground at Mount Pearl, where despite all the filling, smoothing and rolling, the makeshift runway was still somewhat reminiscent of the rugged landscape of Newfoundland itself. And this time the *Atlantic* would have a full fuel load.

Harry and Grieve shook hands with Monty Fenn, Eric Platford and the other members of the Sopwith team, settled into their seats and strapped themselves in. They'd already said goodbye to Raynham and Morgan. This was the moment they'd

Wheels splayed even more with the weight of a full load, the Sopwith Atlantic *rolls across the rough paddock at Glendenning Farm on 18 May, 1919, ready for its date with its transatlantic destiny.*[164]

waited for. The adrenalin would surely have been rushing. Harry looked inquiringly at his companion, who nodded. *Ready.* Harry flicked the switches on the control panel, a mechanic spun the two-bladed propeller, and the V12 engine surged into life. It sat throbbing with held-under power. As the engine warmed to maximum revs, a crowd of about fifty milled excitedly about, keen to see this much talked-about crew and plane finally set off on their long-delayed mission.

Now Harry jerked a thumb in the air and the chocks were pulled away. The *Atlantic* rumbled forward along the roughly prepared field at Glendenning's Farm, carrying with it the hopes of all those who'd been involved in getting it to this point.

Slowly it gathered speed, Harry's hands gripping the controls tight to make sure it stayed straight on the uneven surface. Earlier he'd warned Raynham about the several degrees of 'helm' or pull exerted on a loaded plane while taxiing for take-off on this sort of terrain.

The wind was about 20 mph east-north-east, forcing him to take off diagonally across the L-shaped piece of ground.

On that trajectory the plane would almost nudge the hill at the intersection of the two arms and go close to the drainage ditch that ran along the base of the mound. His hands and ears were alive to the rhythm and sound of the engine, and his eyes were everywhere—on the dials, the ground ahead, the trees, the beckoning sky.

The crowd that was so buoyant a moment ago was hushed now as the plane gathered speed and headed towards the end of the strip, its two wheels splayed with the burden they were carrying.

The Sopwith's wing was only inches from the hill as the plane bumped its way past, gathering speed, and Harry felt the craft roll a little under the weight it was carrying, but the momentum carried it through. Then they were past the drainage channel. Only the trees to clear. He piled on maximum power and hauled on the stick.

There was a flash of green below them as the *Atlantic* leapt into the air, like a steeplechase horse going over a brush fence. To cheers and shouts from the crowd below the big plane climbed steadily into the blue sky. They were safely off the ground.

Harry was pleased: he thought there'd been a respectable distance between the wheels and the trees.[165] Grieve wasn't so sure—he ignored the plane's intercom for a scribbled message to Harry: 'We didn't have much to spare taking off.'[166]

It was around 3.40 p.m. local Newfoundland summer time, Sunday 18 May, 1919.

In Hook, Surrey, it was 6.40 p.m. English summer time the same day. By this time next day, the Sopwith *Atlantic* could be touching down at Brooklands.

Harry deliberately took the plane over the Martinsyde site at Pleasantville, but only he knew if that was to make a final farewell to Raynham and Morgan or to rub in the fact that the Sopwith was in the air ahead of them.

'Look at old Tinsides with a crowd around him,' he said to Grieve, perhaps a little peeved that the *Raymor* had attracted many times the number that came out to Glendenning's Farm.

After seven frustrating weeks, on 18 May 1919 Hawker and Mackenzie Grieve finally headed off over the trees from their makeshift airstrip in Newfoundland on their transatlantic flight to Ireland.[167]

The first most of the locals knew about the Sopwith's take-off was when they heard the plane climbing over their heads at 100 mph. They'd continually heard the mantra that the transatlantic planes needed a westerly for take-off, so weren't expecting to see an aircraft overhead that day. Windows swung open and people tumbled into the streets to watch the *Atlantic* pass over St John's at a thousand feet, thrilled that one of 'their' planes was finally on its way.

'Many a prayer was breathed for their success,' the local paper reported, 'and for their rescue and safety should disaster overtake them.'[168]

Harry pointed the Sopwith east-north-east and, as they passed over Signal Hill, the highest point in St John's, the wireless operator at the Marconi Station let the world know that the first of the Newfoundland starters for the *Daily Mail* prize was finally in the air.

Ahead of the plane Harry could see a dozen white smudges against a dark green background, like sheep grazing in a paddock. But this was no green field, it was the Atlantic Ocean, and the smudges were the fuzzy shapes of icebergs, bobbing their way south to make a nuisance of themselves in the shipping lanes, as the Captain of the *Titanic* had discovered too late seven years earlier.

Now that they'd crossed the coast and were over open sea, they could discard the undercarriage, as planned. Harry gripped the lever beside his seat, looked across at Grieve, then yanked hard. The landing gear was near the plane's centre of gravity, so when it dropped away there was so little difference in the plane's trim that neither of them felt it go. But when they looked over the side they could see the wheels tumbling end over end towards the sea.

They didn't see the splash, however, because as soon as the additional weight had gone, the Sopwith surged forward and the air speed indicator flicked up another seven miles an hour. Home sooner.

Ejecting the undercarriage was not only a way of minimising drag and increasing air speed, it was also a symbolic act of separation from their take-off point, a sign that they'd kicked off the shackles of their enforced residency. There was no going back.

The next time they landed it would be without wheels, and they wanted that to be a sliding touchdown at Brooklands on the Sopwith's wooden skids. Just like the Wright planes used to.

Back at 'Ennadale', Muriel finally received the news she'd been waiting for: this time Harry and Grieve really had taken off and were headed across the Atlantic. She rushed around the house, hanging up the bunting and 'Welcome Home' signs she'd had on hand for weeks. When that was complete, she sat down, suddenly empty, unable to think of anything else to do.

The questions Muriel was no doubt asking were the ones the rest of Britain also likely wanted answered: would Harry and Grieve beat the Americans to Europe? And what about Raynham and Morgan?

When the people of St John's watched the Sopwith head seaward earlier that afternoon, they quickly realised that, if the weather was good enough for Harry and Grieve to lift off, Raynham and Morgan would not be far behind. Within 30 minutes of the *Atlantic's* disappearance out to sea, there was a rush for Pleasantville—cabs, automobiles, 'square-bodies' (pick-up trucks) and dog carts raced each other to the ground, weaving their way through a throng of citizens on foot. The Martinsyde site was closer to town than Glendenning's Farm, and Raynham's later take-off gave more people a chance to reach the place. By departure time, there was an excited crowd of 2000 or more.

Raynham and Morgan were just as determined as Harry and Grieve to beat the Yanks across. They'd looked up as their British rivals passed over Pleasantville late on Sunday afternoon, but Raynham was not fazed. He thought the *Raymor* was about three hours faster than the *Atlantic* over the 1900-mile route and that he'd soon overtake them. To announce their arrival over the Irish coast, he and his navigator planned to throw overboard message bags with trailing streamers.

On its successful test flight a month earlier, the single-engine *Raymor* had a light load and took off into the wind. This time it had a full tank of fuel, and the wind on take-off would be behind it, pushing it along, making it harder for the pilot to keep it under control. Harry had already expressed reservations about the tightness of the site, and on another day Raynham might have waited to see if the wind would turn in their favour. But the Americans were in the Azores, Harry and Grieve were in the air, and the *Raymor* was ready to fly. Time to go.

When the 'chocks away' call came, Raynham put all his experience into getting the red and yellow Martinsyde into the air. As the colourful biplane started to move over the rough and ready strip, it was sitting low to the ground, and it was clear that this time the mass of the aircraft was considerably greater than it was for the trial flight. Nevertheless, it continued to rumble along, gradually picking up speed. One hundred yards, two hundred yards, three hundred yards. But did it have enough pace to get off the ground?

The big crowd held its collective breath. The man Harry called 'Tinsides' thought it was now or never and hauled back on the stick. Just as he did so, the *Raymor's* wheels hits a ridge and the plane bounced upwards, leaping a hundred feet into the air, giving the impression of flight. The powerful Rolls-Royce Falcon engine strained to pull its heavy load skywards.

Raynham and Morgan's Raymor *came to grief as they tried to take off from Newfoundland shortly after Hawker and Mackenzie Grieve.*[169]

The crowd started to clap and cheer. Their enthusiasm turned to shouts of dismay, however, as the Martinsyde suddenly plunged with a thud back to earth. It smashed belly first into the ground, its undercarriage twisting sideways under the impact. The plane's momentum juddered it forward, before it choked to a halt in a soft patch of soil, its nose tilted downwards. White smoke poured from its engine, and the biplane's lower wing was almost flat on the ground. Spectators in suits and hats rushed to help.

Raynham killed the engine and turned off the fuel to reduce the risk of fire, and clambered slowly out. He had cuts and bruises and a bleeding nose. The wind had been knocked out of him in more ways than one, but otherwise he seemed unhurt.

Morgan wasn't so lucky. He'd been leaning out over the right-hand side of the cockpit, watching the plane's progress over the rough ground. When the Martinsyde thumped back to earth, his left cheek slammed into the window frame. Stunned and in shock, he had to be helped from the plane. He was treated by two doctors and a paramedic from the crowd before being taken off to hospital. The navigator ended up with stitches in his cheek and over one eye, and severe bruising of his left shoulder and surviving leg. Worse still, he appeared to be blind in one eye, the same eye where a tiny splinter of shrapnel had lodged during a wartime raid, and he now needed morphine to cope with the pain.

Shortly after the crash, Raynham went back to his room at the *Cochrane*, but later recovered sufficiently to drive himself back to Pleasantville to survey the damage. Although the plane's engine and undercarriage were done for, he declared himself ready to set off again as soon as repairs were made. It seemed like bravado, but—like Harry Hawker—Fred Raynham was not a pilot to give up easily. Nevertheless, it was obvious there were a few hurdles to clear before another attempt was within reach, not the least of which were convincing Martinsyde Aviation that it was a good idea, repairing the plane and finding a new navigator.

It was now up to Harry and Grieve to fly the flag for Britain.

CHAPTER 13

'Making the night less terrible'

As word of the debacle at Pleasantville spread, the Marconi wireless station operator sent a message to alert Harry and Grieve, but received no reply.

Unbeknown to him the *Atlantic's* wireless was out of action. Grieve had tried it soon after take-off and managed to get a spark but the generator wasn't pushing enough current for a transmission. This was ironic, given that on the test flight the generator had burnt out because it was turning too fast. In any case the two men had never built their flight around the wireless, either for messages or for navigation. So the demise of the device was no big deal for them, but it did mean that they didn't know about Raynham's take-off fiasco. Nor did they know whether the Americans had left the Azores on the final leg. They also couldn't call for help in an emergency.

But this was what they'd planned for. The two of them against the elements. No outside help. No outside interference. Certainly no string of warships. They'd do it through their own efforts. Just as Harry had mastered the spinning dive, so crossing the Atlantic was another beast to conquer and ride into exhaustion.

Muriel seemed to accept that. If she sometimes cried in the darkness and cursed her husband for leaving her and Pamela while he went off to pursue his dream, she gave no public sign of it. Much as she sobbed on the day she said goodbye at Euston Station, she also recognised the sort of man she married.

'My husband has talked with me so often about this Atlantic flight that I know all its difficulties and dangers,' she told a reporter. 'He has set his heart on doing it, and I would not say one word to deter him.'[170]

Even though the weeks of separation had taken their toll on both of them, she continued to recognise that her husband was a driven man. For the time being, at least, she was not going to stand in his way.

Grieve was a different sort of person, but he too was committed to this enterprise. His mastery was of a different kind too—of fluctuating ocean currents in the seas of the world, of meticulous navigation for a sea-going platform for aircraft carrier trials, of 'chronometrical and astronomical observation.' Now he was applying his skills and experience as a shipboard navigator to the ebb and flow of the currents of air above the notoriously fickle Atlantic Ocean.

Earlier Grieve had told a *Daily Mail* reporter: 'The machine might get across by steering a compass course, allowing for the various winds, supplied from the limited knowledge of meteorologists. But few reports of the surface winds are available, leaving large spaces on the chart of the weather in which conditions could only be guessed, while the upper air currents are absolutely unknown.'[171] In other words, no one had

any idea how much the Sopwith might be blown off course as it headed across the Atlantic.

In their way, Harry Hawker and Mackenzie Grieve were explorers—not of the physical environment like the pre-war Polar expeditions of Roald Amundsen and Robert Scott, but pioneers of the air, heading into the unknown, unsure of what lay before them, relying on their own initiative to get them through the inevitable challenges. What they could expect was a series of skirmishes and battles, all dictated by weather conditions that were not only unpredictable, but potentially life-threatening. Their armour was a plane they believed in and faith in their own abilities.

There was also another piece of news that would've been of interest to them if they'd had radio contact: while it was true the Americans had reached the Azores, they were in disarray. Only one amphibian, *NC-4*, had managed to reach the Portuguese islands intact. The other two had come down in the sea, and were too damaged to take off again, although both crews eventually reached the Azores. *NC-1's* crew were rescued by a passing Greek freighter while, in a remarkable feat of endurance and navigation, Towers and his crew managed to sail *NC-3* backwards for 53 hours and 200 miles.

Under Navy protocol, the flotilla commander, John Towers, should have taken command of NC-4 for the flight to the European mainland. However, Navy Secretary Josephus Daniels ruled that Putty Read should retain command of the amphibian that the Press had earlier dubbed the 'Lame Duck', for the final leg. Towers would travel by ship.

After damaging their craft while making an ocean landing, the crew of NC-3 managed to sail the crippled amphibian backwards for 200 miles before being taken in tow at Delgado in the Azores.[172]

However, on Sunday 18 May, the day *NC-4* might have taken off on an historic flight to Europe, and the day Harry and Grieve left St John's, the weather across the South Atlantic to Lisbon was decidedly unsettled. It was considered too dangerous for a record attempt by *Nancy-4*, which national pride dictated must succeed. So the final US leap was postponed, leaving a small window of hope for the British team.

Unaware of these dramas, Harry and Grieve were focussed on the task at hand. Unshackled from its undercarriage, the Sopwith soon kicked away from the pockmarked east coast of Newfoundland. It climbed rapidly, still on the east-north-east bearing that should ultimately bring the aircraft back to Brooklands, and Harry back to Muriel.

All being well, the next land the two men would see was the jagged west coast of Ireland.

As they headed further out across the sea, they met one of their old friends—a Newfoundland fog, sitting offshore as if waiting to greet them. Harry pushed the Sopwith through it and upwards, and burst into clear sky, an encouraging find. It was not so good for Grieve, however, who had now lost his view of the sea which helped him calculate the rate of drift. Nevertheless, by the time Harry levelled the plane out at 10,000 feet, the Scot had worked out they needed to allow for a slight northerly wind that was otherwise pushing them ten degrees off course.

For the next few hours, they stayed high under a benign blue arch of sky, riding a few bumps, correcting for the northerly, scoffing coffee and munching chocolate while the engine purred along at a steady 105 mph. The cockpit was chillingly cold, but their oversuits kept them warm. As the sun slid down the sky to hide until it reappeared on the dawn of what promised to be an historic day, Harry smiled to himself. I could just about let the machine fly itself, he thought, and simply hold it on the course Grieve sets for us.[173]

Four hours into the flight, 400 miles from Newfoundland and with 1500 to go, his reverie was broken by a realisation that the sky had begun to fade to purple, as if theatre lights had dimmed. Soon it was a ghostly grey, and they found themselves travelling through an eerie opaque world that brought a strange uncertainty after the clarity of the evening sky they'd been flying across. Uncertainty changed to apprehension when through the gloom they sighted a mountain range of looming black cloud ahead, a boiling mass of peaks and gorges. It was as if they were over the Alps of Europe rather than the Atlantic Ocean.

It looked as if this would be their first major battle.

Newspapers across the world reported the extraordinary developments in the transatlantic race on the weekend of 17–18 May, 1919.[174]

Meanwhile, in a time zone a few hours ahead of them, Muriel was willing the hours to pass. She'd been able to cope with Harry's extended stay in Newfoundland, but now that she knew he was in the air, time seemed to drag. When the last flickering shards of daylight had disappeared, she went over to the window and stared at the darkening sky, waiting for the moon to rise.

The pale yellow orb seemed to have become a symbol for her, a connecting point with Harry, its soft glow hopefully now guiding him home. Despite the solace the sight of the moon brought her that night, as she looked up at the heavens, for the first time she found herself having doubts about the venture she'd given her imprimatur to. 'The moon was waning,' she said later, 'but, despite that, it seemed to make the night less terrible. It was very cold, and I wondered whether it was all worthwhile.'

Earlier, she'd entered in a notebook each of the 22 hours she expected Harry might be in the air from the time of his take-off until he arrived at Brooklands. With the moon now moving slowly across the heavens, she began to cross the hours off, one by one.

Harry was still 1400 miles from his wife when the *Atlantic* reached the billowing pile of black of cloud. With typical self-belief, he decided attack was the best form of defence and plunged the plane straight in, hoping it would soon pop out into clearer skies on the other side. Seconds later, it was so inky black around them that they could have been in a cave. Unseen gremlins were bumping and jiggling the plane. Out of the darkness a scud of rain startled them as it hit the plane, and then was gone.

Harry peered through the blackness, desperate for a glimpse of light that might indicate a way out. But the cloud seemed to mass more heavily around them, hemming the plane in like a steer in a cattle crush. He decided to try to get above the cloud and, with a quick sign to his navigator through the gloom, pulled back on the control stick and arrowed the Sopwith upwards, completely unsighted.

As they climbed, he noticed the water temperature thermometer was also edging upwards. In response he flicked open the tiny metal shutters over the radiator to let in more cold air. The thermometer stopped rising for a moment, then edged its way up a little further and sat there, as if pondering its next move.

But Harry's focus was on getting above the cloud mass, and he kept the Sopwith climbing through the treacly blackness, all the while looking for the feathery edges that might reveal that clearer air was not far off. Grieve meanwhile was looking downwards, seeking a glimpse of the sea that might help his drift calculations. Occasionally a window opened like a skylight in the cloud below to give a dark glimpse of green water, but to the navigator's frustration closed just as quickly.

Eventually Harry was forced to level out at 12,000 feet, the Sopwith's maximum altitude. He jockeyed the plane across the undulations of the seemingly never-ending ranges of cloud, like a cowboy riding the Badlands. Still working blind, Grieve noted each course the plane was on and for how long, and made an estimate of drift, and every time he calculated a new compass bearing, scrawled it on note-paper and held it up for Harry to see. Their 900-mile trial flight from Brooklands hadn't prepared them for this. Would they be on course when they finally emerged into clearer sky?

Harry was still concerned about the radiator. The water temperature was now edging towards boiling point in the thinner air at higher altitude. He pushed the shutters fully open, bringing a rush of cold air from the darkness on to the engine. But the mercury continued to rise.

The experienced pilot thought he'd seen this problem before. He reckoned bits of accumulated rust and solder had probably piled together to block the pump filter, so not enough water was getting through. The trick was to turn the engine off and make a sharp dive, which would have the effect of dislodging the accumulated rubbish and forcing it to the bottom of the inlet. And *voilà!* the intake should be clear.

Nevertheless, even for Harry Hawker MBE, this would be a challenging manoeuvre—a plunge through thick cloud from

12,000 feet with the engine off, towards the ocean somewhere below, before levelling out and restarting the engine mid-air. He'd need the same sort of nerves he showed when he mastered the spinning dive.

Shouting a warning to Grieve, Harry flicked the motor off and dropped the Sopwith's nose sharply. The biplane plunged silently down through the clouds, its propeller spinning wildly from the force of the descent. It dropped 1000 – 2000 – 3000 feet. Then Harry threw the switches, the Rolls Royce engine sprang back into life, and he expertly levelled the aircraft out. So far so good.

But had the manoeuvre had any effect on the temperature? He checked the gauge—it had dropped back, not to where it should be, but at least enough to bring his anxiety down a notch as well. Remarkably, despite the high water temperature, the engine was running smoothly. If he could just keep the plane on an even keel, follow his compass under Grieve's guidance, and hold the temperature steady, he thought they'd make it.

So they pushed on, bumping through the cloud bank, still completely unsighted, no doubt glad of each other's company in their pitch black cocoon.

But Harry's relief was short-lived—the temperature was rising again. When it was again in the danger range, he decided to repeat his earlier manoeuvre, convinced that rubbish had again accumulated across the filter. Down, down they plunged, but when the plane recovered he discovered that this time not only had the temperature not dropped, it had zoomed up to near boiling point.

Next moment a tiny geyser of steam spurted from a pinprick hole in the radiator like a mini-volcano. The water in the cooling system was clearly at a critical level.

CHAPTER 14

Close to boiling point

As Harry wondered what to do about the water temperature, the Sopwith suddenly came out of the cloud mass into a bright night sky. They discovered Muriel's moon was now also shining down on them. The one they hadn't seen since the day they arrived in Newfoundland. Harry was finally able to hold the *Atlantic* steady again, free of major bumps. To add to their delight, the water temperature came to the party by sitting steadily at just below boiling point.

They were flying through wispy cloud, but Grieve immediately set about taking sightings from the stars that glimmered through the gaps like fairy lights in a grotto. When he took off his bulky outer gloves to manipulate his instruments and jot down his calculations, the freezing wind whipped away his silk undergloves, putting him at risk of frostbite. It wasn't so much the loss of the gloves that annoyed the reserved Scot, however, but that the cotton handkerchief tucked in his jacket pocket had frozen stiff.

Working on his charts by the dim lights of the moon and a cockpit lamp, Grieve discovered that during their long sojourn in the cloud bank, the northerly wind had pushed them some 150 miles off course. He held up a new compass bearing for Harry, who immediately swung the plane northwards, against the wind, until they were back on track, somewhere above the transatlantic shipping routes.

Meanwhile, Muriel was still full of hope as she marked off the hours, especially when she realised that morning would soon be breaking over the two fliers. She remembered that the hour of dawn was 'the one hour in twenty-four in which flying always seemed to hold the greatest charm for Harry.'[175]

As Sunday folded into Monday, the dawn's charm was probably lost on her husband, however, because the plane's radiator was still a big problem. If they had to face another cloud bank like the one they'd recently come through, Harry wondered if the engine would hold out. It was like an aching tooth he'd like to ignore but which just wouldn't go away.

Soon afterwards, the very scenario he feared loomed across the sky ahead: another massive black cloud. As before, Harry knew that if they were to stay even roughly on track and make their destination with the amount of fuel in their tanks, he had no option but to take the enemy on. He nosed the Sopwith through the outer curtain of cloud. Immediately the plane was thrown around disconcertedly inside the cloud bank, and he did a quick U-turn. This cloud bank was very different to the previous one—it was a volatile formation formed by violent upcurrents which in turn created strong downward currents on the extremities.

Again the cloud mass was too high for the *Atlantic* to leap over, so he flew back and forth, looking for a chink. Tentatively he tried skirting the main formation, hoping to hurdle a couple of the lower peaks, but the unpredictable currents tossed him backwards like bouncers in a night club. These exertions put pressure on the engine, and again the temperature moved ominously close to boiling point. What's more, the tiny spurt of steam was back.

Harry wished he knew how much of the 17 gallons of Newfoundland water was left in the cooling system, but there was no way of telling. He decided to have yet another go at clearing the filter, although it would mean plunging through the thick layer of cloud that lay beneath them. And somewhere below that cloud bank was the Atlantic Ocean.

Again he alerted Grieve, cut the engine and pushed the control stick forward. Down, down the Sopwith silently plunged once more. They were dropping fast, further and further, still in heavy cloud, when suddenly they burst through the bottom of the cloud bank, and found themselves just 1000 feet above the sea.

Harry quickly tried to restart the engine. Nothing happened. He realised that stopping the engine had also cut off the flow of the small amount of water still left in the cooling jacket. With no coolant, the engine had died.

He managed to edge the Sopwith into a glide but it was still heading rapidly towards the Atlantic. There was just one chance. Harry shouted to Grieve to man the petrol pump to force fuel into the carburettor. The big Scot quickly leaned forward to the pump in front of his seat and began thumping away as if his life depended on it. Which it did. Harry kept trying to restart the engine. Still nothing. The sea rushed towards them.

A crash into the whitecaps seemed inevitable. Harry whacked his navigator on the shoulder and yelled at him to brace himself.

A split-second later, the fuel-charged engine suddenly fired, and with some 20 feet to spare Harry gave it full throttle, the 12 cylinders kicked in, and the Sopwith zoomed upwards. Moments later, they were back at 2000 feet, shaking their heads at how close they'd been to ending their Atlantic attempt right there.

Sitting just under the cloud bank, Harry managed to keep the plane steady, but they knew they were in trouble, with only around half the distance covered. There was simply not enough water circulating around the engine to bring the temperature down. And if the pump choked completely, the engine would cook itself and shut down. *If only we could have slung a bucket overboard and picked up a few gallons as we went along*, Harry thought wryly.[176]

The two men considered their options. They'd survived the challenge of an L-shaped take-off from a sticky airstrip, battled with mountains of black cloud, encountered conflicting winds that had blown them upwards, downwards and sideways, and now they were nursing a near-boiling radiator. Already they'd been across air space no one had ever flown before, and were aware of the reserves they'd had to reach into deep within themselves to get to this point. But they also knew in their souls that while their personal limits had not yet been reached, the fabric of the machine would undoubtedly soon let them down.

'We could still fly for an hour or two with what water we had left,' Harry said. 'But to get to Ireland? No longer within the range of practical politics.'[177]

The two fliers concluded there was only one thing to do: put the Sopwith down on the sea. On the peaks and troughs of the surging Atlantic Ocean. At least that way they'd have some control over the time and place of their landing. Thanks to Grieve's navigational skills, Harry was able to jockey the *Atlantic* back over the transatlantic shipping routes. They decided to try to locate a passing ship and land the Sopwith on

Hawker had incorporated a detachable lifeboat into the Sopwith Atlantic's *design. It looked as if they might have to see if it worked if they had to land mid-ocean.*[178]

the water close by, in the hope they could be rescued before the plane went down.

With a bit of luck and a benign ocean, they might even be able to launch the stubby little lifeboat they'd tested in Newfoundland. This lake was just a bit larger, however, and promised to be somewhat rougher.

Now they stayed at low levels, criss-crossing the transatlantic 'Steamer Lane'. They came face to face with patches of cloud, blustery winds that were growing stronger, and occasional flurries of rain that peppered their open cockpit. The ocean surface was choppy, but Harry was confident he could land on it as long as the wind didn't whip it up further. He was glad they'd discarded the undercarriage. His immediate discomfort was airsickness, a curious affliction for an experienced pilot. He strove to keep the nausea at bay as they kept their eyes peeled through the haze for a vessel that might be their saviour.

Battling a north-easterly that Harry described as 'half a gale',[179] they peered through the low-slung clouds for any sign of a ship. If they could find a vessel, their plan was to put the Sopwith down on the ocean somewhere nearby, and try to stay afloat long enough for the ship to reach them. It was chancy, but the thermometer was close to boiling point.

After close on two hours, no ship had appeared out of the murk to save the souls of the two desperate airmen. Their eyes were probably strained from peering through the mist, and perhaps they sometimes thought they saw a shape only to find it was their minds conjuring up what they so much wanted to see. The wind became stronger and gustier, stirring up the sea and bumping them around. Rain squalls continually peppered the plane from all sides.

In the cockpit, the two fliers couldn't help but notice the ominous increments of the rising thermometer. And Harry was just managing to keep his airsickness at bay.

They kept peering hopefully through the mist, the Atlantic surging not far below. Then, suddenly, through the low drifting clouds, a black shape, which disappeared momentarily, then loomed larger, solidly, crashing up and down in the dark green swell. A ship. A dark-hulled ship of some sort.

His body no doubt taut from the constant criss-cross patrolling of the past two hours, Harry let out a whoop of joy. Grieve too was relieved, but Harry later said tongue-in-cheek that the Scot was 'too constrained by the tradition of the Silent Service' to express any outward emotion.[180] Then the plane was up and over the ship and they could see its name, *Mary*, with 'Danmark' stretched across the hull in bold white letters. A Danish freighter. One of the many small steamers that plied the Atlantic in the wake of Columbus, bridging the old world and the new.

Harry zoomed low over the ship, bringing the crew tumbling out on deck. Not so many months earlier, a low level pass like that over a ship mid-ocean might well have drawn hostile fire. As Harry made another pass, Grieve unholstered the stubby brass-barrelled Very pistol and unleashed three flares. The blood-red lights looped up into the clouds and then floated slowly down towards the sea, briefly bringing a pink glow to the ship's deck.

As the crew crowded the railings, Harry circled the ship once more, then headed off to put the Sopwith down. He thought the reinforced base of the fuselage increased their chances of coming in smoothly, much more so than if the Sopwith was equipped with floats, which almost certainly would have been ripped off in the heavy swell.

Harry took the aircraft about two miles ahead of the *Mary*, flying in the narrow gap between cloud and ocean where they'd spent much of the past couple of hours. Muriel might well have regarded it as one of the earth's 'thin places' where in the Celtic tradition the space between heaven and earth is especially narrow, and the sacred and the secular are said to meet.

On this occasion, her husband turned the plane into the wind for the landing, which gave him more control but also meant coming face-to-face with the choppy waves. It was in these sorts of conditions that *NC-1* and *NC-3* had come to grief in the heavy swell of the same ocean further south. The Australian took the plane lower, heading downwards now, looking for a quieter patch of water, and fighting to control the nausea rising inside him.

A sickly sun smiled briefly through the clouds as Harry lined the biplane up and began the final approach, conscious of the waves leaping up to snatch shark-like at the fuselage. If he could keep the Sopwith on an even keel for the touchdown, it was more likely to stay afloat long enough for them to launch the lifeboat; if the nose went under during the landing, so might they.

The white crests were right in front of them now, and then with a huge splash they were down, the plane bouncing across the peaks. Waves broke over the cockpit and licked hungrily at their rubber suits, and the overheated engine steamed with relief in the cooling sea. Harry throttled back and switched off. They were afloat, thanks to the skill of the pilot and the lack of an undercarriage. The Sopwith settled as best it could in the surging waves, with the part-empty fuel tanks helping keep it buoyant.

Now all they had to do was stay afloat until the Mary reached them.

CHAPTER 15

'And vanished into the blue'

Unaware of the mid-ocean drama, Muriel continued to mark off the hours Harry had been in the air. As the day went on, she began to prepare to head over to Brooklands, hopeful she would soon be reunited with her husband. There was quiet anticipation among the Sopwith representatives, military officers, and government and aero club officials gathered at Brooklands that Monday afternoon, 19 May, 1919. It promised to be a momentous occasion for the future of cross-Atlantic travel and for British aviation.

Muriel and her brother, RAF Captain Laurence Peaty, had driven over from Hook in the Sunbeam. Word had come through that the American fliers were trapped in the Azores by the weather, so *NC-4* had not yet been able to make the final hop. There was still a possibility that Harry and Grieve could claim the transatlantic gong.

Nevertheless there was also an undercurrent of anxiety about the two fliers. No messages had been received; no sightings reported. Based on the reported Sunday departure time from Newfoundland, by Muriel's 22-hour timeline the *Atlantic* should touch down at Brooklands at around 4.30pm. Unlike some others, she wasn't worried by the lack of contact with the plane because she knew Harry and Grieve weren't counting on the wireless during the flight.

But as the afternoon ticked by, concern started to grow. The Royal Air Force sent planes out from its Aldergrove base in Ireland to probe along the transatlantic route, but the pilots came back with nothing to report.

When Muriel crossed off hour number 22, and there was still no sign of the plane, the tension among the waiting group must have been palpable. They all knew that by then the Sopwith's fuel tank would be close to empty. When a full 24 hours had passed without any contact, no one had to say what that meant.

The waiting group reluctantly disbanded. Muriel and her brother returned to 'Ennadale', doubtless disconsolate on a day they should have been delighted.

The hopes of the waiting public had been dashed too. That evening the Air Ministry released an official communique. It confirmed that the pair were five hours overdue and that there had been no news of them since they'd left Newfoundland.

Once again Muriel sought solace from the pale moon, its waning silhouette sitting in the sky like a thin slice of lemon. But this time its soft light didn't seem to make the night less terrible for her.

Around 10 p.m. that evening, she was sitting quietly with her thoughts when the phone rang. It was the Admiralty: the Sopwith had come down in the North Atlantic, just 40 miles off the mouth of the Shannon River in south-west Ireland. Harry and Grieve had survived, and Royal Navy ships were racing to pick them up.

The sense of relief that Muriel must have felt rippled out across her family and friends as the news spread. Her home phone went berserk with messages of delight, and Laurence

volunteered to take the calls. By 2 a.m. he was almost incoherent from talking to exuberant callers. Muriel eventually went to bed 'thoroughly happy and at peace,'[181] but too excited to sleep. Pamela's father was coming home!

Next morning she rushed downstairs to grab the morning papers, her lifeline to Harry's progress. When she opened the first one, probably the sponsoring *Daily Mail* because it most likely would have had the biggest splash about the rescue, staring back at her in big bold letters was the headline: '**HAWKER MISSING – FALSE REPORT OF FALL IN SEA.**'[182]

Muriel was dumbstruck, 'nearly blinded,' she said, by the headline.[183] How could this be? After all the delay, all the build-up, the on-again, off-again take-offs, the welcome news the Sopwith was finally on its way, the worrying lack of contact, and then the relief to hear they'd been found and were about to be rescued. Only to be told that it was all a mistake—her husband and his navigator were still missing. What a mind-numbing, heart-wrenching letdown.

'I do not think I had ever felt so frantic and yet so completely hopeless as when I saw the fatal words,' Muriel said.

The Admiralty confirmed the newspaper report, and apologised: an official request to mariners around the Irish coast to keep a lookout for the Sopwith had been picked up and misinterpreted as a rescue message by French wireless operators, who then relayed it back across the Channel to the British. The truth was that there had still been no sightings or contact.

Newfoundland's St John's Daily Star *had three aviation stories on its front page on 19 May, 1919. Unfortunately, the news of Hawker and Grieve was premature—and wrong.*

The only reasonable conclusion was that the Sopwith had been forced down at sea because it would've been out of fuel by now. Inevitably that meant Harry and Grieve had gone down with it. Muriel struggled to accept that her husband was not coming back to her. While she was grasping at anything that might give her some solace, she remembered something Harry had said to her before he left. 'If things don't go quite right,' her husband had told her, 'never give up hope.'

There and then, Muriel decided she'd take him at his word: 'As there seemed to be two sides to the question whether he was alive or not, and no definite proof of either,' she decided she would 'cling firmly to the belief that he was alive.'[184]

'It's just a case of waiting,' the 23-year-old said.

Tommy Sopwith's wife Beatrix came over to support Muriel during the tumultuous week that followed. British and Australian newspapers were full of the story. 'Few events in recent years have so stirred the imagination of Britons as the great adventure embarked upon by Hawker and Grieve, and if existing fears are unhappily realised, it will be regarded as a national loss,' said one regional Australian paper. 'The prospect of their rescue overshadows all other topics.'[185] The consensus of public opinion and media reports was that Harry could not possibly still be alive. Laurence Peaty took leave from his RAF unit to stay with his sister.

Fellow Australian pilot Sidney Pickles publicly offered his support to Muriel, saying he refused to abandon hope for the pair. He suggested they might have been picked up by a ship without wireless or were afloat on the ocean in their little lifeboat. Shortly afterwards, Pickles himself announced that his pregnant wife had persuaded him to withdraw from his own transatlantic attempt.

A long Tuesday without news slid into a long Wednesday without news—three days without any contact or sign of the two men or their plane. Hope for their rescue began to fade, newspaper reports became increasingly gloomy, and unanswerable questions were asked: If they'd struck trouble, why was there no wireless contact from them? If they'd come down in the sea and been picked up by a passing ship, surely by now the captain would've radioed that in? All that was known was that 'Mr Hawker dropped his undercarriage before he left the land,' the Hawkers' local paper, the Surrey Comet reported (not completely accurately), 'and vanished out into the blue.'[186]

As usual whenever there's a vacuum of information, speculation and rumour abounded: the plane had come down in the sea not far off Newfoundland and so fell north of the main shipping lanes, went one story; the two men had reached Ireland, but under the force of the southerly gale battering the Irish coast that night, they were driven north and came down in the Scottish highlands; or, in a scenario that might have disturbed Muriel: they'd been 'caught in the vortex of one of those frequent cyclonic gales in mid-ocean and were dashed to their doom.'[187] The *Sydney Morning Herald* seemed to have inside information, suggesting that Harry had been lost close to the Irish coast, 'when one hundred and fifty miles was all that separated him from success.'[188]

The papers were rife with this sort of uninformed speculation, and the same 'fake news' was often relayed via wire services to papers across Britain and the world.

On the Wednesday morning after the take-off, Lord Northcliffe, owner of the *Daily Mail*, and sponsor of the transatlantic prize, paid a visit to Muriel Hawker. The press baron, only 54 but not in good health, was genuinely concerned about the loss of the two men and the welfare of their families. He expressed his condolences to Muriel and said that now virtually all hope had gone for the fliers' safe return, he intended to announce in his papers the next day that he would split £10,000 equally between the Hawker and Mackenzie Grieve families. The prize for the transatlantic crossing would remain up for grabs, however.

If he was expecting gracious acceptance of his offer, he had another thing coming. Muriel thanked him for his 'generous gesture', but said she had to refuse it because 'I cannot and will not... believe that my husband is not alive. I am sure that he will soon return to hear of the generosity of the Daily Mail and your personal kindness to me at this time.'[189] She told Northcliffe she was perplexed that the public had given up so easily on her husband and that they didn't understand the sort of person he was.

Northcliffe came away from the meeting overwhelmed by Muriel's confidence that her husband would be returned to her, describing her as 'one of the most remarkable people I have ever talked to.'[190] When the 23-year old wife and mother's response to her visitor's offer was published a few days later in *The Times*, another of the press baron's papers, it touched the heart of a nation. Northcliffe didn't withdraw his offer to her, however, and his newspapers continued to write about Harry's presumed death.

The editor of the *Surrey Comet* was also right behind Muriel, telling readers that Harry had a remarkable 'flying will' and a 'quality of dauntlessness and forcefulness and endurance combined' that doubtless would have carried him through his present trials, 'barring accidents.'[191] It was 'accidents', of course, that were one everyone's mind, but no one was sure about what might have brought about the intrepid pair's downfall.

The 72-hour period within which Harry and Grieve had to complete their transatlantic crossing in order to qualify for the prize officially expired late afternoon on Wednesday 21 May, 1919, without the plane having been sighted. In the Azores, *NC-4* had been expected to have taken off for Lisbon that day, five days after leaving Newfoundland, but it was again delayed, both by weather and engine trouble.

As the time gap since the *Atlantic's* take-off widened, public demand grew for the British Government to 'do something' to find Harry and Grieve. After all, the US Government had been throwing a sizeable portion of its resources at supporting the *Nancies'* efforts. Why couldn't Downing Street do the same? In parliament, Captain W. Elliott railed against the government for being 'lamentably remiss and desperately careless of the country's honour.'[192] This is different, replied the Navy, we don't have the resources to send out ships to search the Atlantic for a missing plane in what is ultimately a private venture. Nevertheless, The Sydney Morning Herald (which had been wrong before on this topic) subsequently reported that 'a fleet of destroyers, tugs and trawlers was scouring a huge triangular area off the west coast of Ireland.'[193]

The Sopwith Atlantic *in Newfoundland with its engine cowl removed, and the twin-bladed propeller prior to the transatlantic attempt.*[194]

Muriel herself visited the Admiralty at the end of that terrible week, but there was nothing new. The only whisper of a sighting had come from the Atlantic cable-layer, *Faraday*, whose crew reported seeing the red light of an aeroplane far overhead in the early hours of Monday 19 May. Sopwith Aviation responded that the *Atlantic* was not carrying lights, so what the crew saw might have been the red flare of the plane's exhaust. But what if it was? The question was: where were Harry and Grieve right now?

To add to the speculation, a bottle was retrieved from the sea three miles south of Narragansett Pier, Rhode Island, with a message inside: 'May 19, 1919. 1:34 a.m. – Accident to plane and I am drifting in a collapsed boat, latitude 51 degrees 36 minutes north, longitude 15 degrees 30 minutes east. HAWKER.'[195] No one took the message seriously.

Most people thought the two fliers were probably at the bottom of the ocean. The *St John's Daily Star* suggested, 'That they are alive unrescued is regarded impossible now,'[196] while on the other side of the world an Australian paper reported, 'Cables received in Sydney on Thursday afternoon state that all hope of rescuing Hawker has been abandoned.'[197]

Even the usually upbeat *Surrey Comet* acknowledged: 'As the days go by, the chances of any news being received … grow less', but said there was still a glimmer of hope because 'until the last tramp steamer that was riding the seas on the line of route taken had come to port, hope would not be abandoned that we may yet see both men alive.'[198]

In *Smith's Weekly* newspaper, Banjo Paterson, the Australian poet best known for *Waltzing Matilda* and *The Man from Snowy River*, was moved to write a lament for Harry's passing, *Hawker the standard bearer*, which ends with these lines:

Though Hawker perished, he overcame
The risks of the storm and the sea,
And his name shall be written in stars of flame,
On the topmost walls of the Temple of Fame
For the rest of the world to see.[199]

Muriel would have none of it, complaining that everyone else had either written Harry off or seemed to be putting a time limit on their hopes—'three days', 'a week'. The young woman refused to yield to the doomsayers, and when Saturday arrived, she defiantly said she could almost feel that Harry was near, and that she had only one more day to wait.

Among those who didn't share her optimism was George V, King of England, who'd been closely following Harry and Grieve's progress. On the same Saturday that Muriel was still full of hope, six days after the pair had vanished into the blue, His Majesty sent her a telegram:

THE KING, FEARING THE WORST MUST NOW BE REALISED REGARDING THE FATE OF YOUR HUSBAND, WISHES TO EXPRESS HIS DEEP SYMPATHY AND THAT OF THE QUEEN IN YOUR SUDDEN AND TRAGIC SORROW. HIS MAJESTY FEELS THAT THE NATION LOST ONE OF ITS MOST ABLE AND DARING PILOTS TO SACRIFICE HIS LIFE FOR THE FAME AND HONOUR OF BRITISH FLYING.[200]

A lesser person might've crumpled when they read those words from the monarch of the land, but Muriel remained unruffled. She said that neither the king's telegram nor Northcliffe's generous offer to make provision for herself and Pamela had changed her conviction that Harry would turn up 'safe and sound'.

In the whole world, it might have been only Muriel Hawker (and perhaps the editor of the *Surrey Comet*) who continued to believe that.

CHAPTER 16

Three magic letters

On Sunday morning 25 May 1919, a week after Harry and Grieve's take-off, Muriel knelt in prayer in St Paul's Church, Hook. This was not the church they were married in, but it was just across the road from 'Ennadale'. It was a warm sunny morning, one that might have encouraged the congregation to think along with the poet Browning that 'God's in his heaven, all's right with the world,'[201] were it not for the two men's disappearance hanging over them.

Earlier that morning Muriel had once again been incensed by what she saw as the pessimism of the British press, which seemed unanimous in reporting that all hope of rescue had passed. 'How can they say "all hope",' she demanded, 'when they don't know what everyone's hopes are?'[202]

The parishioners at St Paul's were offering special prayers that morning for the safe return of Harry Hawker and Mackenzie Grieve. As if to mock them, on the other side of the world the same day the Perth *Sunday Times* reported: 'Any hope of rescue seems to have been abandoned. He is too long overdue to be alive.'[203] In her reply to Lord Northcliffe and her subsequent disdain for the consensus view about her husband's fate, however, Muriel had shown faith in powers and circumstances beyond normal human comprehension. Genuinely uplifted by the church service, afterwards she hurried back across the road, convinced that good news had come while she'd been away. She quickly discovered that nothing had changed.

This was probably the crunch point for Muriel Hawker. All week she'd been strong, arguing against the naysayers, espousing her unrelenting belief in her husband's safe return, rejecting any suggestion that this was an impossible pipe dream. Now, having built up to the point where she had nominated this day as the one her husband would be returned to her, she'd convinced herself that the glow she felt at the church service would be converted into the reality of his reappearance, only to find her hopes dashed again. Was this the time when she would finally yield to admitting that Harry was gone for good?

At the other end of the country, the two men on duty at the Lloyds Coastguard Station on the Butt of Lewis were delighted that the sunshine that was blessing London had extended its warm beams into the far north of Scotland. This remote headland had freezing winters, was officially the windiest place in Britain, and for 300 days a year rain lashed its rugged coastline. Not exactly a tourist paradise.

But today the swell on the often aggressive Atlantic Ocean would hardly have disturbed a floating seagull. Chief Officer William Ingham and Officer George Harding were expecting a quiet shift. No one should need rescuing today.

They were therefore surprised to hear the shriek of a ship's siren, and when they went outside there was a cargo boat steaming towards them, much closer inshore than freighters on the North American-Scandinavian run usually were.

The old freighter was puffing out white smoke and had a single black-topped funnel circled with a light band of grey. There was a sturdy mast fore and aft with davits for loading and unloading cargo. The Coastguard officers could see the ship's name, *Mary*, picked out in white along its blackened rust-streaked hull, and below that, 'Danmark', its country of origin. They recognised it as a solid coal-powered cargo ship, one of the many that had resumed the transatlantic run now that the war was over.

So what brought this old freighter to this windswept headland in the Outer Hebrides on such a sunny Sunday morning?

The ship slowed, and as they watched, signal flags began to slide up its mast. The first one spelled out *M-A-R-Y*, the freighter's name. Then followed the international signal for 'Communicate by wire', indicating to the watchers that the message to follow was important and needed to be sent posthaste to the authorities. Now the ship would really would have had the two officers' attention, and they doubtless watched eagerly as the next flags went up. It was another international signal: 'Survivors on board.'

This message probably puzzled the two men on the shore. Survivors? From where? Another ship? Castaways?

This flag was followed by the international code to indicate that words would follow, spelled out in single letters, three at a time. One could only imagine what went through the officers' minds as they watched to see what would come next, like anxious Scrabble players. Then the first three letters slid up the mast: *S-O-P*. The two men might well have looked at each other, wondering what was to follow.

What came next was a longer word, but its first three letters, *A-E-R*, probably gave it away before the rest of the word followed: *A-E-R-O-P-L-A-N-E*.

S-O-P A-E-R-O-P-L-A-N-E could mean only one thing: *Sopwith aeroplane*. And if the steamer had survivors on board, it must surely be Harry Hawker and McKenzie Grieve.

The *Mary* must be carrying the two men from the missing plane! But what were they doing way up here?

Remote Butt of Lewis lighthouse, north-west Scotland, near the Coastguard Station where the Mary's captain signalled the rescue of Hawker and Grieve, 25 May 1919.[204]

Ingham and Harding were still getting over their surprise when they saw black smoke start to belch from the *Mary's* funnel, and the ship began to turn away, back towards its original path. They were able to see the name of its home port, 'Esbjorg', stencilled in white on its retreating stern as they rushed to put up their own flags before the freighter moved out of range. When their first signal started to rise, they saw the ship slow, then turn back towards the shore.

The Coastguards' flags asked just one question: *I-S I-T H-A-W-K-E-R?*

It probably seemed like an eternity before three magic letters went up the slowly moving *Mary's* mast: *Y-E-S*. Minutes later Chief Officer Ingham was telegraphing the news urgently to Lloyds head office in London. Soon the world would know.

The *Mary*, meanwhile, turned once more and headed out to sea with the two survivors still on board, the captain apparently anxious to reach his destination port in Denmark.

One might imagine that Muriel Hawker was feeling flat, even embarrassed, after her euphoria earlier that Sunday morning. She'd been so sure that good news awaited her, and just the day before had declared she was 'perfectly sure' she had only one more day to wait. Now she had to think about her future and that of seven-month old Pamela. Did Harry still figure in that picture?

Whatever Muriel's thinking, when the phone rang after she had returned from St Paul's that morning she let someone else answer it. Perhaps she'd become so used to disappointment she no longer wanted to pick it up. This time, however, the phone call was for her. It was someone from the *Daily Mirror*, a competitor to Northcliffe's *Daily Mail*, who insisted on speaking only to Mrs Hawker. Muriel was doubtless used to reporters' questions by now, and probably steeled herself for the inevitable queries about how she was coping, did she still believe, etc.

When she took the instrument, she discovered that it was not a reporter trying to fill a column, but the *editor* of the *Daily Mirror*. He told her he had some news for her. 'Your husband is alive,' he said. 'He and Grieve were picked up mid-Atlantic by a Danish freighter, the *Mary*, and the captain signalled the rescue to a Coastguard station in Scotland just a couple of hours ago.' The ship had no radio, he said, so couldn't get a message through until now, a week after their take-off.

And this time, he assured her, the report was true.

True to his calling, in exchange for this astonishing piece of information, the editor asked Muriel if the paper could have an exclusive interview with her. When asked about it later, Harry's wife said she couldn't remember what she'd said in response: 'Probably nothing—but I felt that anyone could do what they liked then.'[205]

Muriel was understandably ecstatic, and rushed out the front door to tack up a simple message on the gate of 'Ennadale': 'Mr Hawker has been found. He was on the boat *Mary*, bound for Denmark.' Apart from the brief details the *Daily Mirror* editor had given her, she didn't know much more. She'd have to wait until Harry returned to get the full story.

Although she constantly claimed to have been expecting it, when news of Harry's rescue came Muriel's spirits were surely at their lowest, when the hope that had risen inside her earlier that morning in church had once more been crushed, when the newspapers were consistently pronouncing her husband dead after a week of no contact and no sightings, when just the day before the King had sent her a message of condolence.

Then suddenly, the tomb was open, the stone rolled away. The premonition she'd had that morning in St Paul's church turned out to be true. It had just been a bit later in coming than she expected.

206

Now she and Laurence jumped in the Sunbeam and headed off to spread the good news. They sped around to the Sigrists' riverside home, where Muriel had spent the day before, and discovered the family had already heard of the rescue. But Fred bounded down the front steps as if he didn't know why she was there: 'What can I do for you?' he asked disingenuously.

Muriel's face was no doubt glowing with relief after a week of uncertainty. 'Oh, jump in,' she said with a laugh, pointing at the river.

And Fred did. Straight into the Thames, clothes and all. Then he proceeded to swim up and down, talking animatedly but incoherently to anyone who would listen. The excitement was contagious, and soon a knot of people had gathered at the Sigrists for a celebratory drink.

Shortly afterwards, Muriel returned home to find 'Ennadale' overrun with reporters. The *Daily Mirror* correspondent was still hopeful of an exclusive interview, but the other reporters insisted they wanted to sit in. In the end, there was no actual interview, just questions and answers.

Asked why she had so much faith her husband would be returned to her, Muriel said, 'I just felt it. I had felt it all the week. Other people had their tails down, but I hadn't.'

As for her 'lucky Sunday': 'It was on a Sunday my husband made his highest flight. It was a Sunday that he started from Newfoundland, and lots of lucky little things, too domestic to be worth telling, have happened to me on a Sunday. But this, of course, is my luckiest Sunday of all!'[208]

A happy Muriel holding baby Pamela after hearing news of her husband's rescue.[207]

Once the reporters had rushed off to file their stories, a spontaneous party erupted in the Hawker household. Muriel worried she didn't have enough to feed everyone, but no one seemed to care what they ate or drank, just as long as they could celebrate. The *Surrey Comet* tacked up notices around the community, and the whole district came alive as the news spread. Local residents cheered when they saw the signs, and slapped one another on the back and hugged each other, as if it was a relative of theirs who'd been saved.

A happy crowd of locals gathered noisily outside 'Ennadale', a friendly police sergeant on hand to discourage them from invading the house to share their joy with Muriel. Instead, they resorted to three hearty cheers: one for Harry, one for the

Danish steamer, and one for Mrs Hawker 'for being as plucky as her husband.'[209]

That evening, plucky Mrs Hawker went back across the road to the church that had given her such a good feeling earlier that day, this time with her sister Evelyn, for a thanksgiving service, led by the Reverend Wood. It was an upbeat occasion, and thanks were given for the 'preservation from the perils of air and deep of Harry Hawker.'

The Reverend Wood took for his sermon theme the parable of the prodigal son: 'For this my son was dead, and was alive again; he was lost and was found.'[210]

After the service, Muriel arrived home to discover that friends had organised dinner at a nearby hotel. A happy convoy of cars sets off, led by Muriel driving the Sunbeam, an Australian flag draped over its bonnet. As they charged down Putney Hill in the summer twilight, a policeman stepped out and waved them to the side of the road—it was a speed trap.

Unlike her husband when confronted by Constable Peverill in Melbourne many years before, Muriel didn't try to run the officer down. She obediently pulled over. When the sergeant in charge saw the flag and recognised the car, however, he waved them on. 'I'd feel like more than a few drinks myself if I was in your place,' he said to Muriel.

She enjoyed the celebratory dinner with friends and family, but had hardly had a minute to herself since the morning phone call from the *Daily Mirror*. What Muriel really wanted was to be reunited with Harry, who was at that moment ensconced on a Royal Navy ship in Scotland.

180 · A great and restless spirit

Hawker and Mackenzie Grieve were transferred from the Mary *to HMS* Woolston *off Scotland's north coast May 1919.*[211]

Earlier criticised for sitting on its hands, when the Navy heard that Harry and Grieve were on the *Mary* and heading for Denmark, they sent out one of their fast destroyers, HMS *Woolston*, from the Royal Naval fleet based at Scapa Flow, Orkney. It was tasked with intercepting the Danish ship. The Navy wasn't going to miss this opportunity, and the much faster *Woolston* caught up with the *Mary* off Loch Eriboll, a picturesque sea loch on Scotland's north-west coast. Harry and Grieve said farewell to the captain and crew who'd looked after them for six days, and transferred to the destroyer, which sped them to Scapa Flow.

That night they slept aboard HMS *Revenge*, as guests of Vice-Admiral Sidney Fremantle. It was exactly one week since they'd left Newfoundland.

When Muriel reached home later that evening, there was a message for her from Harry, sent from HMS *Revenge*. It was the first communication she'd had directly from him since he'd let her knew on 29 March he'd arrived safely in Newfoundland.

'All well; making for home,' the cablegram said. It was the sort of message Muriel might have hoped for all week.

In his sermon earlier in the evening, Reverend Wood had said that the stoicism of Muriel Hawker had come down to faith, hope and love: 'Faith in a man and in his power to fight and conquer, hope almost in the face of despair that joy might yet issue forth from sorrow and peace from sadness—love was the source of both.'[212]

Muriel might well have said, 'Amen' to that.

CHAPTER 17

'The sweetest and most wonderful thing'

Among the claims to fame of Grantham, a large market town in the county of Lincolnshire, in central-east England, is its mention in the Domesday Book. Apple-watcher/scientist Isaac Newton went to school there, and it was also the birthplace of the first female British Prime Minister, Margaret Thatcher. On Tuesday 27 May, 1919, Harry and Muriel Hawker were interested in the town, however, only because it was a major junction on the Edinburgh to London railway line. They were going to make their own history by being reunited there as soon as Harry's train from Scotland pulled in.

This would be the first time they'd seen each other in two months, after a week that had been highly traumatic for both of them—Harry picked up from a choppy sea mid-Atlantic and sitting incommunicado on a sluggish cargo ship; Muriel in high suspense, fighting the sceptics, buoyed by faith.

Harry was on the train because, after overnighting on HMS *Revenge*, he and Grieve had been ferried across to Thurso. It was there, at the northern tip of the mainland, that their rail trip to London began Tuesday morning. The mayor of Thurso showed them clippings of their obituaries in British newspapers, and long-time bachelor Grieve was tickled by a photo of a woman a newspaper claimed was his wife.

As their train headed south, the rescued fliers discovered that the nation had responded to their unexpected and seemingly miraculous return with pandemonium. The editor of *Flight* magazine said, 'It is no exaggeration to say that a thrill of relief passed over all the world.'[213]

At a lunch-time stop at Inverness, Harry protested to the large audience: 'I cannot help feeling in a sort of way that I am here under false pretences insofar as I am not so good as people think I am. The risk I ran was not so great as people think it was.'[214]

But the adulating crowds would have none of it. Thousands lined the route, cheering as the train whistled past villages, towns, and sidings. Bagpipers saluted them from isolated station platforms, and well-wishers tossed so many bouquets that the scent of Lily of the Valley hung heavily in the fliers' carriage. Occasionally a plane circled overhead to add its salute to the excitement of the welcome. Newspapers tried to outdo each other in the exuberance of their headlines.

When the train pulled into Edinburgh station, the waiting crowd of Scots surprised the small police contingent by rushing through the ticket barriers and grabbing Harry as soon as the train ground to a halt. They hoisted him on their shoulders and carted him off to breakfast. A local reporter described Harry as 'the very picture of health, bright and youthful,' whereas the slightly older Grieve looked 'a bit tired and strained.' Further along the track, the crowd at York included an enthusiastic bunch of Australian soldiers, and the station-master had to force his way through to deliver a fistful of telegrams. One of the messages was from the King, inviting the pair to Buckingham Palace.

A short stopover at Newcastle gave Harry the opportunity to say a few words he'd probably been formulating in his head as the train had thundered southwards. 'I am convinced that the public display of appreciation more than repays me for anything I had gone through,' he said, 'and convinces me that the attempt to cross the Atlantic was well worthwhile.'[215]

When the *Atlantic* disappeared, there was criticism of the decision to take off from Newfoundland in what even the Reverend Wood at St Paul's Church called 'unpropitious conditions.' But Harry counter-attacked: 'I have nothing to say about the criticisms of those who think the attempt under the conditions then prevailing was foolhardy, save to say that I do not regret anything I have done, and that under similar circumstances I should act in the same way.'

And it seemed that ultimately, as Muriel had known all along, it was national pride that finally triggered the take-off, the weather relegated to second place: 'The attempt... had to be made, for there was a danger of the honour of being first across the Atlantic being wrested from the old country,' he continued. 'Someone else might succeed where I failed, but I hope that whoever does succeed, the honour will rest with Britain.'

The usually reticent Grieve was just as adamant: 'It was a fine stunt, well worth attempting, and, like Hawker, I have no regrets.'

Both men claimed they were up for the attempt again if the opportunity was still there. They were probably surprised to learn that in the week they'd been away Raynham hadn't got off the ground, and the Americans had still not made the final leap to Europe, but had been trapped in the Azores. Nor had the other contenders in Newfoundland yet made their move.

The first Atlantic crossing was still up for grabs by a British or US crew.

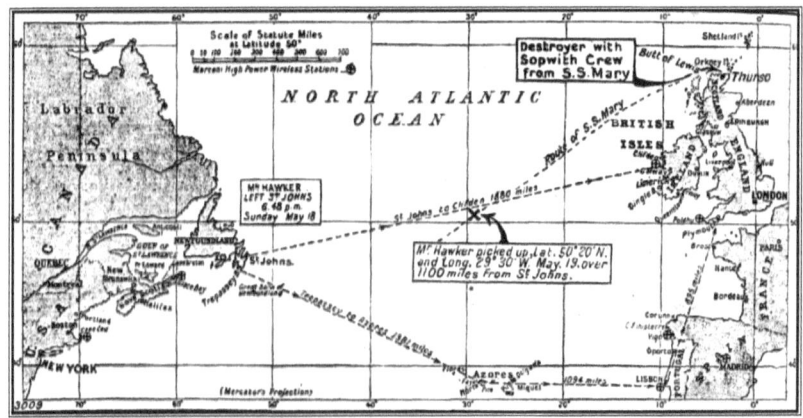

Rough map from Flight *magazine showing the approximate point at which Hawker and Grieve were picked up by the* Mary *mid-ocean 19 May 1919, the day after their take-off from Newfoundland.*[216]

While Harry was contending with massive crowds on his southward rail journey, Muriel had become a celebrity in her own right in London. George V had already sent her a second telegram: 'THE KING REJOICES WITH YOU AND THE NATION ON THE HAPPY RESCUE OF YOUR GALLANT HUSBAND. HE TRUSTS THAT HE MAY BE LONG SPARED TO YOU.'[217]

The monarch's mother, Queen Alexandra, who was born in Denmark, added a personal note to her message: 'I REJOICE THAT A DANISH SHIP RESCUED HIS PRECIOUS LIFE.'

On the Monday that Harry and Grieve boarded the train, Muriel was guest of honour at the premiere of a movie in London that documented Harry and Grieve's preparation and take-off for the transatlantic flight. On her way in the Sunbeam to the Majestic Theatre, Clapham, a short drive from Hook, Muriel found the streets unexpectedly crowded with cars and people. She surmised there'd been some major incident, perhaps a fire, that had brought such gridlock. When she finally reached the cinema, she was astonished to discover that the 'major incident' was Muriel Hawker—the crowds were there to see her.

'I could not believe that they had all come to see us, but it seemed they had,' she said, 'and I am afraid they must had been very disappointed.'

It must have been strange for Muriel to see her husband on the screen that day, when she'd been married to him for 18 months but hadn't seen him in person for eight nerve-wracking weeks. No doubt she was interested in seeing the foggy and snowy island where he was forced to remain for considerably longer than expected, and the rudimentary airstrip must have been an eye-opener in contrast to the well-established Brooklands site. But what thoughts might have been going through her head as she watched the *Atlantic* lift off and head over Signal Hill, to vanish out into the blue, triggering a whole week of anxiety for her, and morbid speculation for the world?

As Harry and Grieve headed south on the Tuesday after they'd left the *Mary*, Muriel was a passenger in Tommy and Beatrix Sopwith's car, sprinting up the Great North Road on the 100-mile trip to Grantham. No doubt she was looking forward to the reunion with her husband—but what was Harry feeling about coming back to his wife without having accomplished the task he'd asked her blessing for?

In his speech at Newcastle he'd paid tribute to her. 'I have been loyally backed up by my wife; and when a man embarks on an adventure of this kind the spirit in which it is taken by his wife counts for a great deal,' he said. 'She has been splendid through it all, and what credit there is for what has been achieved is hers as much as mine.'

Harry was used to winning—breaking aviation records, designing world-beating aircraft, being awarded an MBE, even being first to the Newfoundland starting post for the transatlantic race. How did the much-publicised failure sit with them both?

Would they both agree on 'what has been achieved'? Did Muriel wonder again whether it was all worth it?

When the Sopwiths delivered Muriel to the railway station at Grantham, hundreds of locals and reporters had already gathered. In an effort to give the couple a moment of privacy, the Grantham stationmaster had relinquished his office for the occasion. He escorted Muriel into the little room and headed off to await the train's arrival. It was running 30 minutes late, delayed by the shenanigans of the crowds at platforms along the way.

Hawker and Muriel reunited, Grantham Railway Station, England, 27 May 1919, Mackenzie Grieve on left, Tommy Sopwith at rear.[218]

It's hard to imagine that Muriel sat down, crossed her legs and possessed her soul in patience this time. More likely she was on her feet, aware of the hubbub on the platform outside the door. Doubtless she could hear the noise level rising as the train chuffed into the station and stopped with a loud hiss of steam that was likely drowned out by the roar of the crowd. She could probably hear sounds of pushing and shoving outside as the police and railway officials tried to make a path for Harry through the noisy throng.

Next moment, said Muriel, 'Harry literally fell into the little room where I was waiting.'[219] She had not seen him since the teary farewell at Euston Station on 20 March, over two months earlier.

So after all the build-up, all the trauma of the flight itself, all the ensuing hype, how did Harry react when he was reunited with his wife in the little station-master's office in Grantham? Extraordinarily, according to his wife: 'He just said the sweetest and most wonderful thing I could ever hear'—although she didn't say exactly what that was. He also told her not to cry, but that was probably a battle lost.

They didn't have much more time before the mass of cheerful humanity clamouring at the door burst in. The pair turned to face a wall of cameras, flashbulbs popping like fireworks, photographers desperate for images of the happy couple to splash on the front pages of newspapers across the world. Once the chaos settled, the pair were helped to make their way to the carriage Harry and Grieve had occupied from Edinburgh. As the train headed south again, a single plane took to the air above them, a lone escort for the trip, all the way to London.

CHAPTER 18

Wild about Harry

The crowd began to gather at Kings Cross Station about two hours before the train was due. In order to maintain some dignity for the Mayoral welcome, barricades were erected on the arrival platform. Entry was restricted to ticket-holders, which included wounded English soldiers. The lucky ones with tickets began to fill the waiting area, and happy crowds started to mass outside the barriers. They filled the huge space below the station's opaque arched roof with a swelling level of enthusiastic noise that rivalled the pandemonium of a major football stadium at match time. Tens of thousands more lined the route the two 'heroes' would take to the Royal Aero Club, several blocks away. It was claimed that window seats along the route were selling for 10 to 20 guineas apiece.[220]

As train arrival time drew near, a large contingent of Australian soldiers in uniform marched up, distinctive in their felt slouch hats, and came to a disciplined halt on the roadway beside the station. Police on duty might well have looked askance at them, but the new arrivals, curiously led by a woman and a soldier brandishing an Australian flag, assured those nearby that their role in the reception was 'quite informal' and that they were 'just men who happened to be on leave.'[221]

These troops 'happened to be on leave' mostly because there was a lack of shipping to get them back to Australia,[222] so they were at a loose end. Given Australian soldiers' reputation for having a good time when out of the ranks, bystanders might reasonably have been a little wary of their intentions on this celebratory occasion. The Australian Prime Minister, Billy Hughes, had been based in Britain for over a year, from where he'd been participating in the treaty talks at Versailles.

On learning of Hawker and Grieve's rescue, Hughes had said: 'The flight originated as a test of the capacity of an aeroplane to cross a great space in a new way, but the world sees it as a test of men. Technically, the aeroplane has to be yet proved, but Hawker's attempt proved the men.'[223] It was a perspicacious comment from the PM.

By the time the train pulled in to Kings Cross Station, an estimated crowd of 20,000 had assembled to welcome Harry and Grieve, enough to populate a large Australian country town. The noise rose to a crescendo as the engine shrugged to a steaming halt. The crowd was so thick that railway officials had trouble opening the carriage doors, while on the platform the reception party was hard-pressed to preserve a space for themselves.

From then on, chaos reigned, as Muriel herself recalled: 'As the train drew up at the platform, part of the enormous crowd surged into our compartment. How they knew which one was hard to tell. The civic reception party who were on the platform to give official welcome to the heroes were completely shattered, and I believe it must had been wonderful tactics which allowed the official Mace-bearer to retain the mace in the face of 300 or so Australian soldiers who thought they needed it.'[225]

There was just time for a quick welcome from the official party before the Diggers hustled Harry and Grieve to the

The massive London crowd presses in as Mackenzie Grieve in an Australian slouch hat leans forward over Hawker's shoulder while they sit atop what is probably Harry's Sunbeam car borne aloft, 27 May 1919.[224]

Hawkers' Sunbeam. They'd tied ropes to the car so they could pull it through the streets as part of a procession of vehicles heading to the nearby Aero Club. There were just too many spectators, however, so the high-spirited troops lifted the car on to their shoulders (Muriel reckoned there must had been 40 of them), which was some feat given its size and weight. It seems likely that Grieve, who'd weathered many a rough crossing, sought alternative transport at this point. Other Australian troops formed ad hoc barriers to restrain the surging cheering crowds and help stop people from being trampled underfoot.

Meanwhile, Harry was having a precarious ride in the Sunbeam, and was also worried about damage to the car. So he abandoned his shoulder-borne chariot, crawling across the backs of the soldiers like a sheep dog scrambling over a flock.

After abandoning his lofted Sunbeam car in the crowd, Hawker used a different sort of horsepower to reach the official welcome dinner in London on 27 May 1919.[226]

In the midst of the crowd he came upon a mounted policeman, who happily motioned to him to jump up in front of him on the horse. So a cheerful Harry rode along as a passenger, waving happily to the crowd like a Royal personage, and probably still coming to grips with the huge numbers that were there to greet them. After a short while, the bobby relinquished his horse entirely to the Australian, and Harry continued along in the procession through the cheering masses to the Aero Club on horseback, like a victorious general.

Next day the Times reported that the 'gentle force of organisation' that the Australian troops brought to bear was 'perhaps a trifle irregular and unconventional, but had a great deal to do with preventing any very serious accident to one of the biggest, most excited and ardent, but one of the best-tempered throngs that had ever gathered in a London railway station.'[227] The official welcoming party might have had other views, of course.

Whether through luck or good spectator control, Grieve and Muriel ended up at the Aero Club with Harry, along with Beatrix and Tommy Sopwith and other club members, who were no doubt similarly overwhelmed by the size and exuberance of the crowd. When the inevitable spate of speeches and responses was over, and the Hawkers try to leave, they discovered that the front entrance was blocked by revellers still wanting to catch a glimpse of their heroes, particularly Harry. Sopwith went out on a second floor balcony and appealed to the masses below to clear a path for the Australian pilot, but his words were lost in the good-natured mayhem.

Eventually Harry and Muriel, having said goodbye to Grieve, escaped through a side door. Ten mounted policemen then closely shepherded the Sunbeam (now without its ropes) through the crowd until the car had gathered enough momentum to deter larrikins from jumping on board.

The size of the welcoming crowd in London on 27 May 1919 can be gauged by this photo in the New York Tribune *afterwards. Left inset is Muriel with Pamela.*[228]

ocean.[178]

For the first time in two months, Harry was back at the wheel of the family's home-built car. He and Muriel sped through the fading light to a concert at the Sopwith works at Ham, south-west of London, where he'd promised to make an appearance. Many of these employees would've been involved with the design, development and delivery of the Sopwith *Atlantic* six months earlier. The presumed loss of both plane and crew would've hit them hard. So the miraculous reappearance of Harry was of special significance to them.

When their chief test pilot drove up in his well-known Sunbeam in the middle of the concert at about 9 p.m., the singer on stage stopped mid-note, the pianist broke into *See the conquering hero comes*, and the audience of 800 workers and their families erupted around him. It took some time for them to settle down for the welcome and to listen with cheers to Harry's thanks.

Afterwards, Sopwith staff re-attached ropes to the Sunbeam and insisted on pulling it at a run about two miles to a restaurant at Kingston-on-Thames, where Tommy and Beatrix Sopwith had organised a late supper. Once again Harry had to run a gauntlet of well-wishers keen to shake his hand, but when he reached the restaurant entrance, he was still smiling.

'This is the end of a perfect day,' he said.[229]

It was not quite the end, however, as Muriel had promised the residents of Hook that they'd have a chance to welcome their local hero home. Even though it was almost midnight by the time the Hawkers arrived in the village, it seemed the whole population, boosted by a swag of outsiders, was there to hold her to her pledge. As the car turned into the front gate, fireworks lit up in the shape of 'Welcome Home!' and a long and spectacular fireworks display followed. The local newspaper reported next day that the whole hamlet shook with the ferocity of the cheers for Harry and his wife.

Muriel couldn't get over the crowd's unending enthusiasm: 'It must be a very strange and wonderful experience, even although it lasts but a few days, to be continually the centre of a demonstrative crowd. Crowds waiting to see you leave your house; more crowds waiting at your destination. It could only be the very few who remain unspoiled by such ovations.'[230]

Harry had been up since the early hours, and travelling all day. No doubt exhausted, he nevertheless made another short speech to thank the crowd and the organisers of the fireworks. Still the crowd didn't disperse, and to their delight, Harry, Muriel and Pamela stood and waved from a lighted bedroom window before literally drawing a curtain on the day. 'Thus ended one of the most notable welcomes ever accorded to a hero in this country,' the *Surrey Comet* said the next day.[231]

A few days after their return, King George V awarded Hawker and Mackenzie Grieve the Air Force Cross.[232]

The British public, it seemed, didn't care that Harry and Grieve hadn't made the first transatlantic flight; it was the pair's return from the grave that overwhelmed a war-sick population and had them spilling on to the streets in their tens of thousands. This was not just a 'lucky rescue' story, but one of hope for a people ground down by four years of war that at times seemed unwinnable.

Harry's reappearance after nearly a week was proof that miracles do happen, that in even the deepest ponds of dark despair bubbles of light pop to the surface. It was almost as if the British public were seeking redemption for their almost unanimous lack of belief that the two men would ever be found alive.

Three days after their return to London and eleven days after they'd left Newfoundland, King George V awarded Harry George Hawker and Kenneth Mackenzie Grieve the Air Force Cross.

CHAPTER 19

A restless quest

On the morning of Tuesday 27 May, the day that Harry and Grieve's train was steaming towards a jubilant reception in London, Lieutenant-Commander 'Putty' Read and the crew of *NC-4* had set off for Portugal from the Azores. US warships again shadowed the floatplane's journey.

A big crowd gathered at the Lisbon waterfront, attracted by the publicity the US Navy was pumping out to keep the local Portuguese in touch with the aircraft's progress. Just after 8 o'clock that evening, the USS Rochester sounded its whistle to alert the city to the big seaplane's arrival overhead, and immediately the harbour was alive with the shriek of ships' horns and the wail of sirens. Soon afterwards, *NC-4* touched down on the Tagus River to a colourful and noisy welcome, including a 21-gun salute from the USS Rochester. The Americans had won the race to be first to fly the Atlantic. It was 11 days since *NC-4* had left Newfoundland; Hawker and Grieve had been hoping to complete the crossing inside 22 hours.

Harry respected the *NC-4*'s achievement, but he'd already told the captain of the Mary that he wouldn't have wanted the sort of support the American fliers had because it would devalue the significance of the crossing.[234] At a *Daily Mail* dinner in London two days after the Americans' feat, he said:

The US Navy's NC-4 *amphibian on its way to Lisbon in May 1919 to become the first aircraft to cross the Atlantic. It was the* Nancies' *take-off from Newfoundland that spurred Hawker into action.*[233]

I think that if we had ships every twenty yards apart you people would have looked on it as a joke and not a serious attempt to fly the Atlantic. If you are going to fly the Atlantic you have to weigh it up in your mind whether it is a serious proposition or a do-or-die effort... If you put a ship every fifty miles apart it only shows that you have no faith in your motor or in your machine.[235]

Perhaps not unexpectedly, the national pride at stake in the US and Britain was reflected in the responses of their respective news media to the American achievement. One US newspaper trumpeted it as 'The great Yankee triumph', and the Washington Evening Star proclaimed that 'American ability, American ingenuity, American thoroughness, American nerve have again come into their own.'[236] In Britain, many thought the extent of the assistance provided was excessive, and that the real challenge was to complete the journey non-stop.

The editor of *Flight* magazine summed up the British attitude to the American effort: 'Stripped of its glamour of being the first time an aircraft has crossed the Atlantic, the circumstances of the flight are such as to make it rather less wonderful than the simple record would be. As a matter of fact, the flight has nothing much of the spectacular about it—it was rather a triumph of organisation than anything else.'

Americans were bemused by the attention given to Hawker and Grieve for a flight they didn't finish, compared to their US Navy pilots' considerable achievement in bridging the new world and the old, even if it was in two hops and with a support network.

Despite their reservations about the Americans' transatlantic crossing, the British laid on a spectacular official welcome when *NC-4* flew into Plymouth, England, on Saturday 31 May. It was escorted by three flying boats. The Americans' arrival in the English city was symbolic—it completed a loop that had begun 299 years before, when the Pilgrim Fathers set sail from the south coast port and crossed the Atlantic in the Mayflower to settle in the New World. When they arrived in November 1620 in the north-east of the land that would become the United States of America, they called their new settlement 'Plymouth'.

At the same dinner Harry where had spoken, the Air Ministry's Major-General Seely said that members of the newly formed Royal Air Force

> know the appalling strain of waiting, waiting, waiting, until the weather gets ready, to do this long flight, and many a man with the necessary grit and determination has failed after waiting. We all know Mr. Hawker and Commander Grieve did not fail in this way, and this is the greatest compliment I can pay.[238]

Lt-Commander Read (second left) and the crew of NC-4 *with the Mayor of Plymouth, England, May 1919. They are standing on the 'Mayflower' stone, from which the Pilgrim Fathers embarked for the New World in 1620.*[237]

In the absence of Lord Northcliffe, who was ill, Seely presented Harry and Grieve with a £5000 consolation prize from the Daily Mail. During the general bonhomie afterwards, Harry left the cheque lying on the table and had to be reminded to take it with him.

In the 'large and distinguished company' at the dinner, Muriel was the only woman. She was also present at a Royal Aero Club luncheon the next day, when Tommy Sopwith told his fellow diners that if Harry and Grieve had managed to achieve the crossing, they'd agreed they would divide the prize 70/30 between pilot and navigator. With the consolation prize, however, Harry had insisted they split the award 50/50, because they'd equally shared the risks.

The tongue-in-cheek menu for the Aero Club meal comprised:

Barquettes Hawker

Supreme de Sole Atlantique

Poulet Reine Sopwith

Salade Southern Cross

Timbale de Fraises Northcliffe

Gateau Danois.[239]

As if street parades, fireworks and distinguished dinners were not enough, on the weekend of Saturday 31 May and Sunday 1 June, there was a grand gathering at Hendon Aerodrome of pilots and planes from all over the country. This was also partly a celebration of the Americans' achievement, but also a special attraction at the event was a flying display by Harry himself. What's more, there was an open auction for a joyride with the famous pilot. The hero of the hour arrived on Saturday in a Sopwith Gnu, a two-seater biplane with registration K.101 (later G-EACZ) painted on the side, and Muriel as passenger.

Daisy King bid 60 guineas for a flight in this Sopwith Gnu with Harry Hawker at Hendon on 31 May 1919.[240]

Miss Daisy King made the highest bid at the auction, 60 guineas (£3,300 today), and was rewarded with the first joy flight with Harry in K.101. During the afternoon, he took up several other bid-winners, and then put on his own display in his Sopwith Scooter, K-135. Flight magazine reported that 'his rolls particularly were very neat, the machine finishing the roll horizontal and right way up with the greatest precision.'[241]

Harry Hawker, it seemed, was back in control in the air.

On Sunday he came face-to-face with Lieutenant-Commander Read, the man who beat him across the Atlantic. Initially Harry was part of the official party that greeted the American fliers when they arrived by train from Plymouth to an enthusiastic welcome at Paddington station. He then drove Read in the Sunbeam to a Royal Aero Club luncheon. Later that day Harry came down from his aerial acrobatics at Hendon when the crew of *NC-4* arrived at the airfield by car.

Just two weeks after his Newfoundland take-off and disappearance, at Hendon Hawker met US Navy Commander 'Putty' Read, who led the team that made the first air crossing of the Atlantic in the NC-4 *amphibian.*[243]

The two Atlantic pilots were photographed shaking hands, with the caption, 'Mr Hawker, at Hendon, congratulating Commander Read on his Atlantic flight in the *NC-4*.'[242] Presumably there was no mention of Harry's earlier criticism that the US Navy's effort was not a serious attempt.

Muriel seemed happy enough to accompany Harry to these celebratory events, but the intensity of the past week was getting to them both, and they decided to take a break from London. They headed to a seaside village in the county of Norfolk, 150 miles north-east of the English capital. This was accessible for them by car, but small and quiet enough that it was unlikely anyone would recognise Harry.

The balmy weather was holding, and June was officially the first month of summer, so even in England they could reasonably expect more of the same. They purposely didn't take the Sunbeam, thinking it would be too conspicuous. It seems they also left Pamela with the nanny. Their subterfuge seemed to work—they enjoyed a private evening together, and next morning a long walk along the seashore.

As they came back to the village for lunch, however, heads started to turn, and tongues started to wag. A small child made the first move, approaching Harry with an autograph book. The word spread quickly, a trickle became a stream, and by evening it seemed the whole village was lined up outside the hotel with autograph books. Muriel thought that *not* using the Sunbeam might have been a giveaway, because that's what you'd do if you were trying to pretend you weren't who you were, right?

They fled to the nearby town of Cromer, but the rural grapevine was again active, and before long there was another crowd outside their hotel—'quite a terrifying spectacle', Muriel said.[244] She was not enjoying this adulation at all, and again they left town. For the next few days, they drove around Norfolk, making only one-night stops to help keep the autograph hunters at bay.

On 15 June 1919, shortly after the Hawkers' return to London, Captain John Alcock and Lieutenant Arthur Whitten Brown in their modified Vimy IV claimed the *Daily Mail* prize for the first non-stop aerial crossing of the Atlantic Ocean. Taking off from Lester's Field, near St. John's, Newfoundland, they landed unceremoniously some sixteen hours later in a muddy farm paddock in Clifden, Ireland. A week later at Windsor Castle

King George V dubbed each of them Knight Commander of the Most Excellent Order of the British Empire. The Secretary of State for Air, Winston Churchill, presented Alcock and Brown with the £10,000 *Daily Mail* prize.[245]

Alcock and Brown take off from Lester's Field, Newfoundland, in July 1919 on their way to Ireland to claim the first non-stop flight across the Atlantic.[245]

Harry Hawker is a classic example of the adage that it's not failure that defines you, it's how you respond to failure. There's no doubt Harry was deeply affected by having to abort the transatlantic attempt. The fact that an American crew was first across, even if they did make a stopover on the way, no doubt rubbed salt into the wound. He was pleased that a British pair eventually conquered the distance in a single flight, but it was doubtless hard for him not to think that it could've been him and Grieve lining up for those knighthoods. If only that radiator had behaved itself.

Shortly afterwards, Harry said that, while he and his navigator were deeply touched by the reception they'd experienced back in Britain, 'we are completely agreed that the whole of this business was utterly undeserved and out of all proportion to what we had tried—and failed to do.'[246]

'All the welcomes and demonstrations were unexpected by Harry,' Muriel said. 'Having failed to do what he set out to do, [he] had thought of creeping home and getting to work on another machine as quickly and with as little fuss as possible, with a view to making a fresh start.'[247]

CHAPTER 20

Feelings of qualm

Harry started what Muriel described as 'looking round for other fields of achievement'[248]— not 'employment', or 'activity', but 'achievement'. The 30-year-old wanted to rinse his mouth of the taste of failure, and he soon set out again on his restless quest for speed and adventure.

For the moment, Sopwith couldn't offer Harry employment to match his ambition. Over the course of the war, the company had produced more than 16,000 aircraft, under its own name or in partnership, making a nice profit, and no doubt adding a healthy sum to Harry's bank balance.

Understandably, orders for military machines had now tailed off. Tommy Sopwith, wary of rushing

Like other aviation companies of the time, Sopwith were not backward in promoting their wartime achievements, with production in Britain, France and Italy, as this 1920 advertisement shows.[252]

into the production of commercial or recreational aircraft before a market had developed, tried to diversify, initially moving from the production of wartime planes to aluminium cooking utensils. Swords into ploughshares.

Harry wasn't impressed: 'Saucepans! Where do I come in?' I never thought I should live to find myself in a job that [cookbook author] Mrs Beeton could do better than I.'[250]

When the company subsequently settled on the partnership to mass produce motorbikes as well as turn out a small number of private-venture civilian aircraft, using existing military designs, Harry could make a more significant contribution. He came of age designing and racing motorbikes back in Australia, and was able to provide his expertise for this new Sopwith venture. For the moment, however, he was interested in other competitive pursuits.

In June, just a month after his rescue from the Atlantic, he attempted to enter the 1919 'Victory' Aerial Derby, a handicap event that required contestants to fly two circuits each of some 100 miles around the city of London, starting and finishing at Hendon. The race was initiated pre-war by the *Daily Mail* but was now sponsored by the Royal Aero Club.

Harry's aircraft of choice was a Sopwith Snapper, one of three prototypes built for the British Government at the end of the war. However, the Snapper was fitted with an ABC Dragonfly engine, which was originally developed under government contract for military use and a year after the war still officially classified as 'secret'. The government refused him permission to use it in the race, so reluctantly he had to withdraw.

Undaunted, he made a bid shortly afterwards for a place in Britain's Schneider Cup team. The Schneider Cup, more properly the Coupe d'Aviation Maritime Jacques Schneider, was

Feelings of qualm · 211

an annual prize initiated by its namesake, a French financier, balloonist, speedboat and aircraft enthusiast, for the winner of an international seaplane race over a set triangular course. The race was first held in 1913; October 1919 saw the first post-war event, which was open to all nations. Only three countries had entered, however: Britain, France, and Italy, and there were four contenders for the three places on the British team.

This time Harry's mount was a specially designed single-seater Sopwith amphibian biplane with a 450 hp engine and a top speed of 170 mph. The cockpit of the seaplane was so tight he had to wear a close-fitting sweater to squeeze into the space. This almost proved his downfall at its first trial when the biplane tipped forward on its floats and plunged its nose under the chilly waters of the River Test in Hampshire, with Harry inside. He managed to wriggle his body free, like a butterfly emerging from a cocoon, and yelled to the mechanics to grab the tail before the Sopwith went completely under.

After manhandling the plane to shore, they discovered the floats (which Harry had designed) had been fitted too far back on the machine. So they loaded the amphibian

Hawker lauded the engine of the Sopwith-Jupiter seaplane he flew in the Schneider Cup in October 1919, but it was the floats that caused him most problems.

on a truck to take it back to the Sopwith works for a refit, only to find the truck wouldn't start. No worries, Harry said, and he zipped over to Southampton where his Sunbeam was garaged, drove it back to the disabled lorry, and hooked the big car to the front of the truck.

He then headed off for the Sopwith plant 'at a speed that must have made the lorry driver's hair stand on end,' Muriel said admiringly,[251] apparently more impressed with her husband's driving than concerned about his close call with drowning.

Muriel Hawker might not have been quite as restrained a few days later, however, when Harry almost drowned *her*. The Schneider Cup race was being held at Cowes, on the Isle of Wight, but the plane was housed at Hythe, 30 miles away on Southampton Water. Harry, Muriel and Pamela, along with Muriel's younger sister, Evelyn, were staying at Southampton, across the River Test from Hythe. With typical flair, Harry commuted from the hotel to the plane at Hythe each day on *Kangaroo II*, his own two-seater high-speed hydroplane.

On 3 October, he flew to Cowes to try out the Sopwith. By now one of the original four British contenders had dropped out, so Harry's plane was an automatic acceptance, but he still needed the practice run. The waters of the Solent, the strait separating the Isle of Wight from the mainland, were placid this day, but as he was coming in to land after his first loop, one of the floats struck a partly-submerged object. Almost immediately, the plane began to sink. Only a rowboat quickly pushed beneath the craft helped the amphibian reach shore.

Harry decided he'd take both floats back to Hythe on *Kangaroo II* for repair. Muriel was not impressed: 'This hydroplane was designed to carry two people at speed, and not as a useful conveyance for friends and baggage, so it was with feelings of qualm that I took my seat beside Harry, my sister on my knee, two floats securely tied on the bows, and two men at the stern.'[252]

It was early autumn, and Muriel and Evelyn were dressed for a social outing on a cool evening, in coats and furs, not a sea voyage. Fortunately Pamela wasn't with them.

As they set out at dusk along the Solent, every movement of the passengers sent a tremor through the little craft. Harry kept calling out, 'Trim the boat,' as if he were piloting a plane through thermal currents. When the overloaded speedboat reached the end of the Solent, he swung it left into the mouth of Southampton Water, a manoeuvre that exposed the hydroplane to the incoming surge of the open sea. Almost immediately a wave caught the unstable craft and flipped it over, tossing them all into the chilly water.

Muriel could feel her clothes becoming waterlogged, and realised they could be in a serious predicament. 'The first few minutes one swims with much gusto,' she said, with an undertone of concern, 'but things get very heavy after a little while and a kind of effort was required to keep up.'[253] (Somewhat like being married to Harry, perhaps?)

One of the mechanics couldn't swim but fortunately managed to cling to one of the floats. Harry bobbed up near his wife and started a roll-call to check that everyone was okay. Meanwhile, two quick-acting Australian soldiers on the shore grabbed a beached rowing boat and rowed rapidly out to the splashing group. Muriel and her sister were about to climb aboard when the rowers suddenly turned about and headed even more quickly back to where they'd came from. They'd realised almost too late they'd forgotten to put the bung in the bottom of the boat.

Fortunately a launch turned up soon after and rescued all five passengers, and Harry towed the hydroplane to shore.

It was nine o'clock that night by the time Harry finished repairing the drowned magneto in *Kangaroo II's* engine, and they headed off across the wide expanse of Southampton Water in the dark, this time without the floats. Half-way across, the magneto gave up again, and Harry had to tether the boat to an anchored vessel so he could work on the engine in the dark. When they finally reached Hythe, Muriel and Evelyn travelled back to their hotel on the Southampton steamer, taking advantage of the heat in the engine room to dry off their coats and furs.

Harry turned up at the hotel about 11 o'clock, his wet clothes still clinging and soggy. Whether Muriel gave him sympathy or the edge of her tongue isn't known, but it was these sorts of escapades that she had to accept in being married to Harry. As with the transatlantic attempt, she seemed to have come to a position where she would tolerate his need for speed, though sometimes with 'feelings of qualm'. On the occasion of the dunking in Southampton Water, more was at stake than Muriel probably realised—she would soon discover that, at the time she was dogpaddling for her life in open waters, she was in the early months of pregnancy with their second child.

A week later, with the Sopwith repaired, Harry and the other contestants arrived at Cowes for the Schneider Cup competition, only to find they had to contend with factors outside their control. In Muriel's opinion: 'The new floats were procured, but the actual race itself was a fiasco.'

Feelings of qualm · 215

The Sopwith Schneider seaplane passed through the seaside crowd on its way to its launching point in Cowes where Hawker competed unsuccessfully for Britain in the Coupe d'Aviation Maritime Jacques Schneider in October 1920.[254]

Once again, unpredictable weather was the problem. Fogs rolled in and out of the competition site at Cowes, creating havoc with flight planning, and perhaps reminding Harry of his Newfoundland experience. The organisers seem to be in two minds about whether to postpone the event or not, confusing competitors and spectators alike. Eventually the three British planes lined up, but Harry didn't take off when he should have because his new floats were leaking. So he held back starting the engine until the last possible moment to avoid pushing water into them.

When he did take off, and while all three British planes were in the air, a fog bank shuffled back in. One British pilot surrendered to the lack of vision and landed prematurely. Soon after, the second plane tipped its nose into the water as it touched down, bringing the rescue boat charging. This left Harry and the Sopwith as the only remaining British entry. He didn't last long—as he came down, the plane's floats filled so quickly with water that he was forced to land close to the beach so the mechanics could pull the aircraft to shore before it sank.

So ended the British tilt at the 1919 Schneider Cup.

Meanwhile, the two French planes withdrew without lifting off, leaving just a single Italian plane to claim the prize. So the large British crowd, bemused by the day's developments, was left to watch one foreign plane complete its required circuits. When the Italian pilot eventually brought his aircraft down, however, he was disqualified because on every one of his circuits he had failed to round a particular marker boat. The race was declared null and void, and there was no winner. It was not one of British aviation's better days.

Nevertheless, this was the sort of life Harry was now pursuing, usually with Muriel close by. He was a man of means after his demanding, but profitable, wartime service with Sopwith, and still earning a salary. The board of Sopwith Aviation and Engineering decided that from mid-November that year, Harry would receive 25% of any cash prize won in flying competitions, in addition to his salary, but that any trophies would become the property of the company.

One personal opportunity Harry had been hoping for after the Schneider Cup disappointment had shut down quickly. He and Muriel had planned to go on a deer shoot in Scotland with Tommy Sopwith. However, a national railway strike in late September and early October 1919 put paid to that, much to Harry's great disappointment. He'd gone hunting in Scotland in autumn the previous year, as the war was going out with a whimper, and on that occasion had killed two royal stags (a male deer with 12-point antlers) in one day.

In the winter of 1919–20, however, Harry was at a loose end, still looking around for 'other fields of achievement.' Muriel observed that there was not much flying to be done at that time of year 'and the prospects of it recovering its pre-war popularity not very hopeful.'[255]

The family probably spent many hours in the warmth of the indoors at 'Ennadale' as they prepared for the arrival of their second child, due in May. No doubt Muriel read Harry a lot of books.

Perhaps looking to identify areas elsewhere in which civil aviation might have some prospects, in February 1920 Harry had proposed to the Sopwith Board a tour to Australia. He had suggested leaving in October, taking with him four biplanes and two monoplanes. The board asked the Sales Manager to follow this up as part of a possible joint venture with Larkin Aviation in Australia. The trip never eventuated, however, possibly because a very different opportunity came along for the renowned aviator.

In the Spring, Louis Coatalen, chief designer at the Sunbeam Motor Car Company, invited Harry to test drive the company's new six-cylinder racing car in a forthcoming race. This speedster had been designed for the Indianapolis 500 event in the United States, a 500-mile race held at the Indianapolis Motor Speedway. Harry had driven his own Sunbeam only on the open road, and had no experience of track-racing, but he jumped at the chance. It's likely the two had first met when Harry sought the engineer's advice a few years earlier when the Australian had fitted the Sunbeam aircraft engine into a Mercedes chassis.

The car Harry was invited to race was a 4.9-litre open-wheeler, with a pointed wasp-like tail. Thin leather straps held down its heavily riveted silver bonnet, which had 'Sunbeam' stencilled on it in prominent blue lettering. The car's initial public outing would be at the first Brooklands race meeting since the war, on the Whit-Monday holiday, 24 May 1920.

There was a shadow hanging over Harry's venture into motor-racing, however—in February that year racing driver Josef Christiaens was killed in a similar car when it hit a curve and overturned during a demonstration run outside Sunbeam's headquarters at Wolverhampton. If the now very pregnant Muriel Hawker had the same 'feelings of qualm' about motor racing as she had on the overloaded hydroplane, at that time she kept them to herself.

CHAPTER 21
Finished with failures

When race day at Brooklands arrived on Monday 24 May, there was an overwhelming response from motor enthusiasts to Britain's first post-war competition. To them it was another sign that normality was being restored, a reassurance that all hadn't been lost during the four-year racing drought, when war seemed to suck the essence out of life.

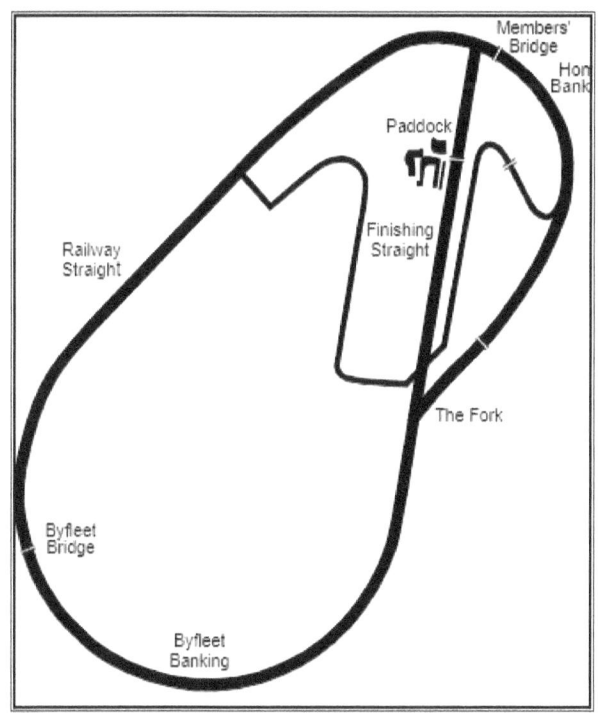

Brooklands was a 2.75-mile (4.43 km) motor racing circuit near Weybridge in Surrey, England which also enclosed the airstrip where Harry Hawker learnt to fly. The racing circuit ran anti-clockwise, and one of Hawker's racing cars burst a tyre at high speed on Railway Straight. On at least two occasions he flew planes under the Members' Bridge.[256]

'From the bottom of the Test Hill to the entrance to the course the track was lined on both sides with packed masses of cars,' the local paper reported, 'while the Hill was crowded with people breathlessly following the fortunes of their favourites as the burnished bonnets of the great cars glittered like shooting stars round the great track.'[257]

Earlier Harry had driven up to the factory at Wolverhampton to check out the 4.9 litre speedster he'd be driving on the track. He came back impressed with the company's operation, and afterwards had a couple of test drives of the car at Brooklands. 'The Sunbeam people do the whole thing properly,' he told Muriel.[258]

Prior to this, all Harry's experience at Brooklands had been in planes, flying in and out of the airstrip that sat inside the racing circuit. Now he was about to drive a car at high speed on an unsealed banked concrete track 100 feet wide and three and a quarter miles long, and hope that he was ahead when the final chequered flag came down. If he stuck to the dotted black strip known as the Fifty Foot Line that was painted along the centre of the track, theoretically he could take the banked corners without turning the steering wheel.

Today, however, he was up against some experienced racing drivers, although the break caused by the war had no doubt left all of them a little rusty.

Muriel was disappointed not to be able to go to the track to see her husband drive in his first races, but it was less than a week since the couple's second child was born. The new baby happened to arrive 12 months to the day from Harry's take-off date in Newfoundland, 18 May. To maintain the link even more closely, they named their new daughter Mary, after the Danish 'trudging lollypop' that had rescued her father mid-Atlantic. No doubt Queen Alexandra would have been pleased by the gesture.

The races on the Brooklands program were short—three, five or ten laps. Father-of-two Harry was in the first race, the Short Lightning Handicap, where he was beginning from scratch. From the start he made good ground, but as he snuck up on an Opel on a rough part of the track, the Sunbeam jumped out of gear. Harry immediately thrust it back into gear but didn't realise he'd put it into second instead of third. Intent on passing, he pushed the no-doubt complaining engine up to 100 mph in second gear, and the rev counter needle zoomed well into the red before he changed into third.

Hawker peers over the windscreen of the six-cylinder Sunbeam at Brooklands circuit on Monday 24 May, 1920, in his first attempt at car racing. He went home ecstatic that night, with two wins under his belt..[259]

But there was no stopping him now, and he set out with a roar in pursuit of the lead car. He caught it at the top of the straight to go on and win, with an average speed of just over 98 mph. Afterwards, a mechanical check revealed that jamming the gear lever in second at high speed for a short burst fortunately hadn't damaged the engine.

Buoyed by his success, Harry set out just as determinedly in his second race, the Long Lightning Handicap. This time he weaved his way through the pack over a longer distance to beat the others home by a length, to the delighted cheers of the large crowd. His fastest lap for the day on the banked concrete track was close to 107 mph—about the cruising speed of the Sopwith *Atlantic*.

Naturally Harry was overjoyed with his doubly successful debut as a racing car driver, and was bubbling when he went home to his wife and two daughters that night. Muriel described it intriguingly as 'the first day of complete success he had ever had,' and seemed as happy about it as he was.

Harry told her he felt his luck had changed and that he was 'finished with failures, glorious or otherwise.'[260] Twelve months after the event, the premature end to his Atlantic adventure clearly still rankled.

Harry's car racing debut so impressed Louis Coatalen that Sunbeam invited him to drive their newest race car, a 350hp V12 monster, in the midsummer meeting at Brooklands on 26 June, a month later. This was a huge honour for him, a big step-up in motor racing. Under the bonnet the 16-feet-long open wheeler had four times the capacity of the Sunbeam he drove to success at Brooklands. Muriel described this second Sunbeam as 'the largest car in the world' at the time.[261]

She also noticed a change in her husband: 'This new form of speed had got well hold of Harry,' she said.²⁶² One result was his decision to tune the engine of their own home-built Sunbeam to racing pitch. He spent hours in his home workshop, stripping the car of its mudguards, lights, windscreen and anything else he thought might slow it down, and finessed the engine for maximum performance.

*Hawker found another outlet for his need for speed on the curved bank of the Brooklands Raceway.*²⁶⁴

In a trial of the revamped car at Brooklands, he managed to shred half the rubber off a front tyre on the rough banked track in a series of spectacular skids, but nevertheless pushed the home-built Sunbeam up to a top speed of 107 mph. Fast enough for him to think about having the car properly streamlined.

That was, until the 350 hp Sunbeam arrived at Brooklands and he took the new speedster out on the track for the first time. When he arrived home that evening, Muriel was amused to see him begin returning their own Sunbeam to its original condition, replacing everything he'd earlier stripped off in search of a better performance. He also ordered four road tyres for the car. In response to his wife's quizzical look, he said with conviction, 'A car only capable of under 110 mph is only fit for a touring car.'[263]

Harry never tried it on the track again. It seems he'd decided that only a purpose-built car was good enough for 'real' racing.

On the morning of 26 June he set out from home in the Ford ahead of Muriel so he could have a practice run in the big Sunbeam before the main race. It was a car with plenty of grunt, handsome with its black snout, long white bonnet and stubby pointed tail. The crowd on this fine summer morning was keen to see what it could do. On his trial run, Harry sat upright in the single-seater, and soon urged the speedo over the hundred mark. It was all looking very positive for the main event.

Still on his practice run, as he came around on the banking under the Members' Bridge, he began to push the sleek-looking car faster. Soon it was well past 110mph. If he could sustain it, he'd be heading towards an unofficial lap record.

He pushed harder on the accelerator, at exactly the same time as the front off-side tyre blew. The Sunbeam lurched to the right as the axle bit into the concrete track, and Harry fought to control the car as the momentum pushed it along Railway Straight. It was close to the right-hand fence now, and the newly recruited driver wrestled with the wheel, trying to push the big car to the left, but at 80 mph the screeching, clattering axle wouldn't be swayed. The car continued to hurtle alongside the high corrugated iron fence, rejecting Harry's efforts to wrest it away.

Finished with failures · 225

Hawker's 12-cylinder Sunbeam after its skirmish with a corrugated iron fence at Brooklands racetrack, 26 June 1920.[265]

Finally, after another 400 yards car and barrier merged in a grinding, screeching climax. Metal fence panels peeled off like an iron roof in a cyclone, and the Sunbeam careered off the track and over a four-foot drop. It came to a stop, right-side up, with a paling jammed through the spokes of one front wheel.

Unaware of the little drama taking place on the track, Muriel was in the family Sunbeam in a queue of cars making their way into the Brookland grounds. As she awaited her turn, a passing spectator yelled out to another driver in the queue, 'Hawker's crashed in the Sunbeam in practice!'

Muriel immediately leapt from the car and rushed across the paddock towards the track. Her mind was awhirl with what might have happened to Harry, and she could hardly think straight as she charged towards the entrance. She was still dazed by the news when she suddenly came upon her husband, standing waiting for her at the track gate. The sight of him unhurt was such a surprise and relief after the possibilities that had been whirling through her head that she was stunned into silence.

Unaware Muriel had heard about the accident, Harry carried on as if nothing had happened, and asked her where the car was. 'You don't usually walk to Brooklands,' he said with a smile.[266]

'And you don't generally wait patiently just at the gate for me to come,' Muriel said, waiting for him to tell her the news.

Harry finally came clean, but he downplayed the incident: 'I've just blown a tyre off the Sunbeam and shan't be able to race today, so I've nothing on earth to do.'

It was only later that Muriel learnt the truth about 'just blown a tyre off the Sunbeam': 'So much for coming off the banking at the fastest part of the track with a flat tyre at something over 110 miles an hour, crashing through a fence, and jumping a ditch on the other side,' she said in exasperation.[267]

And she wasn't reassured when she saw a newspaper headline next day: 'Hawker, the man who won't be killed!'[268] She learnt from that report that when the first responders reached Harry after the accident, he was shaken, but all he'd wanted to do was talk about how well the Sunbeam had been going before the tyre burst.

Despite her declared support for her husband's endeavours, it was clearly not easy for Muriel to live with his continuing urge to push the boundaries, and it would not be long before she openly expressed her concern.

Hawker performed 'many extraordinary evolutions' in the Sopwith Swallow at the RAF Aerial Pageant at Hendon on 3 July, 1920.

Harry would get to have another crack at driving the big Sunbeam at Brooklands in August 1920, but in the meantime went back to his old love, flying. On 3 July he executed 'many extraordinary evolutions', performing loops, rolls and spins in his Sopwith Swallow runabout. His was one of the many acts at the Hendon RAF Aerial Pageant, which attracted a huge crowd. 'Aviation has never had such a day as it experienced last Saturday,' *Flight* magazine reported.[269]

Three weeks later, Harry ended up in a flying contest he wasn't originally planning to enter. He'd decided that Sopwith didn't have a plane that was up to scratch for the 1920 Aerial Derby at Hendon, so instead he agreed to again perform acrobatics in the Swallow to entertain the crowd while the competitors were out on the course. The thought of doing more loops, rolls and spins while his fellow pilots were out competing must have niggled at him, however. 24 hours before the event, he decided he'd enter the race in a Sopwith Rainbow, registration G-EAKI.

This was the machine he'd flown as an amphibian in the 1919 Schneider Cup, now modified as a land plane. Ironically, the original engine had been replaced by the ABC Dragonfly, now no longer classified as an official secret. When word got out that Harry Hawker was in the 1920 Derby, newspapers declared him the 'dark horse' and bookies made him race favourite.

It was a handicap race. In a field of 16, Harry would be 13th away, so there were three potentially faster planes against the Sopwith Rainbow. One of these was a Martinsyde Semiquaver, which normally would have pitted him against his old friend and competitor Fred Raynham, but 'Tinsides' had to withdraw

Wearing his trademark 'backwards' beret, Hawker checks out the Sopwith Rainbow he entered late in the 1920 Aerial Derby. A mistake at the finish cost him a place.

[Sopwith Rainbow, copyright Brooklands Museum.]

because of a knee injury, and had been replaced by another pilot. On scratch in the race was the Nieuport Goshawk that had recently established a new British speed record, a plane that some 12 months later would come to be inextricably linked with Harry Hawker.

During the two circuits required for the 1920 Aerial Derby, each covering 100 miles around London, several entrants didn't make it to the finish line. The Rainbow was going well, and at the end of Harry's two circuits the always competitive Australian was in line for a place. Unfortunately he failed to realise that last year's rules had changed. Instead of making a circuit of the pylons around the airfield, he flew across the middle and was disqualified. Except for that mistake at the finish, he would've taken second outright place in the Derby and third in the Handicap. One can only imagine his chagrin when he discovered his error and its consequences. Did he consider this another 'glorious failure'?

However, there was a shadow hanging over Harry that was much more serious than where he placed in the Aerial Derby. Muriel knew that for the past few weeks her husband had been in agony from pain in his back. Trying to sleep had been torture for him, but he'd been determined to carry on as if nothing was wrong. It was a stubbornness that would have dire consequences.

CHAPTER 22

'Precarious activities'

Muriel believed Harry's back pain originated before she met him, when he crashed into the sea off Dublin in August 1913 while flying with Harry Kauper as the lone entrants in the Seaplane Circuit of Britain. Kauper broke his arm in that incident, but Harry reportedly was not injured. Muriel thought otherwise.

She also knew about another crash her then husband-to-be had had in October 1913 when competing for the British Empire Michelin Cup, an endurance race for British machines. Flying a Sopwith biplane, Harry took off from Brooklands and was not far off the ground when a gust of wind caught the plane. An errant wingtip hooked the bank of the River Wey, a tributary of the Thames, and the plane went down alongside the waterway. Fortunately Harry wasn't badly injured and quickly clambered out, but he did hurt his back.

Three weeks after that incident he had another crack at the endurance record, but was forced to retire with a severe headache, possibly because his recovery from the earlier crash was not as complete as he'd thought. Or perhaps at the age of 24 he was already beginning to paper over the cracks of his seeming infirmities.

Subsequent accidents no doubt contributed to the problems he suffered with his back later in life—the abrupt landings in Albury and Ballarat in the Sopwith *Tabloid* on his Australian visit in early 1914; the spectacular dive in the Sopwith *Scout* into a clump of trees near Brooklands on his return to Britain a month or so later; and the strain of rescuing his plane from a snowy field in France just before his wedding in November 1917.

Now, just as Harry was starting to find new outlets for his inner fire, the problem re-emerged one evening in June 1920, not long after his car racing debut, and before the Aerial Derby. Shortly before he was due to drive the big Sunbeam, and with a commitment to forthcoming flying displays, the 31-year-old staggered into the house from his workshop. He told Muriel he'd been doing some heavy lifting and now had excruciating pain in his back. Soon his spine was so stiff he couldn't bend.

Harry promptly consulted a medical specialist—whom Muriel disparagingly referred to as 'a famous bonesetter'[270]—who told him that the problem was 'adhesion of muscles'. The doctor said the only solution was to break the muscles away and so loosen the adhesion. This turned out to be a painful procedure, but week after week Harry submitted to it, all the time continuing to race cars and fly planes.

He had a particularly hectic schedule in August 1920. In addition to driving the 350 hp Sunbeam at Brooklands, he was committed to flying a Sopwith Antelope (see poster) in an Air Ministry speed and reliability trial; he'd also accepted an invitation to take part in international speedboat races for the first time, competing for the British International Trophy (B.I.T.) at Cowes.

'He was hardly fit to be walking about,' Muriel said, 'and certainly not to be flying and racing, but with that indomitable courage and determination to go on as usual, he refused to give up any part of his work.'

The only way Harry could keep his multiple commitments at the dispersed venues across southern England was to dash between them in his Sopwith Scooter. He based the runabout at Martlesham, north-east of London, the site of the Air Ministry trials. Muriel stayed 200 miles away at beachside Bournemouth, south-west of London, with the two girls. She referred to them as 'the two babies', although Pamela was now almost two years old; Mary was close to three months.

Around this time Muriel became much more nervous about what she now came to describe as Harry's 'precarious activities'.[272] It's not clear whether this was because of the two children, her husband's severe back pain, his move into car racing, or a combination of all three. She was particularly

Harry and Muriel Hawker with their two children, Pamela and baby Mary, in the grounds of their house in Hook, Surrey.[271]

concerned about his having another crack at driving the big 350hp Sunbeam at Brooklands, scheduled for Monday 2 August.

'The narrow escape which he had with this car at its first public appearance on the track,' Muriel said, 'perhaps accounted for the unsportsmanlike attitude I took up on the occasion of its second.'

To this point Muriel had been very supportive of her husband's need for speed, and in their earlier days had enjoyed their on-road skirmishes with other speedsters. But now she was having reservations about the lifestyle he'd chosen, particularly when she thought he might have bitten off more than he could chew.

In the weeks leading up to the second race in the Sunbeam, Muriel overheard snatches of conversation ('catching stray sentences, as one does in the paddock [at Brooklands]') suggesting that Harry could be putting himself in danger. She grew increasingly anxious when she heard people who knew about car racing saying that the big new machine was too fast for the Brooklands track. Muriel also knew that his back pain hadn't gone away.

She kept her fears bottled up until Harry arrived to spend the weekend before the Monday race with her and the two girls at Bournemouth. Unable to constrain herself any longer, Muriel told Harry she was afraid he was going to crash if he drove in the race. She begged him not to take part.

'I only succeeded in thoroughly upsetting him,' she said.[273]

Harry was astonished. He'd never seen his wife like this. 'I expect the unusualness of my attitude worried him,' she said afterwards, 'since it was the first time I had tried to deter him from any of his precarious activities.'[274]

He was also very angry. 'Can't you see the position you're putting me in?' he said. 'What excuse would I have for pulling out at the eleventh hour? That my wife was afraid I might crash? No, my commitment stands!'

'You do whatever you feel you have to,' she said, 'but don't expect me to go and watch you.'

Harry left Bournemouth on Sunday for commitments in London, and on the morning of the race next day, Muriel continued to pray that something would happen to prevent his driving the car.

But her resolve not to watch his races faltered. When she reached 'Ennadale', her need to see what happened on the track got the better of her, and she headed off to Brooklands to watch the two races Harry was entered in.

She was late arriving, however, and was delighted to discover that his first race had been cancelled because a heavy rain shower had made the track too greasy. She found Harry working on the car with Louis Coatalen. Her husband looked up in surprise as she approached. No doubt recalling their Bournemouth discussion, he quickly tried to reassure her. 'I did some laps on the track in the car this morning and it was running beautifully,' he said.

A 350hp Sunbeam of the type that Hawker raced at Brooklands in June and August 1920. This was the car that Muriel had overheard described as 'too fast for the track.'.[275]

Nevertheless, Muriel was still anxious about him driving. By the time the cars rolled out for Harry's second race, the 24-year-old had worked herself up into what she described as 'a perfect example of the panicky old woman.'[276] The words 'too fast for the track' were echoing in her ears. She still hoped something would happen to stop Harry taking part, whatever the fallout.

It was a handicap race, and the Sunbeam was off scratch, so all the other cars were flagged away ahead of Harry. Now it was his turn, and Muriel's heart was likely in her mouth as the big black and white car sat throbbing with understated power, waiting its chance. Harry's eyes were on the starter. The flag fell. Harry floored the accelerator.

Then nothing. The car sat there, unmoving. The famous Harry Hawker had stalled the engine on the start line.

It was too late to restart it. The 350hp Sunbeam was out of the race. After all the publicity, all the speculation about the car and its driver, neither of them made it on to the track that day.

Muriel didn't feel the elation she'd expected, though. 'I knew that, although I had got what I prayed for, I had failed him,' she said, 'and his disappointment afterwards was my punishment.'[277]

But, no doubt to her surprise, Harry didn't make any connection between his failure to start and the opposition Muriel had expressed to him. He simply called it 'damn bad luck', and made no further mention of what she'd said earlier about him pulling out of the race. When he dropped her at the station next morning to catch a train to where the speedboat races were being held, his mind was on the next event. 'See you at Cowes tomorrow for the B.I.T [British International Trophy],' he said. 'It will be some fun.'

Muriel was generous in her praise of her husband's response to what had happened at Brooklands : 'He was always the real kind of sportsman—a good loser,' she said.

As it happened, he didn't get another chance to drive the big Sunbeam. In other hands it would go on to set a Brooklands lap record and then the land speed record over a mile at almost 130 mph. A few years later the world-famous racing driver Malcolm Campbell would buy the 350hp V12 Sunbeam from Coatelen, paint the body blue and give it a new name, *Blue Bird*, and push the big car to a new world land speed record.

To add to the disappointment that Harry no doubt felt after the Brooklands debacle, the British International Trophy (BIT) speedboat races on 10 and 11 August 1920 didn't turn out to be the fun he'd anticipated either. The BIT was more commonly known as the Harmsworth Cup. It had been established in 1903 by Alfred Harmsworth or, as he was better known, Lord Northcliffe, also sponsor of the transatlantic race.

There was a huge crowd at Osborne Bay on the Isle of Wight, most of them hoping to see a British win over their American opponents in an event that was last run just before the war. Harry was rated a big chance because he was behind the wheel of the most powerful boat of the five entrants, the 39-foot *Maple Leaf V*, with four whopping 450 hp Sunbeam engines.

Maple Leaf V, *shown here on a practice run, and driven by Harry Hawker, was no match for the two lightweight American entries in the 1920 Harmsworth Cup.*.[278]

Unfortunately for him and the British supporters, the power didn't translate into speed. *Maple Leaf V* leapt in the air on take-off, possibly due to uneven weight distribution of the engines, and never regained its equilibrium. Predictably, its take-off jump earned the Australian's boat the nickname, 'Kangaroo'. An expert commentator of the day said:

> Someone once said that, given sufficient power, he could make a grand piano fly, but whatever the truth of this assertion as applied to aerodynamics, one need only have seen this, the most formidable of the British team in action, to be convinced that such is not the case with boats. *Maple Leaf V*, with her four Sunbeam motors aggregating one thousand

eight hundred horse-power, had power enough to make her fly, but there was something lacking, without which as fine a power plant as was ever installed in a hydroplane was unable to produce the desired results. Whether it was the angle of the planes, the position of the steps, or the placing of the engines; or a combination of all three, it is impossible to say, but the fact remains that she did not take advantage of her power.[279]

Harry managed to move into second place at one point, but couldn't maintain it, and *Miss America* surged across to win, with the other American boat in second place.

Despite his loss on the water, it seems that in this environment Harry was in elite company. A photo of him on board a yacht at the time shows him in much smarter garb than the 'indifferent' clothes he wore in Newfoundland.

Hawker in smart garb on board ship during the British International Trophy speedboat races at Cowes, August 1920.[280]

Around the Brooklands car race and the several days of the B.I.T event, Harry managed to fit in his commitment to the Small Commercial Aircraft Competition at Martlesham Heath, Suffolk. To encourage innovative aircraft development, the Air Ministry was offering prizes totalling £64,000 for speed and reliability, for flying slow and fast, for economy and for a plane's ability to fly itself. With an eye on the commercial market, Sopwith entered the single-engine Antelope, which was fitted with armchairs in an enclosed cabin for two passengers behind the pilot's compartment. It even had a temperature control for the passenger cabin, an innovation Harry and Grieve might have appreciated over the Atlantic.

In the speed tests, Harry managed to keep the plane to a low of 43 mph and push it to a maximum of 110 mph, and in the 'uncontrolled' test, the Antelope 'flew for five minutes by itself.'[281] However, for overall speed and reliability, the Sopwith biplane came second to a Westland Napier, winning a runner-up prize of £3000.

So Harry's three challenges in August, in the air, on the sea and on the racing track, all had disappointing outcomes for him—the racing car was a non-starter, the speedboat came third in the B. I. T., and the Sopwith plane was pipped for first place. Did he regard these as more 'glorious failures'?

Underneath all these activities, Harry's back pain hadn't gone away—he'd just been trying to ignore it. Muriel suggested getting a second opinion. A back specialist looked at the X-rays (a procedure discovered only 25 years earlier) and advised Harry that he had two options. The first was to lie flat on his back for two years; the second was to have an operation to graft new bone onto his spine, and then spend twelve months on his back, recovering. And if he did nothing at all? The specialist said Harry's back would eventually reach a point where he would be completely immobile.

It was a sobering prognosis for the famous pilot, racing car enthusiast, and speedboat driver, with his constant need for speed. 'Place Hawker anywhere he could get his hands on a machine, and you simply couldn't keep him on the ground,' an aviation writer once commented.[282]

Yet, this doctor wanted to do just that—keep him not only on the ground, but on his back. How would Harry survive either of these treatments? How would Muriel cope with Harry if his wings were clipped?

'Poor Harry!' she said.[283]

But what about poor Muriel?

As the couple reviewed their options, someone suggested that Harry should try Christian Science treatment. This set of beliefs and practices was developed in the 19th-century by Mary Baker Eddy, who argued that sickness was 'an illusion that could be corrected by prayer alone.'[284] Her treatments, however, encompassed the disciplines of science, theology, and medicine. While the Hawkers were considering whether to pursue this approach, Mackenzie Grieve, on hearing of Harry's back problems, coincidentally wrote to him, urging him to give Christian Science a go, apparently unaware the Hawkers were already thinking about it. He told Harry of instances in his own family where people had been cured by following the sect's practices.

'Well, if it's good enough for old Mac,' Harry said to Muriel, 'it's good enough for me!'[285]

So Harry studied Christian Science beliefs and adopted the treatment methods they advocated. The result, according to Muriel, was 'magical'.[286] She said the pain in his back, which doctors had told him needed radical treatment, went away 'not gradually, but immediately.'

She claimed that Harry was able to bend his back again with no problem, and put on the weight he'd lost over the previous two months of pain, medical examinations, and unsuccessful treatment. He became, according to Muriel, 'his own cheery self again.'[287]

'We all know so little and profess so much,' Muriel said, 'and yet ninety-nine out of a hundred Christian people will back any guessing human doctor against their God when bodily adjustments are necessary, and smile with amusement when the odd one seeks and receives his Maker's help.'[288]

Muriel would continue to believe that Christian Science practices cured her husband, even when her whole world turned upside down.

CHAPTER 23

'We're really beginning to go now!'

September 1920 brought more opportunities for Harry to go fast, especially now that his back was apparently working freely again. Unable to jazz up his old Sunbeam to racing standard, he'd bought himself a new four-cylinder car, the A.C. (the initials of its manufacturer, Automobile Carriers), and was keen to break the track speed record for a light car. He thought he'd have a go during the autumn meeting at Brooklands on 4 September, in a race designed for 'standard' cars.

When the A.C. was lined up in the marshalling area with the others, however, there was a last-minute protest. Although the manufacturer regarded Harry's car as a 'standard sports model', the other drivers, aware of Harry's reputation and the likely power of the A.C., convinced the organisers that his new car was more 'sports' than 'standard'. Harry was forced to withdraw.

'If the mount had been a Mr. Brown's entry it would probably have been allowed to race,' Muriel caustically commented.[289]

The Australian had never been known for giving up, however. At the final race meeting for the year, on September 25, he turned up with a different car, from the French car-maker,

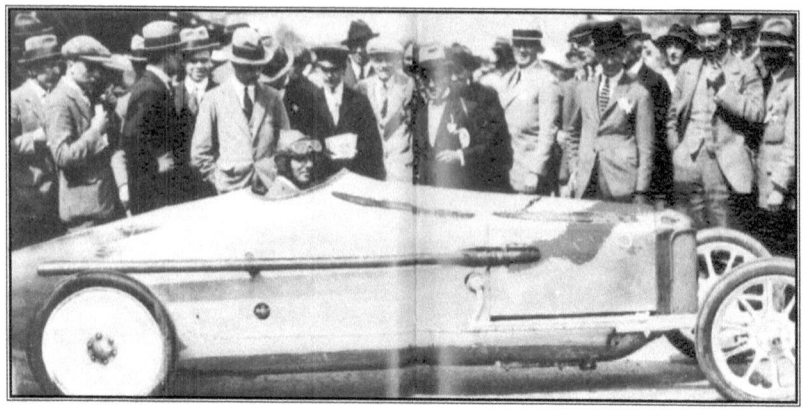

Hawker in his AC racing car at Brooklands after creating a new world speed record, June 1921.[290]

Doriot, Flandrin and Parant (D.F.P.). Muriel described it as 'a perfectly ordinary 4-cylinder D.F.P. car.' Harry had recently become a partner in a D.F.P. agency in Australia, so was keen to give this one a public tryout for promotional purposes. However, the handicapper at Brooklands had 'a wonderful knack of letting the light in on dark horses,' according to Muriel,[291] and on this occasion gave the D.F.P. a hefty time penalty. The result was that Harry's car was coming up the finishing straight about the same time as the entrants for the next race were heading to the start line.

Once again Muriel thought Harry's reputation for fast driving went against him: 'So much for a name,' she said wryly.

Observers might have made a similar comment when Sopwith Aviation and Engineering Company went out of business in September 1920, and re-emerged not long afterwards with a new title.

After its post-war move into motorcycle production, Sopwith had gone on to produce over 2000 powered bikes. But it was a competitive market, and the company struggled to be viable, especially when in June 1920 the British Government introduced a new corporation tax on limited liability companies. It also raised the Excess Profits Tax on wartime production back to its previous level of 60 per cent. These moves had severe implications for Sopwith Aviation and Engineering as a very successful wartime manufacturer. The company decided to pay out its creditors and go into liquidation. The closure came just in time to deny Harry entry into the Gordon Bennett Air Race at Etampes, France, where he'd been scheduled to fly the Sopwith Rainbow again, alongside two other British fliers, including his old friend, Freddy Raynham.

On the face of it, the closure of the original company must have been a big blow to Harry, who had built so much of his life around it. 'Harry knew every man and woman in every department of the Sopwith works,' his friend Andrew Lang said, 'and in his great, loyal heart, anything that emanated from the hands of the Sopwith work people was the finest thing it was possible to get. He lived for Sopwiths... and speed.'[292]

Harry didn't come away empty-handed from the shutdown, however. Although the Sopwith company had disappeared, before year's end a new one was formed to take on some of the same tasks. The Hawker name was at the forefront. Harry joined with Tom Sopwith and Fred Sigrist and two engineers to form the H.G. Hawker Engineering Company. Sopwith and Sigrist had

been very well paid in their previous roles, and Harry himself had been earning some £30,000 a year (almost £1.5 million today), so they were well placed to invest in the new company. H.G. Hawker Engineering immediately purchased the assets of the now bankrupt company, including the rights to Sopwith aircraft designs.

Tommy Sopwith disingenuously suggested that the new name was 'to avoid any muddle if we had gone on building aeroplanes and called them Sopwiths—there was bound to be a muddle somewhere.'[293] It seems more likely that he wanted no suggestion that the new company was simply a renaming of the old one, and hence still liable for wartime taxes.

Nevertheless, the new company quickly won a contract for restoring RAF Sopwith Snipes damaged in World War 1. It also produced several varieties of motor-bike of its own design, beginning with the 292cc two-stroke, two-speed lightweight 'Hawker', with technical advice from the new model's namesake. A feature of the bike was automatic lubrication: 'You fill the sump with lubricant,' a promotional poster proclaimed, 'and the running of the engine forces the oil to every point of friction.'[294]

Nevertheless, motor-bike production was a drastic change for both the company and their most famous employee. At its peak Sopwith Aviation employed more than 5000 people; now it had fewer than 20. In this difficult period, Harry sometimes worked on the bench alongside the fitters, and test-rode bikes around the company's factory site. It was a full circle for the man who had cut his teeth on building and racing motorcycles with his mates as a teenager back in Australia. Now, in their early 30s, Tommy Sopwith and Harry Hawker rode the new machines in motorcycle races on London tracks, with some success. But it

The newly named H.G. Hawker Engineering Company in 1921 began producing motorbikes using its famous pilot's name.[295]

was a comedown from the machines that for the past eight years they'd been riding in the sky.

Meanwhile Harry continued to pursue his obsession with winning races and creating records in his A.C. In track practice, he pushed the car faster and faster, but he was forever modifying the engine. 'From the moment he brought the car home,' Muriel said, 'there was little rest for all concerned with it, his own energy and enthusiasm being enormous.'[296]

There were times when Muriel wished her husband wasn't so obsessed. One day when she'd towing home the broken-down A.C. from Brooklands for what seemed the hundredth time, she said to him, 'Let's burn the thing and buy a motor car!'[297]

Harry wasn't fazed. 'Never mind,' he said cheerfully, 'we're really beginning to go now!'

When they arrived at 'Ennadale', he proceeded to spend all night in the workshop pulling down the motor and restoring it, with short breaks for coffee and cake. Muriel might have known that he'd never take her suggestion seriously. And it does seem that his back wasn't troubling him, given the amount of time he was spending in his workshop on modifications to his various cars.

Harry also owned a Rolls-Royce, from the company that manufactured the Eagle engine fitted to the Sopwith *Atlantic*. Typically, he couldn't resist modifying the luxury vehicle by replacing the car's body with one of his own design. He also had no hesitation in using it as a workhorse, and on one occasion transported the A.C.'s engine strapped to the back of it.

24-year-old Muriel herself drove a Minerva saloon, a luxury Belgian-made car that was a favourite of Hollywood stars and moguls of American industry. It was generally regarded as the equivalent of a Rolls Royce but not as expensive. Muriel said the downside of owning a Minerva in the Hawker family was that hers 'degenerated into a travelling workshop' for the A.C. She claimed the Minerva always followed Harry's A.C. proudly to Brooklands, 'complete with tow-rope and spares, and nearly always, less proudly, preceded it home, connected by the rope.'[298]

Muriel Hawker drove a Belgian-made Minerva saloon, an earlier version of the 1925 one pictured here.[299]
These luxury cars were about half the price of the British-produced Rolls Royce. She complained that Harry turned hers into a 'travelling workshop'.

Despite Muriel's scepticism about the A.C., Harry was convinced it would be the first light car to break the 100 mph barrier. Thanks to the streamlining he'd undertaken in consultation with the car's engineer and designer, John Wellman, he'd already pushed it to around 90 m.p.h. on the track.

When it first appeared at a Brooklands race meeting at Easter 1921, the sleek aluminium speedster attracted a lot of attention as a genuinely streamlined light racing car. Once again the handicapper had a say in the outcomes of the two races Harry entered, with the A.C. second both times. Although the car still hadn't reached the magic 100 mark, Harry's initiative won the H.G. Hawker Engineering Company orders for streamlined racing car bodies.

Harry had a couple of small race wins soon after, but he still couldn't push it up to the magic 100. He continued beavering away, no doubt with Muriel's Minerva still as his support vehicle.

At the Brooklands midsummer meeting on 3 June, 1921, Harry finally achieved his goal: the four-cylinder A.C. reached a top speed of 105.14 m.p.h. on the cambered track. It was a new world speed record for a 1.5 litre car. 'Even the lay Press showed some sort of enthusiasm for the latest achievement,' Muriel chortled afterwards.[300]

Harry had previously held national records for flying faster, higher and for longer; now he had an international one for road racing. There's little doubt he would've liked to have added the transatlantic crossing to his triumphs.

Later that month the ever-faithful Muriel was sitting in the grandstand at Brooklands timing Harry on a practice run in the A.C. for a race meeting the next day. As he came into Railway Straight, where earlier he'd had a lucky escape when the Sunbeam blew a tyre, he had the open-wheeler up around the 100 m.p.h. mark.

Suddenly something rose up in front of him and smashed into his face.

Out of control, the car careered down the sloping track. Its front wheels hit the encircling three-foot concrete wall head on, and the car's momentum pushed it grindingly right over the low parapet. Without any guidance from the hapless driver, the A.C. finally came to rest right side up in the long grass beside the track.

Muriel had seen the car slide down the track and disappear in a cloud of dust. One of the spectators near her shouted, 'Hawker's off the track! He'll need his luck now!'

Ever since his rescue from the Atlantic, Harry seemed to have had an aura of luck around him, and even during the war his colleagues thought he had some sort of fortune shining on him. Muriel no doubt hoped it was still with him as she ran down the steps of the grandstand. In the paddock she grabbed a lift with Sunbeam's Louis Coatalen. They found Harry standing alongside the track, his goggles smashed and his face covered in blood.

Harry wiped his face with a handkerchief while at the same time asking for help with the car. The aluminium bonnet hadn't been strapped down properly and had come loose mid-lap. It had whipped back, striking the hapless driver in the face and smashing his goggles.

Leave it to us the responders said, but Harry insisted on staying until the A.C., its front wheels severely buckled, was back on

the track. Once again Muriel towed the streamlined car home with her Minerva, and once again Harry stayed up all night repairing it. He was cheered to see that it was not as badly damaged as he'd feared, despite the rough path it had taken. It was typical that it wasn't the crash that worried him, but he was very annoyed about his smashed goggles.

Harry's back still seemed to be holding out, and next day, 25 June, he was in the thick of it again at Brooklands. This time engine trouble puts the A.C. out of contention. Nevertheless, his lifelong dream of speed pulled him onwards: he now had his eye on setting a record for a light car of 120 mph.

In the midst of this hectic life, it seemed that at age 32 Harry hadn't lost his boyish sense of the ridiculous. One week-end he and Muriel were staying with her parents at West Ealing, and Harry enlisted her brother Laurence's help for a practical joke on the Peatys' cook. The two snuck downstairs after everyone else was in bed. An hour later, when Harry returned to Muriel's side, he refused to tell her what the pair had been up to.

In the morning, when the cook went to open the dark-painted door into the kitchen, an entrance she knew so well, she was confronted instead by a gleaming white one. The previous night, Harry and Laurence had gone to the trouble of swapping the white door in the drawing room with the dark one leading into the kitchen. The cook couldn't make out what was going on. Convinced she was being made a fool of, she quit on the spot. Hopefully she reconsidered when Harry and Laurence confessed.

But Harry would soon be back to the serious business of air racing. He had entered the 1921 Aerial Derby, a time trial over two 100-mile circuits around London, beginning and ending at Hendon Aerodrome. There was a prize of £500 for the overall winner, with lesser amounts for the first three places in the handicap competition. It was a popular event with the public, and 100,000 spectators were expected, paying between one shilling and five shillings for a place in the enclosure, or four pounds forty shillings for a private box. Harry's participation would be a drawcard in itself.

He'd been disqualified in the previous year's Derby because he didn't follow the landing rules at the end of the race, so he was especially keen to do well in this one.

And for the first time since before the war he'd be flying a plane that wasn't built by the Sopwith company

CHAPTER 24

Brave and ageless

On Saturday 9 July, 1921, a telegram arrived at the Hawker home, addressed to Harry: 'Machine ready for flying Tuesday afternoon.'

The telegram was from Henry Folland, designer of the single-seater Nieuport Goshawk, the plane Harry was going to fly in the 1921 Aerial Derby. This particular Goshawk was already famous—just over 12 months earlier, Major Leonard Tait-Cox had flown it to a new British air speed record of 166.5 mph (268 kph). The Derby would be held on Saturday, 16 July, and Harry was anxious to get a feel of the machine in advance to see what it was capable of.

National honour was at stake because a French aviator held the *world* record, which was now edging towards 200 mph. Harry was hopeful of making a dent in that, especially as his rivals from across the Channel would be taking part in the Derby.

He set off from 'Ennadale' on the Tuesday afternoon, weaving through the thickening London traffic on his two-stroke 'Hawker' motorbike,[301] newly minted at the company that now bore his name. When he arrived at Hendon Aerodrome, Henry Folland greeted him, and took him over to where the Nieuport Goshawk was being rolled out of its shed. The machine was resplendent in its racing livery of bright blue and yellow checks, a far cry from the drab colours of the wartime aircraft of just a few years earlier. The Goshawk hadn't had much flying time since it had broken the British speed record the previous year, but had recently been overhauled in preparation for its Derby challenge.

Registered as G-EASK, the stubby biplane was powered by a 320 hp ABC Dragonfly engine. Ironically, this was the same type of engine that Harry had wanted to use two years before, in the 1919 Aerial Derby, but which at that time was still officially secret.

The afternoon sun was still bright as Harry climbed into the open cockpit and started the engine. Britain was remarkably dry

Saturday 9 July 1921 was Hawker's first time in the powerful Nieuport Goshawk, G-EASK. He sat in the cockpit at Hendon Aerodrome for 30 minutes, listening to the engine and waiting for it to warm up. When the famous pilot took off, by intention or neglect he didn't fasten his seat belt...[302]

and sunny that mid-summer. The long, soft twilight would give him plenty of time to test out the plane. A light northerly wind was unlikely to trouble the master pilot.

He sat listening to the engine for a while, then leaned out to tell Folland that it was misfiring, probably due to a weak magneto. They both knew this was not a major problem, because the other two magnetos could carry the load if they had to. Nevertheless, Harry ran the engine for another 30 minutes, until he was satisfied it was running smoothly enough for a take-off. As he taxied up the runway, by intention or neglect he didn't bother fastening his seat belt.

Harry warmed the engine a little longer then sped down the runway and lifted the Goshawk into a clear blue sky. The plane was only just airborne, however, when the engine cut out, but immediately restarted. Under Harry's ministrations, it spluttered a few times and resumed its regular beat. The heart of a novice aviator might well have followed a similar path, but for a pilot with Harry's experience this was a minor blip. He might have made a mental note of this tiny example of 'the shoe pinching', but it's unlikely he became flustered over such a detail.

The familiar mosaic of the city of London would have fanned out below him as the plane climbed in a wide arc to the left of the airfield. Harry hadn't done much flying that year, but now he was back in the environment he loved. The bird after which the plane was named, the goshawk, is known for its speed and manoeuvrability, and the famous pilot was no doubt sniffing the air in anticipation of the battle in a few days' time. A dream of speed.

On the ground below, people stopped to watch and point as the sun caught the colourful aircraft, lighting it up like a tiny blue and yellow star as it zoomed up into the brilliant summer sky. At that moment anyone might have believed that nothing could hold back this famous pilot and his winged capsule from creating a new world record in a few days' time. In those few sun-filled seconds, anything was possible.

Then, in one terrible moment, the Goshawk's spectacular arc ended abruptly, as if it had hit a glass wall in the sky. The plane's tail waggled erratically and it lurched to the left.

Next minute, it began to plummet in a steep dive. The engine that was designed to pull the streamlined plane to mind-boggling speeds through the air was now wrenching it rapidly earthwards.

To the watchers below, this didn't look like something the pilot intended. Their worst fears were realised when they saw a burst of red flame leap from the engine. Orange tongues of fire streamed back along the fuselage, then just as quickly disappeared. There was no reprieve, however—the plane continued to plunge downwards, nose first.

Years earlier, Harry Hawker had managed to escape almost unscathed when he wrangled his Sopwith Scout out of a spinning dive over Brooklands. On that occasion he crash-landed in a copse of trees. This time his legendary luck seemed to have eluded him as the plane headed rapidly towards the earth below.

Suddenly, a glimpse of salvation. Just 50 feet above the ground, he managed to flatten out the dive, turning the plane to the left over a grassy field. Above the Atlantic, Harry had been able to zoom the aircraft upwards moments before it hit the water. This time the plane was going way too fast for that sort of manoeuvre. Horrified bystanders thought they could see the pilot standing in the open cockpit.

Moments later the Goshawk smashed into the ground, belly first, splintering the undercarriage and bursting into flames. It bounced forward, igniting another explosion, before finally sliding to a flaming stop some seventy-five yards from its impact point.

Somewhere along this fiery path Harry was catapulted from the open cockpit. He landed about fifty yards away, minus his shoes and socks.

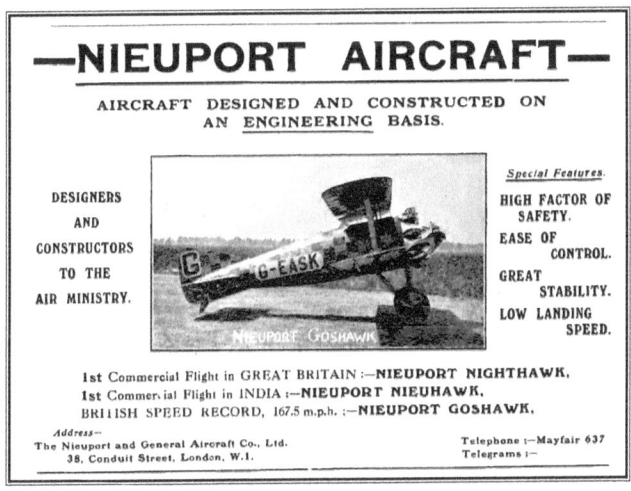

The Nieuport Goshawk in which Harry Hawker made his final flight, on 9 July, 1921. It was painted in bright blue and yellow checks.[303] *Its official British Speed Record was 166.5mph.*

Bystanders rushed over to where he lay. They found him alive, but unconscious. He had a fractured neck, right ankle and left forearm, and there were patches of raw skin on his arms and legs from burning petrol. His brown leather shoes were lying 90 yards away, severely charred except for the parts that would've been jammed against the rudder bar. Around him, the grass had ignited, dry from London's hot spell of weather, and firemen from a fortuitously passing Hendon Fire Brigade truck quickly quenched the flames.

Apart from the fractures and burns, the rescuers realised that the famous pilot was suffering severe internal injuries. These first responders did what they could, but ten minutes later 32-year-old Harry George Hawker MBE AFC was dead.[304]

He never would know if he could fly faster than the French.

News of Harry Hawker's death flashed across the world. Tributes flooded in from politicians and friends, and even the British media itself: 'The whole press unites in sorrow and mourning for Mr Harry Hawker.'[305] There was a similar tribute from the French press, which 'expresses its greatest regret at the death of Harry Hawker, and pays homage to his skill and bravery.'[306]

The acting Australian Prime Minister, Sir Joseph Cook, said he'd met Harry at a dinner after he 'came back to life' post-Atlantic and had been impressed by his 'bright, alert, intelligent manner.'[307] Cook said Harry was 'a typical Australian, full of courage and full of resource.' King George V, who in his second telegram to Muriel just over two years before had said, 'Long may he be spared to you,' now had to tell her the nation had lost one of its most distinguished airmen, and that the loss of her husband was 'irreparable'.[308]

This time there would be no miraculous return.

At Harry's funeral on Monday 18 July, 1921, a huge crowd, silent and bare-headed, lined the short route from St Paul's Church, Hook, to the cemetery, 'as if the remains of a national hero were being laid to rest.'[309] Resting on the coffin were a bouquet of carnations from Muriel, and flowers from Pamela, who would soon be three years old, and from Mary, 14 months. Leading the funeral procession was Harry's beloved Sunbeam, covered in wreaths and driven by Muriel's brother, Laurence. The wreaths came from all over the world, including one from Mackenzie Grieve and another from Billy Hughes, who had earlier suggested the transatlantic crossing was more a test of men than of machines.

A special area of the cemetery was set aside for Harry's grave, which was marked out with evergreen shrubs and flowers from the Hawkers' own garden across the road.

Muriel's brother, Laurence Peaty, drove the wreath-laden Hawker Sunbeam at the head of the funeral procession.[310]

There were conflicting reports about the way Harry Hawker had died. Some observers suggested the plane was at 6000 feet when it began its plunge. Others claimed the pilot had jumped from the cockpit just before the plane hit the ground. There was also an allegation that the aircraft's wings had been shortened to make the plane faster and that this could've been an aggravating factor. 'Absolutely untrue,' Goshawk designer Henry Folland retorted.

Fellow fliers cast doubt on any explanation other than a catastrophic incident because they believed Harry would have survived anything else. Andrew Lang, a friend since his Melbourne days, said: 'One could rest assured that Harry fought it out to the last. He was not the type of man to jump from a machine to certain death when there was a fighting chance with his machine.'[311]

Harry himself had earlier said, 'If I must die in the air I hope I would be flying high. It would be easier.'[312]

Two inquiries were set up to investigate the circumstances of the crash, one an official coronial inquiry into his death, the other by the Air Ministry's Accident Investigation Branch.

The official inquest into Harry's death was conducted by Dr G Cohen at Hendon Town Hall on Sunday 17 July, just five days after the accident. Henry Folland attested to the airworthiness of the Goshawk, and said he personally checked it after the overhaul about a month prior. Various witnesses to the crash described what they saw, including a young girl, Edith Cantlief, as explained in the coroner's report:

> When the machine crashed there was an explosion. The machine rose again and again crashed, and there was a second explosion. After the second explosion there were "lumps" flying from the machine. One of the "lumps" flew to the spot where Mr. Hawker was afterwards lying, and she supposed that the 'lump was him.'[313]

Tellingly, it was Muriel's father, not Harry's wife, who formally identified the body.

At the inquest, once again the state of the pilot's health became a focus. Dr Eric Gardner, the general practitioner Harry originally consulted, told the Coroner that a London specialist had diagnosed tuberculosis disease in Hawker's spine 18 months earlier (which, Gardner said, had subsequently been proven by the discovery in the post-mortem of an abscess on the spine). He said that Harry had refused to accept the specialist's recommendation to give up flying. This account tallies with Muriel's story of that time, leading to the Hawkers' decision to undertake Christian Science treatment.

Gardner said that Harry didn't realise the seriousness of his condition. He claimed that when their paths had crossed on Easter Monday that year, Harry had 'jeered' at him, saying that he'd done well without the treatment the doctor had recommended. Gardner said he told the famous pilot he regarded that as a temporary remission.

The haemorrhage discovered in the post-mortem occurred either in the air or on impact, Gardner said, with the former the more likely. The general practitioner said that his theory was that Harry was seated when the plane hit the ground and was thrown forward 'and his chin struck something, which threw his head back and broke his neck.'[314]

The Coroner dismissed the notion that the plane caught fire mid-air, accepting expert opinion that the flames witnesses had seen would've been those normally expected from open exhaust ports. As Dr Cohen saw it, the Goshawk caught fire when it hit the ground. He concluded that Harry Hawker 'died of injuries caused by the smashing to the ground of the aeroplane in which he was flying, and of which he had lost control owing to his physical disability.'[315] The official verdict was 'Death by misadventure.'

Harry had earlier given his own verdict: 'All accidents are due to carelessness, or something going wrong with the machines—the motors or the mechanism. Eliminate carelessness, and you only have defective material or construction; but these too are but the result of some elements of carelessness.'

It seems that 'death by misadventure' was not in his lexicon, but he also hadn't allowed for the possibility that the 'defective material' might not be in the plane, but in the pilot.

Hawker's grave memorial reminds us he had just nine remarkable years in aviation.

In their mechanical inspection of the wreckage, the Air Ministry investigators found that the float chamber cover of one of the carburettors was completely unscrewed, leading them to conclude petrol had splashed out on to the engine, causing a fire. Nevertheless, the evidence also suggested Harry had been able to extinguish the flames. The cause of the crash, according to the

Air Ministry investigators, was that Harry hadn't been able to land the plane, 'owing to physical disability caused by burns and spinal haemorrhage.'[316] A post-mortem examination had found extensive tuberculosis disease in Harry's spine, and doctors had concluded that a large adjacent abscess had burst. Experts said that haemorrhaging in the spine would have brought intense physical pain and likely caused rapid paralysis of the legs.

The Accident Investigation Branch concluded that while Harry might have been able to make an emergency landing despite the fire, the sudden and painful eruption in his spine had incapacitated him, causing him to lose control.

In the House of Commons, the Secretary to the Air Ministry acknowledged his department was aware that Harry Hawker was suffering from tuberculosis, but that a medical examination in December 1920 had justified the renewal of his licence. That licence expired in June 1921, meaning that at the time of his death Harry technically was flying without a licence.

As if that made any difference.

As the editor of *Flight* said, 'When ill health should have kept him on the ground he still continued to fly, not so much, perhaps, because he underestimated his illness, as because his restless nature would not suffer him to sit still and "take things easy".'[317]

Muriel Hawker was incensed by the Coroner's verdict and the Accident Investigation Branch's conclusions. In a letter to the *Daily Mail* a few days after the inquest, she said her husband had been 'perfectly well', and that his back was 'completely cured and had given him no trouble for 12 months.'[318] In the absence of actual proof of the cause of the accident, she said, it was not right to attribute it to physical disability. Muriel declared that the 'stigma' of the finding was 'repugnant' to her.

Twelve months later, in a book about Harry's life and work, Muriel detailed the success of the Christian Science treatment and made no mention at all of the Accident Investigation Branch's findings or the Coroner's verdict. What she did say about the crash was:

> Exactly what happened or what was the cause will never be known, but it seems probable that something serious, which, Harry realised, might cause a fire, occurred while he was fairly high over Burnt Oak, Hendon; and it was evident that he proceeded to land, but was unable to do so before the machine took fire. As the aeroplane struck the ground the petrol tank exploded. That Harry died instantaneously there is no doubt, for his body, terribly fractured, was found some 200 yards away.[319]

Muriel mourned Harry's passing, but she didn't regret the lifestyle they'd had. How dare people persist in suggesting 'that a man with dependants should not continually risk his life unless they were securely provided for,' she said.[320] The editor of the *Lincoln Star* newspaper in the US claimed Harry's death 'emphasizes the price of daring too much and too often.'[321]

But despite her earlier fears about his venture into car racing, the widow of the famous aviator said she was all for Harry taking risks: 'Never would I understand why a man of a hazardous career should have to choose between that career and the comforts of his own home, and possible parenthood, because of a fearful dread of a premature parting which was allowed to exist.'[322] To the very end, Muriel Hawker stood by her man.

On the Sunday before he died, he'd said to her, 'Let's go out alone like we used to do and not take anyone with us.'³²³

And they did.

In a eulogy in *Flight* magazine, the editor said it was Harry's 'indomitable spirit' that set him apart from other expert pilots: 'Within a small exterior—not an insignificant one, for his extraordinary will power and energy prevented it from being insignificant—he had a great and restless spirit, a driving force which made it imperative for him to be up and doing.'³²⁴

His fellow flier on the aborted Atlantic attempt, Mackenzie Grieve, had given his own verdict of Harry's capabilities while they were still in Newfoundland: 'To my mind he is an ideal pilot, with unlimited pluck, unfailingly good judgment, and what is equally to the point, an inexhaustible supply of good spirits. In his handling of an aeroplane I am tempted to believe that he takes advantage of some sixth sense which allows him to become an integral part of the machine.'³²⁵

Even the Americans, whom Harry had openly criticised for their 'safe' passage to Europe, were in awe of his prowess. One US writer suggested he had 'an ability to draw a line between sheer recklessness and prudent daring' and that 'what would be recklessness in another had in his case simply been good craftsmanship because of his consummate skill and wonderful nerve and vitality.'³²⁶

An Australian contemporary of Harry Hawker who knew him well, summed up his picture of the world-famous pilot:

'He never struck me as being young, though he was still little more than a lad at the time of his death; but he was never old either. He was the spirit of early aviation, brave and ageless.'³²⁷

POSTSCRIPT
'A shoddy, trudging lollypop'
— How the *Mary* rescued Harry Hawker and Mackenzie Grieve

As they sat in the plane's wave-drenched cockpit in the middle of the Atlantic Ocean, through the waves and drifting fog that day after their Sunday take-off, Harry Hawker and Mackenzie Grieve snatched glimpses of the *Mary* as it ploughed towards them. Although their rubber suits were keeping them dry, 12-foot waves were crashing over the plane, and they decided to launch the lifeboat. They hadn't been able to practise releasing the tiny craft in their Newfoundland lake tryout, but now the clips snapped open easily in the foaming sea. Clutching on to the pitching plane, together they turned the little wooden dinghy right way up, and lowered it into the choppy water.

Then they physically abandoned the Sopwith *Atlantic*, the plane in which they'd hoped to create history, and scrambled into the punt, which was bouncing around in the swell.

Although the *Mary* was on its way, it was fighting against heavy seas. The ship was fully loaded with a grain cargo it had picked up in New Orleans, so was low in the water. Its engine was designed for a slow, steady trip across the Atlantic, not for a short sharp rescue mid-way. Finally the captain manoeuvred the *Mary* within 200 yards of the pitching Sopwith and held it there as steadily as he could, but his crew struggled to launch the ship's lifeboat in the big seas.

When they finally managed to get the boat into the water, the big Danes took to the oars and headed determinedly towards the two stranded men. It was tough going, however, and they fought to make headway, like a surf club crew heading out through the breakers. This was no seaside jaunt, however, and it took the seamen an hour-and-a-half to reach the downed fliers. Just as they got there, a big wave flung the *Mary's* lifeboat against the plane's fuselage. But the sailors were able to keep their boat still enough for Harry and Grieve to jump across from their little punt.

The lifeboat was attached to the *Mary* by a line, and with the crew again rowing furiously, the sailors on board began to haul rescuers and rescued back to the ship. A lifeline indeed. Even then, it was another 30 minutes before everyone was safely on board the Danish freighter.

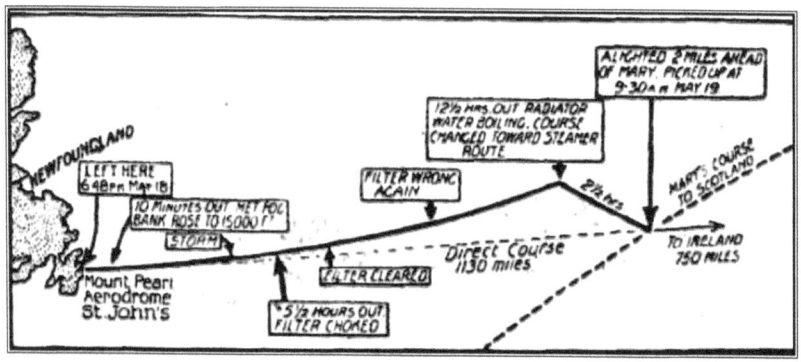

Rough map from Flight *magazine of the Sopwith* Atlantic's *path from the point of departure to the pick-up of Hawker and Grieve by the captain of the* Mary.[328]

The Captain introduced himself. His name was Adolph Duhn and he spoke good English. 'Another hour and you would have gone down,' he said.[329]

By now the weather was closing in fiercely around them, and the sea was churning. The two men hadn't recovered much of what was in the plane, and had come aboard coatless, hatless and bootless. The mailbag of specially franked mail was also lost, although Grieve still had possession of the (slightly damp) letter from the Governor of Newfoundland to King George V. As for the plane itself, Captain Duhn expressed regret that, even if it was possible in the prevailing conditions, they didn't have the equipment required to lift it on board.

At this point the flight wasn't overdue at Brooklands, but Harry and Grieve were anxious to advise the world that they were safe. Sorry, said Captain Duhn, but the *Mary* has no wireless—while at sea it had no way of communicating with another vessel or shore station except by flag. We're on the edge of the trade routes, he told the two fliers, so we should soon come across another ship with wireless.

The weather, which had so dominated Harry's and Grieve's lives for the past two months, then stepped in to mess up their plans once again. Within half a day of the rescue, the storm that had been playing tag with them finally erupted in full mid-Atlantic fury. The captain decided to alter course to try to skirt the worst of it.

The *Mary's* top speed was only about nine knots at the best of times; loaded with freight and heading into gale-force winds, it was down to around a miserly one knot. What's more, the diversion would take them away from the main shipping lanes, which meant they were unlikely to meet another vessel anytime soon. So, while Muriel counted down the hours at Brooklands, Harry and Grieve were bunked down mid-Atlantic on a Danish tramp steamer that had no wireless, was making miniscule progress north-eastwards, and had little chance of crossing paths with another ship for some time.

American poet Percy Mackaye later put the episode into verse:

> 'Twas Danish Mary picked them up
> Out of the air and sea;
> A shoddy, trudging lollypop
> A traipsing slatternly.
> The cry rang north, the cry rang south:
> 'The vanished, where are they?'
> But Danish Mary shut her mouth
> And shuffled on her way. [330]

Captain Duhn at first assumed his unexpected guests were American, and Harry had the feeling that he wished they were. Like the captain of the Greek freighter who rescued the crew of *NC-1*, Duhn knew nothing of the race across the Atlantic, and seemed unimpressed by the endeavour.

'We were struck by the casual manner in which he took the whole business,' Harry said later, 'as if it were an everyday affair to take airmen out of the Atlantic.'[331]

For their part, Harry and Grieve were exhausted when they boarded the *Mary*. They felt no elation at being rescued. After the intensity of the flight and the drama with the radiator, along with Harry's airsickness, all they wanted to do was sleep. It seems that even the Newfoundland take-off itself was an anti-climax for them, perhaps because their hands were forced by the Americans. When they first arrived in St John's, they'd given themselves two weeks to prepare for departure. This had turned into almost two months, and the waiting had dragged on them, their enthusiasm seemingly fluctuating in line with the weather reports.

'We had been waiting for so long,' Grieve said afterwards, 'we felt callous about the whole thing.'

For six days the *Mary* plodded north-east through unforgiving seas, making for the northern tip of Scotland, which it would skirt before turning south into the North Sea and towards its destination, the port of Horsens, Denmark. The captain and crew were extremely hospitable, and once their new guests had benefited from an initial sleep, and Harry's stomach was not so queasy, they passed the time chatting to the captain or reading novels from his English language collection. Given Muriel's assessment of his reading ability, scanning those novels must have been a challenging task for her husband.

With the ship completely incommunicado, Harry and Grieve had no idea how their transatlantic competitors were faring. They'd seen the crowds gathered around Raynham and Morgan's plane as they went over late Sunday afternoon, and might have assumed the Martinsyde was in the air close behind them, and had now had likely won the *Daily Mail* prize. Similarly, they thought all the *Nancies* had made it to the Azores, and as the *Mary* chugged its way through heavy seas, they might have believed that their American rivals had surely by now claimed the honour of being the first to cross the Atlantic.

As they discovered when they finally made landfall, neither of these assumptions was true.

What might Harry have been thinking about Muriel and Pamela as he sat in his cabin struggling with his English novels? Did he think of the many times he'd sat with her in their lounge room while she'd read to him from his favourite books, the ones she thought were 'boy's own'? Did he wonder what she was thinking as days went by without word, and whether she'd remembered what he'd said to her before he left: 'If things don't go right, never give up hope.'

Had she managed to do that, or had she succumbed to despair, thinking that Pamela was going to grow up without a father?

As the days passed and they remained so far off the normal shipping lanes that they sighted no other ships, Harry and Grieve must have been feeling as they had in Newfoundland—that they could but 'possess their souls in patience, and wait.' Captain Duhn was not inclined to seek out a port to drop them off, because that would take him out of his way, and he had a schedule to keep and was himself keen to reach home and be reunited with his young wife. It was not until the ship's track brought them closer to land, the wild islands off north-west Scotland, that he took the opportunity to divert briefly towards a Coastguard station where he could send a visual signal.

The protruding tail of the Sopwith Atlantic, *found by the USS* Lake Charlottesville *two weeks after Hawker landed the plane mid-ocean..*[332]

Even then he did not tarry long, and perhaps it was the two fliers who encouraged the captain to turn back to see the question from the shore, IS-IT-HAWKER?, and send up the final Y-E-S. It was not long afterwards that Muriel heard the news, the Navy flashed into action, and the whole nation went berserk.

A Newfoundland fisherman later retrieved the undercarriage that Harry and Grieve had discarded over the sea as they left Newfoundland, and reportedly donated it to a local museum. Two weeks after the plane left, an American steamship, *Lake Charlottesville*, came across the wreckage of Harry and Grieve's Sopwith mid-Atlantic, the partly stripped tail protruding vertically from the ocean like a marker buoy. The ship's captain salvaged the plane and some of the mail, and transported it to England, arriving in Falmouth on 28 May. Representatives of the Sopwith company, the *Daily Mail* and Selfridges Department Store purchased the remains of the *Atlantic* through the Receiver of Wrecks. It was transhipped from the SS *Lake Charlotteville* and transported to London, where it was displayed on the roof of Selfridges in Oxford Street for some time.

It was claimed that a three-cent stamp recovered with the wreckage and overstamped 'First Transatlantic Air Post April, 1919', sold in London not long after for £210 in aid of a Newfoundland war charity.[333] Another stamp from the same batch sold in London in 2015 for £16,000.[334]

An examination of the radiator apparently found no sign of the accumulated debris that Harry thought had caused the over-heating problem. Other suggestions included that the

One of the 3-cent stamps recovered from the Sopwith Atlantic sold for £16,000 (almost AUD$30,000) in 2015.[335]

opening and closing vents on the radiator had been inserted the wrong way round or were wrongly labelled, resulting in the opposite effect to what Harry had intended, or that the carburettor had iced up, a little-known phenomenon in 1919, but which Alcock and Brown had experienced on their successful flight.

The Board of Trade in Britain awarded pieces of silver plate to Captain Duhn, skipper of the *Mary*, and distributed money to the ship's crew, in appreciation of their rescue of Harry Hawker and McKenzie Grieve.

In the year after her husband's death, Muriel Hawker wrote a book, *H. G. Hawker, Airman: His life and work*. 'With his words still fresh in my memory, that, should anything ever happen to him, the one thing to do was to get work which would occupy my mind,' she said, 'I took upon myself the task of writing my husband's life.'[336] Her intention was 'to convey some idea of the great work and spirit of one who attempted much, and, although crowned by few successes, was never for one moment discouraged.'

Harry's MBE and his Air Force Cross were later stolen from Muriel's home in England along with a number of his trophies.[337] He left £5437 in his will, the equivalent today of a little over a quarter of a million pounds.[338]

Muriel later remarried, twice, and died in West Sussex in 1983, aged 87, having outlived all three husbands.

 Under the chairmanship of Tommy Sopwith and from 1923 with the design expertise of Sidney Camm, the H. G. Hawker Engineering Company maintained the strong reputation for innovation and quality that Sopwith Aviation had developed during World War I. The Hawker Hart, a two-seater biplane light bomber, was one of their early successes. In 1935, the company bought up other firms to form the Hawker Siddeley Aircraft Company, which was responsible for a string of successful aircraft in World War II, including the Hunter, Tempest, Typhoon, and Hurricane.

As the company continued to evolve, the last use of the Hawker name was from 1963 to 1976, when the firm's title was modified to Hawker Siddeley Aviation. In 1977 the former H G Hawker Engineering Company became British Aerospace; in 1999 it took its current name, BAE Systems.

In England, the impressive Kingston Aviation Centenary Project acknowledged the contributions of the more than 30,000 individuals who designed and built aircraft for the Sopwith, Hawker, Hawker Siddeley and British Aerospace organisations based in Kingston upon Thames from 1912 to 1992.[339] Among the most well-known names in the Hawker stable across the years are the Hawker Hart, the Hawker Hurricane of World War II fame, and the Hawker Hunter.

In addition to having his name perpetuated for decades through successive companies and a string of successful aircraft, Harry Hawker has been honoured in other ways. In November 2014, he was inducted into the Australian Aviation Hall of Fame. More than 2000 people gathered at the Moorabbin Airport at Mentone in Victoria in 1969 for the dedication of a memorial to Harry Hawker, and 20 years later the airport was renamed 'Moorabbin (Harry Hawker) Airport' (although the addition now seems to have lapsed on the airport's website).

In 1978, Australia Post released an 18-cent stamp depicting his portrait.

And in memory of the Australian aviation pioneer, in 2007 Kingston University London opened a £4 million 'Hawker Wing' at its Roehampton Vale Campus for engineering teaching staff and students.

In recent times, Hawker family members have set up a website, 'Harry George Hawker: Australian pioneer aviator', www.harryhawker.com.au, 'to recognise and celebrate Harry's achievements as an aviator, aircraft designer and engineer.' James Dale is active in promoting the life and achievements of Harry Hawker and in identifying useful resources.

Commander Kenneth Mackenzie Grieve, A.F.C., R.N., retired from the Royal Navy in March 1920, ten months after the transatlantic attempt. On 14 June, 1923 he married Janet Baddeley at the Parish Church, Dibden, England. The couple had a daughter and subsequently moved to Canada, where the

Mackenzie-Grieve family had farming interests. Mackenzie Grieve died in Canada in 1942, aged 62.

In Newfoundland, Vice-Admiral Kerr and his crew wanted to have a crack at beating Alcock and Brown's time in their four-engine modified V/1500 bomber. However, in early July the Handley-Page Company decided they'd had enough and directed them to fly to the United States. Because of engine trouble, running short of fuel, forced landings and extensive repairs, their journey south via Nova Scotia and New York to Ohio eventually took the crew seven months.

With Lieutenant Charles Biddlecombe as his new navigator, Frederick Raynham took off again from St John's for a transatlantic crossing on 17 July 1919, a month after Alcock and Brown's successful bid. This time he lifted the Martinsyde 120 feet off the ground. Again the plane came crashing back to earth, however, and was seriously damaged. Both crew escaped injury, but Raynham finally gave up. On his return to England, he went on to have a distinguished flying career, including a stint as a test pilot with H. G. Hawker Engineering.

Harry Hawker spent only nine years of his short life in aviation. However, that nine years spanned an era of a demanding world war and a rapidly emerging industry. Both developments quickly took advantage of his remarkable abilities as a test pilot and aircraft designer. Corporately, Hawker's leadership in aviation had an immediate impact on Sopwith Aviation and its successor companies at the time. That legacy has echoed down the years though the companies that evolved from the robust start provided by Hawker and his associates. It is fitting that so many planes in the decades since his death have borne the Hawker name.

---

1 *Flight* magazine, 5 June 1919

ACKNOWLEDGEMENTS

Just as it takes a village to raise a child, so it takes a motley crew to produce a book. This particular book has been in process for some years, and has gone through several iterations (and numerous titles).

Helping it along the way with incisive critical comments have been my Griffith University colleagues Ann Kelly and Mark Tyler and my writer friend Karen Lee.

I've also valued the ongoing encouragement of my family, in Brisbane, Sydney and Launceston, for my writing endeavours. Also of fellow creative Maree Reedman.

I'd also like to acknowledge the support and advice I've had in various ways with archival resources while writing *A Great and Restless Spirit*. These include Dave Robinson at Aviation Ancestry, Beatrice Meecham at Brooklands Museum and David Hassard at Kingston Aviation, UK, along with Tim Felce (Airwolfhound) for the great Sopwith Camel image on the front cover.

In Australia, James Dale and others have done a formidable job in setting up a dedicated website and identifying Hawker-related material in the invaluable Trove collection. Libraries have been impressively prompt in providing high-res images for inclusion, all of which are carefully attributed in the book.

I'm very grateful to Anne Hamilton at Armour Books for offering me a contract to publish *A Great and Restless Spirit*, and for some keen-eyed editing. Beckon Creative has lived up to its name with the amazing cover and overall book design.

My wife Cheryl generously continues to tolerate the hours I spend at my laptop. While I was writing this book, she also listened without too much eye-rolling whenever I dropped fascinating (!) anecdotes about Harry Hawker into our conversations.

Ultimately, of course, responsibility for this book rests with me. I'm conscious there are readers who know a lot more about planes, racing cars and speedboats than I do. Also, family members undoubtedly have more intimate knowledge of aspects of Harry George Hawker's and Muriel Alice Peaty's lives. I acknowledge my limitations in those respects, and hope you won't seize too strongly on the errors and omissions.

There are various accounts elsewhere about Harry Hawker's life, but I wanted to bring his story together in a different way. I've tried to be both creative and respectful, to weave in the special part that Muriel played, and to re-examine his underlying health issues. I leave it to readers to decide how well I've succeeded.

D.R. Dymock

Books

Allen, H. *The story of the airship (non-rigid): A study of one of America's lesser known defense weapons*, 1942, The Lakeside Press, R. R. Donnelley & Sons Company, Chicago.

Babington-Smith, C. *Testing time: the story of British test pilots and their aircraft*, 1961, Harper & Sons, New York.

Blackmore, L. K., *Hawker: One of aviation's greatest names*, 1990, David Bateman, Auckland.

Bloomsbury [Publishing], *Hurricane*, 2018, Osprey Publishing.

Bosher, J. 2012. *Imperial Vancouver Island: Who Was Who, 1850–1950*. Berry Books.

Bramson, A.1990. *Pure luck: The authorised biography of Thomas Sopwith, 1888–1989*, Patrick Stephens, Sparkford, Somerset.

Burns, B.J. *The flying firsts of Walter Hinton: From the 1919 Transatlantic flight to the Arctic and the Amazon*. Jefferson, NC: McFarland & Co., 2012.

Crotty, D. A. *Flying Life: John Duigan and the first Australian aeroplane*, Museum Victoria, 2010.

Gwynn-Jones, T. *The air racers: Aviation's golden era 1909–1936*, 1983, Lansdowne Press.

Kenneth Grieve, Royal Navy Service Record, National Archives' reference ADM 196/45/219, Kew, UK.

King, H.F. *Sopwith aircraft 1912-1920*, Putnam, London.

M. Hawker, *H. G. Hawker, airman: his life and work*, Hutchinson & Co., London, 1922.

McCaffery, D. *Air Aces: The lives and times of twelve Canadian fighter pilots*, James Lorimer & Co, Toronto. 1990.

Motor Boating Magazine — Export and Commercial Boat Number, September 1920, https://books.google.com › books › about › MotorBoating.

Nevin, D. (2004). *The pathfinders*, Time-Life, UK.

Rosie, G. (2012) *The Flight of the Titan: The Story of the R34*, Birlinn Ltd, Edinburgh (e-book)

Rowe, P., 1977. *The great Atlantic air race*, London: Angus and Robertson.

Weintraub, S., 2013, *Young Mr. Roosevelt: FDR's Introduction to War, Politics, and Life*, Hachette, UK.

Wilbur, T. *The first flight across the Atlantic*, 1969, Naval Historical Center, Washington.

Newspapers and journals

'Aeolus', *Flight*, 12 June, 1914.
A marrying month: Four interesting weddings, *The Sketch*, 21 Nov 1917, 161, www.illustratedfirstworldwar.com/item/a-marrying-month-four-interesting-weddings.
'Atlantic Flight', *The Port Macquarie News and Hastings River Advocate*, 24 May, 1919, 4.
'Aviator Hawker aloft', *The Leader*, Melbourne, 11 Apr 1914, 39.
'Aviators expected to start flight across Atlantic Ocean today', *St John's Daily Star*, 12 April 1919, 1.
BAE Systems, 'Sopwith Aviation Company', www.baesystems.com/en/heritage/sopwith-aviation-company
Bingham, A. 'The Original Press Baron: The Role and Legacy of Lord Northcliffe', 2013, The University of Sheffield. Retrieved from: https://docplayer.net/39526242-The-original-press-baron-the-role-and-legacy-of-lord-northcliffe-adrian-bingham-senior-lecturer-in-history-the-university-of-sheffield.html.
'British airmen coming to try Atlanticflight', *New York Times*, 19 March 1919, www.nytimes.com/1919/03/19/archives/british-airmen-coming-to-try-atlantic-flight-steamer-was-bringing.html.
Canadian Enyclopedia, Mount Pearl, 2015, www.thecanadianencyclopedia.ca/en/article/mount-pearl.
Castle, I. 'London, Bombing of', '1914-1918-online. *International Encyclopedia of the First World War*, 2016, https://encyclopedia.1914-1918-online.net/home.
'Commander Read's wife confident of his ability to fly across Atlantic', *Dubuque Telegraph Herald*, 30 May, 1919, 4.
Crouch, T. 'In the Museum: Dangerous crossing', *Air and Space Magazine*, November 2010, https://www.airspacemag.com/history-of-flight/in-the-museum-dangerous-crossing-58604113.
'Editorial comment', *Flight*, 5 June, 1919, 723.
'Fatal flight', *Daily Standard*, Brisbane, 15 Oct 1921, 7.
Field, L. Harmsworth Trophy, 1920, www.lesliefield.com/races/1920_harmsworth_trophy_miss_america_wins.htm.
'Flight began this afternoon', *St John's Daily Star*, 12 April 1919, 1.
'French Press Tribute', *The Maitland Daily Mercury*, 16 Jul 1921, 5.
Friedman, H. & Friedman, A. 'The admiral and the aeroplane', *Aeroplane*, May 2004, 82–87.
'Great British Achievements VI', *Motor Sport*, December 1946, 11.
'Harmsworth Trophy', *Time Magazine*, Monday, Sept. 9, 1929.
Harry Hawker and the British Empire Michelin Cup, 'Historic Wings', http://fly.historicwings.com/2012/10/harry-hawker-and-the-british-empire-michelin-cup/
'Harry Hawker, the Britisher who took chances like a yank', *Literary Digest*, Vol 7, 7 June 1921, Funk and Wagnalls, New York, www.oldmagazinearticles.com/pioneer_aviator_harry_hawker_magazine_article#.XHtS-MAzbIU.
'Harry Hawker', *Grace's Guide to British Industrial History*, www.gracesguide.co.uk/Harry_Hawker.
'Harry Hawker', *Sydney Mail*, 20 Jul 1921, 10.
'Harry Hawker's Grave', *Newcastle Sun*, 20 July, 1921, 1.
'Harry Hawker's death: press mourns the tragedy', *Recorder,* Port Pirie, 16 Jul 1921,

3.
'Hawker killed', *Sydney Morning Herald*, 14 July 1921, 9.
'Hawker & Grieve in London', Barrier Miner, Broken Hill, 28 May 1919, 1.
'Hendon welcomes Atlantic flyers', *Flight*, 5 June, 1919, 731.
'Heroes of the air', *The Argus*, 2 June, 1919, 7.
'His death emphasizes the price of daring too much and too often: Another falls', newspaperarchive.com/lincoln-star-jul-20-1921, 6.'
'Last week one of aviation thrills', *St John's Daily Star*, 23 May, 1919, 1.
'Late Harry Hawker', *National Advocate*, Bathurst, 16 Jul 1921, 2.
'Late Mr Harry Hawker', *Brisbane Telegraph*, 20 July, 1921, 6.
'Legendary figure', *Daily Advertiser*, Wagga Wagga, NSW, 15 Jul 1921, 2.
'Lieut Com Read's own story', *Boston Sunday Globe*, 1 June, 1919, 191.
'Married', *Flight*, June 21, 1923, 334.
M.G.D. ,'The grit of Harry Hawker', *West Australian*, 23 November 1940, 7.
'Mrs Hawker's steadfast faith', *The Times*, 27 May, 1919.
Morley, D. 'Great ties to Uncle Harry', *Air Force*, Vol. 58, No. 10, June 16, 2016, 15, www.defence.gov.au/publications/newspapers/raaf/editions/5810/5810.pdf.
Pitt, J. & Pitt, R. 'Mount Pearl', June 12 2015, www.thecanadianencyclopedia.ca/en/article/mount-pearl.
Read, J. 'Leon Trotsky visited St John's', 2016, www.pressreader.com/canada/the-telegram-st-johns/20160919/282003261893635.
Sheehy, T. 'Hawker, Harry George (1889–1921)', *Australian Dictionary of Biography*, National Centre of Biography, Australian National University, http://adb.anu.edu.au/biography/hawker-harry-george-6605/text11375, published first in hardcopy 1983.
'Success of Hawker's two-stroke', *Examiner,* Launceston, 25 Jun 1921, 3.
'The Daily Mail Atlantic Prize', *Flight*, 21 November 1918, 1316.
'The great Atlantic adventure', *Surrey Comet*, 21 May, 1919, 6.
'The late Harry Hawker', *Kalgoorlie Miner,* 15 Jul 1921, 5.
'The NC-4, First across the Atlantic', www.historynet.com/aviation-history-three-us-flying boats-were-the first-to-fly-across-the Atlantic-in-1919.htm.
'The passage of the Atlantic', *Flight*, 25 July, 1918, p. 835.
'The passing of Harry Hawker', *Flight*, 21 July, 1921, 494.
'The RAF Pageant', *Flight*, 8 July, 1920, 705.
The Times, 18 October 1910, 1 & 6; *Daily News* (London), 19 October 1910, 1.
'The transatlantic flight: Hawker and Grieve retrieved', *Flight*, 29 May 1919, 694.
'The Wellman Disaster', *Progress*, VI (3), 2 January 1911, 20.
'Trans-Atlantic flight', *The Maffra Spectator,* 22 May, 1919, 3.
Trueman, C., '1916 And World War One', historylearningsite.co.uk. ,6 Mar 2015.
'Wait for loved who sailed into upper air and disappeared', *St John's Daily Star*, 21 May, 1919, 1.
'Wife waits confidently', *St John's Daily Star*, 22 April 1919, 1

Selected websites

'1914-1918-online', *International Encyclopedia of the First World War*, https://encyclopedia.1914-1918-online.net/home/

Aviation ancestry database of British aviation advertisements, www.aviationancestry.co.uk/

'Harry George Hawker, Australian pioneer aviator', www.harryhawker.com.au.

'The ultimate car page', www.ultimatecarpage.com/txt/6045/2/Sunbeam-350hp-V12.html

Christian Science, www.christianscience.com

History Learning Site, historylearningsite.co.uk.

History of St John's, www.stjohns.ca/living-st-johns/your-city/st-johns-history/history-st-johns.

Horrie Miller, www.saam.org.au/wp-content/uploads/2014/04/SAAM-Profiles-HORRIE-MILLER.pdf.

Kingston Aviation Day by Day, www.kingstonaviation.org/sopwith-day-by-day

Kingston Aviation, 'The attempt by Harry Hawker to fly across the Atlantic Ocean, May 1919 - as reported by the Surrey Comet', www.kingstonaviation.org/resources/from-the-surrey-comet/1919---atlantic-crossing-attempt

Memorial University of Newfoundland, https://collections.mun.ca/digital/collection/arch

Monthly report of the meteorological office, UK, May 1919, www.metoffice.gov.uk/binaries/content/assets/mohippo/pdf/j/q/may1919.pdf

www.eastsussexww1.org.uk/defending-sussexs-shores/

www.findagrave.com/memorial/24672707/harry-george-hawker#

www.historylearningsite.co.uk/world-war-one/the-western-front-in-world-war-one/christmas-1915-world-war-one/

www.historyplace.com/worldhistory/firstworldwar

www.kingstonaviation.org/sopwith-day-by-day.

www.surreyinthegreatwar.org.uk/places/surrey/kingston/hook.

1 'The passing of Harry Hawker', Editor, *Flight* magazine, 21 July, 1921, 494.
2 *Manitowoc Herald News*, 20 July 1921, 2.

CHAPTER 1: 'HIS ONE DREAM WAS SPEED'

3 ' M. Hawker, *H. G. Hawker, airman: his life and work*, Hutchinson & Co., London, 1922, 182.
4 Library of Congress, Goerge Granthan Bain Collection, Public domain, via Wikimedia Commons.
5 Ibid.
6 The Project Gutenberg eBook of H. G. Hawker, airman: his life and work, by Muriel Hawker, www.gutenberg.org/files/64793/64793-h/64793-h.htm#Page_30
7 'Harry Hawker', Sydney Mail, 20 Jul 1921, 10.
8 www.gracesguide.co.uk/images/8/88/Im070310MCJ-Argyll2.
9 Ibid.
10 Ibid.
11 Ibid.
12 Ibid.

CHAPTER 2: GENIUS UNLEASHED

13 'Harry Hawker', *Sydney Mail*, 20 Jul 1921, 10.
14 https://maas.museum/inside-the-collection/2009/12/02/first-powered-flight-in-australia-episode-3/
15 State Library of Victoria, mp015781.
16 *Aeroplane* magazine, 13 June, 1912. www.aviationancestry.co.uk.
17 'The passing of Harry Hawker', *Flight*, 21 July, 1921, 494.
18 M. Hawker, *H. G. Hawker,* 46.
19 *Flight*, September 20, 1913. www.aviationancestry.co.uk
20 Quoted in M. Hawker, *H. G. Hawker*, 229.
21 *Flight* magazine, 2 August, 1913.
22 *Daily News*, Perth, 3 January 1914, 7.
23 Common daywear for men at the time, worn for business and leisure, comprising a jacket and trousers in plaids, checks, stripes and tweeds.
24 *Harry Hawker in Australia*, nla.gov.au/nla.obj-2442691591, 2.
25 A diary of Sopwith Aviation Company activities through 1914, www.kingstonaviation.org/sopwith-day-by-day/1914.
26 National Library of Australia, nla.gov.au/nla.obj-2442691591
27 Quoted in 'A diary of Sopwith Aviation Company activities through 1914', www.kingstonaviation.org/sopwith-day-by-day/1914.
28 ibid.
29 'Harry Hawker's Biplane', *Harry Hawker in Australia*, nla.gov.au/nla.obj-2442691591, 4.
30 Quoted in 'A diary of Sopwith Aviation Company activities through 1914', www.kingstonaviation.org/sopwith-day-by-day/1914.
31 National Museum of Australia, nma-47655282-001-wm-vs1_o3
32 ibid.
33 'Harry Hawker's Biplane', *Harry Hawker in Australia*, nla.gov.au/nla.obj-2442691591, 4.
34 Albury Library Museum, ARM 16.104

35 M. Hawker, *H. G. Hawker,* 159.
36 G. Payne, '"Arry 'Awker'", 'Aeolus', *Flight*, I5 May 1914, quoted in M. Hawker, *H. G. Hawker*, 128.
37 Library of South Australia, PRG280_1_8_123
38 'Aviator Hawker aloft', *The Leader*, Melbourne, 11 Apr 1914, 39.

CHAPTER 3: 'A SORT OF INSPIRED LIGHT'

39 Quoted in 'A diary of Sopwith Aviation Company activities through 1914', www.kingstonaviation.org/sopwith-day-by-day/1914.
40 The Project Gutenberg eBook of H. G. Hawker, airman: his life and work, by Muriel Hawker, www.gutenberg.org/files/64793/64793-h/64793-h.htm#, facing p. 56.
41 M.G.D. 'The grit of Harry Hawker', *West Australian*, 23 November 1940, 7.
42 A. Bramson, 1990. *Pure luck: The authorised biography of Thomas Sopwith, 1888–1989,* Patrick Stephens, Sparkford, Somerset, 56.
43 Quoted in C. Babington-Smith, *Testing time : the story of British test pilots and their aircraft,* 1961, Harper & Sons, New York, 66.
44 M.G.D. ,'The grit of Harry Hawker'.
45 *The Queenslander*, 2 August 1919, 26, State Library of Queensland, LQ IE1791946_FL1794228.
46 Based on an account in Aeroplane, 1 July 1914, quoted in L. K. Blackmore, *Hawker: One of aviation's greatest names*, 1990, David Bateman, Auckland, 107–8.
47 Quoted in L. K. Blackmore, Hawker, 112.
48 Ibid.
49 National Library of Australia, nla.obj-144916118-m.
50 Based on and rewritten from an account by early aviator Horrie Miller (Blackmore, *Hawker*, 112–3). For more on Miller, see www.saam.org.au/wp-content/uploads/2014/04/SAAM-Profiles-HORRIE-MILLER.pdf.
51 Ibid.
52 M.G.D. ,'The grit of Harry Hawker'.

CHAPTER 4: LIKE A WILL-O'-THE-WISP

53 Ibid.
54 www.kingstonaviation.org/sopwith-day-by-day/1915.
55 'Photographic memories: Sqn Cdr Frederick Rutland', *Navy News*, October, 2011, 12, www.royalnavy.mod.uk/-/media/royal-navy-responsive/images/navynews/archivepdfs/2010s/2011/navy-news-october-2011-issue-687.
56 Quoted in www.kingstonaviation.org/sopwith-day-by-day/1916; entry for 4 March, 1916.
57 M. Hawker, *H. G. Hawker*, 184.
58 Quoted in www.kingstonaviation.org/sopwith-day-by-day/1915; entry for 14 November, 1915.
59 www.kingstonaviation.org/sopwith-day-by-day/1915.html; entry for 21 December, 1915.
60 Quoted in www.kingstonaviation.org/sopwith-day-by-day/1916; entry for 9 March, 1916.
61 M. Hawker, *H. G. Hawker,* 185.
62 Flight magazine, 8 April, 1916, 9376.
63 M. Hawker, *H. G. Hawker*, x
64 M. Hawker, *H. G. Hawker,* 186.

65 M. Hawker, *H. G. Hawker*, 185.
66 Bonhams Auctions, www.bonhams.com/auctions/24733/lot/421.
67 'Harry Hawker', *Sydney Mail*, 20 Jul 1921, 10.
68 Ibid.

CHAPTER 5: NO RESPECTER OF FOOLS
69 M. Hawker, *H. G. Hawker*, 197.
70 www.kingstonaviation.org/sopwith-day-by-day/1917; entry for 16 May, 1917.
71 'Harry Hawker', *Sydney Mail*, 20 Jul 1921, 10.
72 Ibid.
73 A. Bramson, *Pure luck*, 87.
74 Airwolfhound, CC BY-SA 2.0 <https://creativecommons.org/licenses/by-sa/2.0>, via Wikimedia Commons.
75 The Project Gutenberg eBook of H. G. Hawker, airman: his life and work, by Muriel Hawker, www.gutenberg.org/files/64793/64793-h/64793-h.htm#Page_94.
76 M. Hawker, *H. G. Hawker*, 175.
77 In her biography of Hawker, Muriel says the date was 14th November, but this appears to be an error. The official records show 17th November.
78 A marrying month: Four interesting weddings, *The Sketch*, 21 Nov 1917, 161, www.illustratedfirstworldwar.com/item/a-marrying-month-four-interesting-weddings.
79 *The Sketch*, 21 Nov 1917, 161, www.illustratedfirstworldwar.com/item/a-marrying-month-four-interesting-weddings-bpc000005_19171121_01_0007.
80 Build a gasifier, www.build-a-gasifier.com/wp-content/uploads/2014/08/Buick-GasBag.jpg.
81 www.kingstonaviation.org/sopwith-day-by-day/1917; entry for 19 December, 1917.

CHAPTER 6: A POST-WAR PROPOSITION
82 M. Hawker, *H. G. Hawker*, 198.
83 Image: Biblio.com, www.biblio.com/book/automobile-engineer-volume-x-technical-journal/d/1330889159.
84 Ibid.
85 A. Bramson, Pure luck, 96.
86 www.kingstonaviation.org/sopwith-day-by-day/1918; entry for 14 July, 1918.
87 *Flight* magazine, 5 June, 1919, 731.
88 'Harry Hawker', *Sydney Mail*, 20 Jul 1921, 10.
89 M. Hawker, *H. G. Hawker*, 28.
90 M. Hawker, *H. G. Hawker*, 194.
91 M. Hawker, *H. G. Hawker*, 195.
92 Airportjournals.com/theres-no-substitute-for-cubi-inches-a-short-history-of-aero-engine-race-cars.
93 Harry Hawker, wife & child, copyright Brooklands Museum.

CHAPTER 7: WAITING FOR THE FUTURE TO UNFOLD ITSELF
94 M. Hawker, *H. G. Hawker*, 199.
95 Internet archive, archive.org/details/atthewar00nortiala.
96 *Flight* magazine, 28 August, 1913, 893.
97 In 2013, pilot Jeff Boyling recreated the flight in a Catalina seaplane (without the crash!), to celebrate the 100th anniversary of Hawker's 'Circuit of Britain'.
98 *Flight* magazine, 25 July, 1918, 837.
99 *New York Tribune*, 15 June 1919, 2.

100 *Flight* Magazine, July 1918, quoted in www.kingstonaviation.org/sopwith-day-by-day/1918; entry for 25th July, 1918.
101 *The Illustrated London News*, 24 May 1919, 742.
102 *Flight* magazine, 28 November, 1919, www.aviationancestry.co.uk.
103 www.kingstonaviation.org/sopwith-day-by-day/1919; entry for 3 January, 1919.
104 www.kingstonaviation.org/sopwith-day-by-day/1918; entry for 12 November, 1918.
105 *Flight* magazine, 8 January, 1920, www.aviationancestry.co.uk.
106 M. Hawker, op cit.
107 National Library of Australia, nla.obj-140831687-m.

CHAPTER 8: 'MILDLY SURPRISING TO DOWNRIGHT UNPREDICTABLE'

108 Image: Memorial University of Newfoundland, Geography Collection of Historical Photographs of Newfoundland and Labrador, 03.01.001: Harbour Views, St. John's. Ships in heavy ice in the harbour.
109 Climate, St John's, Newfoundland & Labrador, https://stjohnsnewfoundlands.weebly.com.
110 Map: nzhistory.govt.nz/files/documents/waw-maps/Newfoundland_final.pdf.
111 'Aviators expected to start flight across Atlantic Ocean today', *St John's Daily Star*, 12 April 1919, 1.
112 *Decatur Herald*, 19 March, 1919, 1.
113 Hawker and Grieve, *Our Atlantic attempt*, 40.
114 Coll-137 Geography Collection. 07.01.004: St. John's Environs. Buildings on Glendinning's Farm, Mount Pearl, April 1919, Archives and Special Collections, Memorial University Libraries.
St John's, Newfoundland and Labrador.
115 M. Hawker, *H. G. Hawker*, 200.
116 Image: theogm.com/2012/08/24/bridie-molloys-keeping-our-irish-legacy-alive-and-well.
117 Hawker and Grieve, *Our Atlantic attempt*, 42.
118 Memorial University of Newfoundland, Geography Collection of Historical Photographs of Newfoundland and Labrador, 31.01.031: St. John's and Environs. Glendenning's Farm, Mount Pearl, May 1919.

CHAPTER 9: 'POSSESS OUR SOULS IN PATIENCE'

119 M. Hawker, *H. G. Hawker*, 253.
120 Hawker and Grieve, *Our Atlantic attempt*, 41.
121 *The Illustrated London News*, 24 May, 1919, 742.
122 The Project Gutenberg eBook of H. G. Hawker, airman: his life and work, by Muriel Hawker, www.gutenberg.org/files/64793/64793-h/64793-h.htm#Page_122.
123 State Library of Victoria, a04580.
124 'Flight begins this afternoon', *St John's Daily Star*, 12 April 1919, 1.
125 *New York Times*, 12 April 1919, 1.
126 'Flight begins this afternoon', *St John's Daily Star*, 12 April 1919, 1.
127 National Aerospace Library, www.aerosociety.com/news/the-great-transatlantic-race.
128 *New York Times*, 12 April 1919, 3.

CHAPTER 10: A GAME OF CAT AND MOUSE
129 Memorial University of Newfoundland, 01.04.002: New Gower Street, St. John's. View looking east; snow covered street with horse and cart, ca. 1925.
130 'Harry Hawker, the Britisher who took chances like a Yank', *Literary Digest*, Vol 7, 7 June 1921, Funk and Wagnalls, New York, 1.
131 Ibid.
132 'Wife waits confidently', *St John's Daily Star*, 22 April 1919, 1.
133 'Wagers he will be in England Easter Monday', *San Diego Union and Daily Bee*, 20 April 1919, 1.
134 Memorial University of Newfoundland, Geography Collection of Historical Photographs of Newfoundland and Labrador, 05.04.007: Aviation, St. John's. Raynam and Morgan's "Raymor," April-May 1919.
135 *Daily Sketch*, National Aerospace Library, www.aerosociety.com/news/the-great-transatlantic-race.
136 Quoted in R. Watkins, 'Sundstedt, Swedish Naval Officer, Who Seeks to Fly Overseas,' *The Sun*, February 23, 1919.
137 Hawker and Grieve, *Our Atlantic attempt*, 44.
138 Memorial University of Newfoundland, Geography Collection of Historical Photographs of Newfoundland and Labrador, 24.02.002: Ships and other Vessels. "Waiting for the Fog to Lift" : Schooners in full sail, pre-1908.
139 M. Hawker, *H. G. Hawker*, 219.
140 'Trans-Atlantic flight', *The Border Mail and Riverina Times*, 29 April 1919, p. 2, quoting Daily Mail.
141 M. Hawker, *H. G. Hawker*, 220.
142 Hawker and Grieve, *Our Atlantic attempt*, 41.
143 Hawker and Grieve, *Our Atlantic attempt*, 44.
144 Memorial University of Newfoundland, Geography Collection of Historical Photographs of Newfoundland and Labrador, 03.01.016: Harbour Views, St. John's. View of the harbour from Signal Hill, post-1892.
145 Ibid.

CHAPTER 11: NOT WITHOUT A STRUGGLE
146 Quoted in P. Rowe, *The great Atlantic air race*, McLelland and Stewart, Toronto, 1977, 64.
147 Quoted in in Rowe, *The great Atlantic air race*, 88.
148 *The Illustrated London News*, 24 May, 1919, 744.
149 Hawker and Grieve, *Our Atlantic attempt*, 45.
150 Image: Bain News Service, publisher, Public domain, via Wikimedia Commons.
151 Quoted in P. Rowe, *The great Atlantic air race*, 119.
152 *WSS Pictorial News*, 7 June, 1919, Princeton University Posters Collection, Archives Center, National Museum of American History.
153 Quoted in 'A diary of Sopwith Aviation Company activities through 1919', www.kingstonaviation.org/sopwith-day-by-day/1919, 15 May, 1919.
154 S. Weintraub, *Young Mr. Roosevelt: FDR's Introduction to war, politics, and life*, 2013, Hachette, UK, 119.
155 M. Hawker, H. G. Hawker, 253.
156 E. Magnani, *The U.S. Navy's Curtiss NC-4: First Across the Atlantic*, 2002, history.net.com.
157 T. Wilbur, *The First Flight*, 9.
158 Ibid.

290 · A great and restless spirit

CHAPTER 12: 'MANY A PRAYER WAS BREATHED FOR THEIR SUCCESS'
159 'Harry Hawker, the Britisher who took chances like a Yank', *Literary Digest*, Vol 7, 7 June 1921, Funk and Wagnalls, New York, 1.
160 Grieve in Hawker and Grieve, *Our Atlantic attempt*, 97.
161 Quoted in M. Hawker, *H. G. Hawker*, 231.
162 Quoted in 'Harry Hawker, the Britisher who took chances like a Yank', *Literary Digest*, Vol 7, 7 June 1921, Funk and Wagnalls, New York, 1.
163 Ibid.
164 Archives and Special Collections, Memorial University Libraries. St John's, Newfoundland and Labrador, mun.cacdmrefcollectionarch.
165 Quoted in M. Hawker, *H. G. Hawker*, 245.
166 Ibid.
167 National Library of Australia, nla.obj-140831244-m.
168 'Last week one of aviation thrills', *St John's Daily Star*, 23 May, 1919, 1.
169 National Library of Australia, nla.obj-140832928-m.

CHAPTER 13: 'MAKING THE NIGHT LESS TERRIBLE'
170 'Wife waits confidently', *St John's Daily Star*, 22 April 1919, 1.
171 Quoted in M. Hawker, *H. G. Hawker*, 234.
172 USN, Public domain, via Wikimedia Commons, upload.wikimedia.org/wikipedia/commons/7/7f/Curtiss_NC-3_Azores_1919.jpg.
173 Hawker and Grieve, *Our Atlantic attempt*, 49.
174 *Aeronautics*, National Aerospace Library, www.aerosociety.com/news/the-great-transatlantic-race.

CHAPTER 14: CLOSE TO BOILING POINT
175 M. Hawker, *H. G. Hawker*, 240.
176 Hawker and Grieve, *Our Atlantic attempt*, 54.
177 Hawker and Grieve, *Our Atlantic attempt*, 55.
178 The Project Gutenberg eBook of H. G. Hawker, airman: his life and work, by Muriel Hawker, www.gutenberg.org/files/64793/64793-h/64793-h.htm#Page_142.
179 M. Hawker, *H. G. Hawker*, 241.
180 Hawker and Grieve, *Our Atlantic attempt*, 57.
181 M. Hawker, *H. G. Hawker*, 254.

CHAPTER 15: 'AND VANISHED INTO THE BLUE'
182 Quoted in M. Hawker, *H. G. Hawker*, 254.
183 M. Hawker, *H. G. Hawker*, 254.
184 Ibid.
185 'Trans-Atlantic flight', *The Maffra Spectator*, 22 May, 1919, 3.
186 'The great Atlantic adventure', *Surrey Comet*, 21 May, 1919, 6.
187 'Wait for lover who sailed into upper air and disappeared', *St John's Daily Star*, 21 May, 1919, 1.
188 'Harry Hawker', *The Sydney Morning Herald*, 23 May 1919, 9.
189 'Mrs Hawker's steadfast faith', *The Times*, 27 May, 1919.
190 Ibid.
191 'The great Atlantic adventure', *Surrey Comet*, 21 May, 1919, p. 6.
192 Quoted in 'Hawker missing', *Goulburn Evening Penny Post*, 22 May, 1919, 4.
193 'Harry Hawker', *The Sydney Morning Herald*, 23 May, 1919, 9.
194 Aldrich, Arthur F. (Ed.): *The Rudder*, Volume XXXV, June 1919, 291, The Rudder Publishing Company, New York, Wikimedia Commons.

Endnotes · 291

195 *Washington Times,* 25 May, 1919.
196 'Last week one of aviation thrills', *St John's Daily Star,* 23 May, 1919, 1.
197 'Atlantic Flight', *The Port Macquarie News and Hastings River Advocate,* 24 May, 1919, 4.
198 'The Atlantic adventure', *Surrey Comet,* 24 May, 1919, p. 7.
199 A. B. Paterson, 'Hawker the standard bearer', *Smith's Weekly,* 24 May 1919.
200 M. Hawker, *H. G. Hawker,* 255.

CHAPTER 16: THREE MAGIC LETTERS
201 Robert Browning, 'Pippa passes'.
202 M. Hawker, *H. G. Hawker,* 255.
203 'Harry Hawker's fate', *Sunday Times,* Perth, 25 May 1919, 6.
204 Nessy-Pic, CC BY-SA 3.0 <https://creativecommons.org/licenses/by-sa/3.0>, via Wikimedia Commons.
205 M. Hawker, *H. G. Hawker,* 255.
206 *New York Tribune,* 15 June, 1919, 2.
207 Ibid.
208 'Airmen's Atlantic adventure', *Surrey Comet,* 28 May, 1919, 7.
209 Ibid.
210 Ibid.
211 National Library of Australia, nla.obj-140832693-m.
212 Ibid.

CHAPTER 17: 'THE SWEETEST AND MOST WONDERFUL THING'
213 'Safe!', *Flight,* 29 May 1919, 689.
214 Quoted in M. Hawker, *H. G. Hawker,* 260.
215 M. Hawker, *H. G. Hawker,* 264.
216 *Flight* magazine, 29 May, 1919, 694.
217 M. Hawker, *H. G. Hawker,* 256.
218 Library of Congress, Bain Collection, LC-B2- 4948-6.
219 M. Hawker, *H. G. Hawker,* 266.

CHAPTER 18: WILD ABOUT HARRY
220 'Hawker & Grieve in London', *Barrier Miner,* Broken Hill, 28 M May 1919, 1.
221 'Australian soldiers and their hero', The Times, 28 May, 1919, 1.
222 D. Dymock, 'Non-military enjoyment': adult education for Australian troops abroad in World War One, Studies in the Education of Adults, Vol. 29, No.1, 1997, 11–24.
223 Quoted in 'Heroes of the air', *The Argus,* 2 June, 1919, 7.
224 SA Library, PRG280_1_20_355
225 M. Hawker, *H. G. Hawker,* 266.
226 National Library of Australia, nla.obj-141220645-m.
227 'Australian soldiers and their hero', *The Times,* 28 May, 1919, 1.
228 *New York Tribune,* May 1919, 2.
229 *Surrey Comet,* 28 May, 1919, 7.
230 M. Hawker, *H. G. Hawker,* 267.
231 *Surrey Comet,* 28 May, 1919, 7.
232 *Flight* magazine, 29 May, 1919, 695.
233 US CoastGuard, Public domain, via Wikipedia Commons.

CHAPTER 19: A RESTLESS QUEST
234 M. Hawker, *H. G. Hawker,* 244.
235 Quoted in M. Hawker, *H. G. Hawker,* 280.

236 Quoted in in P. Rowe, *The great Atlantic air race*, 181.
237 *The Queenslander*, 2 August 1919, 26, State Library of Queensland, LQ IE1791946_FL1794228.
238 M. Hawker, *H. G. Hawker*, 277
239 M. Hawker, *H. G. Hawker*, 281
240 *Flight* magazine, 5 June, 1919, 729.
241 'Hendon welcomes Atlantic flyers', *Flight*, 5 June, 1919, 731.
242 Ibid.
243 *Flight* magazine, 5 June, 1919, 731.
244 M. Hawker, *H. G. Hawker*, 284.
245 Unknown author, Public domain, via Wikimedia Commons.
246 Hawker and Grieve, *Our Atlantic attempt*, 59.
247 M. Hawker, *H. G. Hawker*, 268.

CHAPTER 20: FEELINGS OF QUALM
248 M. Hawker, *H. G. Hawker*, 291.
249 *Aeroplane* magazine, 25 February, 1920, www.aviationancestry.co.uk.
250 M. Hawker, *H. G. Hawker*, 309.
251 M. Hawker, *H. G. Hawker*, 285.
252 M. Hawker, *H. G. Hawker*, 286.
253 M. Hawker, *H. G. Hawker*, 287.
254 Sopwith - Schneider 1 EAKI, Copyright Brooklands Museum.
255 M. Hawker, *H. G. Hawker*, 291.

CHAPTER 21: 'FINISHED WITH FAILURES'
256 Image: BrooklandsCircuitLayout.png:Spiderlounge at en.wikipediaderivative work.
257 Quoted in M. Hawker, *H. G. Hawker*, 291.
258 M. Hawker, *H. G. Hawker*, 291.
259 Harry Hawker on 6cyl Sunbeam Race 6 BARC meet 24.5.1920, copyright Brooklands Museum.
260 M. Hawker, *H. G. Hawker*, 292.
261 Ibid.
262 Ibid.
263 M. Hawker, *H. G. Hawker*, 293.
264 Harry Hawker in a 150hp Sunbeam racer on Members Banking c.1920, copyright Brooklands Museum.
265 The Project Gutenberg eBook of H. G. Hawker, airman: his life and work, by Muriel Hawker, www.gutenberg.org/files/64793/64793-h/64793-h.htm#Facing page_312.
266 Ibid.
267 M. Hawker, *H. G. Hawker*, 294.
268 Ibid.
269 'The RAF Pageant', *Flight*, 8 July 1920, 705.

CHAPTER 22: 'PRECARIOUS ACTIVITIES'
270 M. Hawker, *H. G. Hawker*, 188.
271 The Project Gutenberg eBook of H. G. Hawker, airman: his life and work, by Muriel Hawker, www.gutenberg.org/files/64793/64793-h/64793-h.htm#Page_300.
272 M. Hawker, *H. G. Hawker*, 299.
273 Ibid.

Endnotes · 293

274 Ibid.
275 Paul Hermans, CC BY-SA 3.0 <https://creativecommons.org/licenses/by-sa/3.0>, via Wikimedia Commons.
276 Ibid.
277 M. Hawker, *H. G. Hawker*, 300.
278 *Motor Boating*, Sept 1920, 10.
279 W. W. Nutting, 'When Miss America Won The Harmsworth Trophy', *Literary Digest*, 18 September, 1920, 71. http://www.lesliefield.com/races/1920_harmsworth_trophy_when_miss_america_won.
280 The Project Gutenberg eBook of H. G. Hawker, airman: his life and work, by Muriel Hawker, www.gutenberg.org/files/64793/64793-h/64793-h.htm#Page_300.
281 M. Hawker, *H. G. Hawker*, 298.
282 'Aeolus', *Flight*, 12 June, 1914.
283 M. Hawker, *H. G. Hawker*, 188.
284 Christian Science, 2019, www.christianscience.com/what-was-christian-science/beliefs-and-teachings.
285 M. Hawker, *H. G. Hawker*, 188.
286 Ibid.
287 Ibid.
288 M. Hawker, *H. G. Hawker*, 189.

CHAPTER 23: 'WE'RE REALLY BEGINNING TO GO NOW!'

289 M. Hawker, *H. G. Hawker*, 303.
290 *Motor Sports Magazine*, October 1948, 48-49, www.motorsportmagazine.com/archive/article/october-1998/48/harry-hawker-aviator-racing-driver.
291 Ibid.
292 'Harry Hawker', *Sydney Mail*, 20 Jul 1921, 10.
293 Quoted in 'Harry Hawker', *Grace's Guide to British Industrial History*, www.gracesguide.co.uk/Harry_Hawker.
294 Advertisement, 'Hawker', *The Motor Cycle*, 23 June 1921, 52.
295 *The Motor Cycle*, 23 June, 1921, www.aviationancestry.co.uk.
296 M. Hawker, *H. G. Hawker*, 310.
297 Ibid.
298 M. Hawker, *H. G. Hawker*, 312.
299 Classic Motors, classicmoto.rs/auto/minerva-ad25-limo-1925-hm3SUI.
300 M. Hawker, *H. G. Hawker*, 313.

CHAPTER 24: BRAVE AND AGELESS

301 Photo: Bonhams Auctions, www.bonhams.com/auctions/17260/lot/366. The one pictured sold for £4,485 (AU$8,334) in 2009.
302 ©FlightGlobal, Rights Managed License.
303 *Aeroplane* magazine, 6 April, 1921, www.aviationancestry.co.uk.
304 Air Ministry, Accidents Investigations Branch, Civil Accident C-43, in Blackmore, Hawker, 210-213.
305 'Harry Hawker's death: press mourns the tragedy', *Recorder*, Port Pirie, 16 Jul 1921, 3.
306 'French Press Tribute', *The Maitland Daily Mercury*, 16 Jul 1921, 5.
307 Quoted in 'The late Harry Hawker', *Kalgoorlie Miner*, 15 Jul 1921, 5.
308 'Late Harry Hawker', *National Advocate*, Bathurst, 16 Jul 1921, 2.
309 'Late Mr Harry Hawker', *Brisbane Telegraph*, 20 July, 1921, 6.

310 The Project Gutenberg eBook of H. G. Hawker, airman: his life and work, by Muriel Hawker, www.gutenberg.org/files/64793/64793-h/64793-h.htm#Page_318.
311 'Harry Hawker', *Sydney Mail*, 20 Jul 1921, 10.
312 'Legendary figure', *Daily Advertiser*, Wagga Wagga, NSW, 15 Jul 1921, 2.
313 'Fatal flight', *Daily Standard*, Brisbane, 15 Oct 1921, 7.
314 ibid.
315 Quoted in 'The passing of Harry Hawker', *Flight,* 21 July, 1921, 494.
316 Air Ministry, Accidents Investigations Branch, *Civil Accident* C-43.
317 'The passing of Harry Hawker', *Flight*, 21 July, 1921, 494.
318 'Harry Hawker's Grave', *Newcastle Sun*, 20 July, 1921, 1.
319 M. Hawker, *H. G. Hawker*, 317.
320 M. Hawker, *H. G. Hawker*, xi.
321 'Another falls', *Lincoln Star*, 20 July 1921, p.6, newspaperarchive.com/lincoln-star-jul-20-1921-p-6.
322 M. Hawker, *H. G. Hawker*, xi.
323 M. Hawker, *H. G. Hawker*, 185.
324 'The passing of Harry Hawker', *Flight*, 21 July, 1921, 494.
325 K. Mackenzie Grieve, 'Some notes on the run', in H. G. Hawker and K. McKenzie Grieve, *Our Atlantic attempt*, Methuen & Co., London, 103.
326 Quoted from 'The New York World' in 'Harry Hawker, the Britisher who took chances like a Yank', *Literary Digest,* Vol 7, 7 June 1921, Funk and Wagnalls, New York, 1.
327 M.G. D. 'The grit', 7.

POSTSCRIPT

328 *Flight* magazine, 29 May, 1919, 694.
329 Ibid.
330 P. Mackaye, 'Danish Mary', quoted in *The Newfoundland Quarterly,* 1919-20, 5.
331 M. Hawker, *H. G. Hawker*, 243.
332 National Library of Australia, nla.obj-140832827-m.
333 *Flight* magazine, 2 October 1919, 1324.
334 P. Fraser, '1919 Newfoundland Hawker 3c stamp makes $25,000', Postage Stamps, 26 February, 2015, www.paulfrasercollectibles.com/blogs/postage-stamps/1919-newfoundland-hawker-3c-stamp-makes-25-000.
335 P. Fraser, '1919 Newfoundland Hawker 3c stamp makes $25,000', Postage Stamps, 26 February, 2015, www.paulfrasercollectibles.com/blogs/postage-stamps/1919-newfoundland-hawker-3c-stamp-makes-25-000.
336 M. Hawker, *H. G. Hawker*, ix.
337 D. Morley, 'Great ties to Uncle Harry', *Air Force*, Vol. 58, No. 10, June 16, 2016, 15, www.defence.gov.au/publications/newspapers/raaf/editions/5810/5810.pdf.
338 Inflation calculator, www.bankofengland.co.uk/monetary-policy/inflation/inflation-calculator.
339 Kingston Aviation, www.kingstonaviation.org.

INDEX

A
A. C. (car), 243, 247, 249-50
ABC motorcycles, 85
Aerial Derby
 1919, 210
 1920, 228-9
 1921, 252-3
Albury, 23-4, 232
Alcock, Captain John, 84, 125, 205-6, 274, 277
Allies WWI, 4, 66, 69
Argyll (car), 7, 9, *image*: 8
Ashfield, Reg, 30
Austro-Daimler, 37, 39, 50, *image*: 51, 53
Azores, 78, 124, 127, 131-3, 143, 145-6, 161, 167, 199, 271

B
BAE Systems, 275
Ballarat, 25, 232
Biddlecombe, Charles, 277
Blériot, Louis, 11, 74
Blue Bird, 237
Bournemouth, 235
British Aerospace, 275
British Empire Michelin Cup, 231
British International Trophy (B.I.T.), 232, 237, *image*: 238
Brooklands, 14, 18, 27-8, 30, 32, 34, 40, 48, 53, 60, 86-7, 105, 136, 161, 219-20, 222, 224, 234-7, *image*: 157
Busteed, Harry, 10
Butt of Lewis, 172
Butt of Lewis lighthouse, *image*: 174

C
Camm, Sidney, 275
Caramut, Victoria, 7, 10
Central Powers, 4
Chicago USS, 128-30

Christian Science, 241-2, 261, 264
Churchill, Winston, 206
Clements, Lieutenant L. J., 110, 112
Coatalen, Louis, 217, 223, 236, 250
Cohen, Dr G (coroner), 260-1
Coil, Lieutenant Commander Emory, 129, 131
Cook, Sir Joseph, 258
Cowes, 212, 214-5, 237, 240
Curtiss, Glenn, 123

D
Daily Mail, 16, 66, 72-4, 76, 117, 122, 124, 138, 144, 162, 166, 199, 202, 205, 210, 263, 273
Daily Mirror, 176-7
Dale, James, 276
Daniels, Josephus, 123
De Fraga, Cecil, 10
de Little, Ernest, 7
Diggers Rest, 12
Doriot, Flandrin and Parant (DFP car), 244
Duhn, Captain Adolph, 268-270, 272, 274

E
Edinburgh, 184
'Ennadale', 65, 98, 139, 162, 170, 176, 178, 217, 236, 254

F
Fenn, Monty, 55, 57, 94, 97
Ferdinand, Archduke Franz, 33
Flight magazine, 15, 78, 100, 111-2, 134, 184, 186, 201, 204, 227, 265, 268
Folland, Henry, 226, 232
Fremantle, Vice-Admiral Sidney, 162

G
Gallipoli, 5, 38, 45
Gardner, Dr Eric, 261
Gordon Bennett Air Race, 26, 245
Grantham, 183, 188

H
H. G. Hawker Engineering Company, 245, 249, 275
 Hawker motor-bike, 246, *image*: 247, 253
Handley-Page V/1500 biplane, 84, 125, 277, *image*: 126
Harbour Grace, 125
Harding, Officer George, 173
Harmsworth Cup. *See* British International Trophy
Hawker aircraft
 Hart, 275; Hunter, 275; Hurricane, 275; Tempest, 275; Typhoon, 275
Hawker Siddeley Aircraft Company, 275
Hawker Siddeley Aviation, 275
Hawker, Harry
 aircraft design, 17, 30, 36, 38, 41, 47,49, 55, 67, 77,82, 211, *image*: 157
 Australian Aviation Hall of Fame, 275
 Australian visit, 18-26, 232
 awards, 66, 198, 274
 car racing, 9, 217, 220, 222ff, 234ff, 243-4, 249-50, 268.
 cause of death, 260-1, 263-4
 characteristics, 9, 39, 49, 51, 54, 61-2, 65, 103, 115, 119-20, 132, 209, 222, 247, 251, 265
 early years: childhood, 5-7, growing up, 7-10.
 children, 71, 220, 233, *image*: 71, 234
 crashes, 24-5, 31, 53, 76, 160, 231, 250, 257
 eulogies, 258, 265
 father, 5, 19, 23
 final flight, 253-8
 financial position, 63, 65, 67-8, 85, 114, 216, 246, 274
 health, 26, 29, 53, 59, 75, 229, 231-2, 241-2
 honeymoon, 62
 looping the loop, 28, 30, 42
 mother, 5
 relationship with Muriel, 4, 37, 39, 45-6, 48-50, 68, 73, 77, 86, 88, 121, 187, 189, 205, 214, 225, 235, 264-5, 271
 rescue, 267-273, *image*: 186
 return after transatlantic attempt, 180-197, *image*: 188, 193, 194, 195.
 siblings, 5, 59
 speedboat racing, 232, 237-239, *image*: 238
 spinning dive, 31, 34-36, 56
 transatlantic attempt, 72,76, 91-170, *image*: 93, 97, 101, 104, 105, 110, 135, 137, 157, 164, 165, 169
 wartime role, 40-42, 66-67, 71
 wedding, 58-62, *image*: 60
Hawker, Muriel, 1-4, *image*: 2, 178
 attitude to Harry's risk-taking, 233-7, 243-4, 263-4
 book, 274
 honeymoon, 62
 later life, 274
 parents, 36-7, 43, 260
 during Harry's absence – transatlantic attempt, 144, 148, 159, 161-2, 164, 170-2, 175-6
 wedding, 58-62, *image*: 60
Hendon Aerodrome, 28, 49, 181, 203, 204, 227, 254
Hook, Surrey, 65, 68, 136, 196
Houdini, Harry, 12
Hughes, Billy, 170, 231

I
Ingham, Chief Officer William, 173
Inverness, 184

K
Kangaroo II, 212
Kauper, Harry, 11, 14, 16, 18, 23, 41, 75-6, 231
Kerr, Vice-Admiral Mark, 84, 125, 277
King George V, 66, 170, 186, 197, 206, 258, 269
King, Daisy, 203
Kings Cross Station, 191
Kingston (-on-Thames), 40, 42, 46, 196
Kingston Aviation Centenary Project, 275
Kingston University London, Hawker Wing, 276

Index · 297

L
Lake Charlottesville, 273
Lang, Andrew, 7, 8, 10, 11, 51-2, 54, 67, 245, 260
Larkin Aviation, 217
Lisbon, 101, 124, 199

M
Mackaye, Percy, 270
Mackenzie Grieve, 80-81, 136, 166, 198, 241, 259, 265, 270, 276-7, *image*: 180
Maple Leaf V, 238, 213, *image*: 238
Mary, 158-9, 173-6, 180, *image*: 186, 268
Mauretania, 78, 125
Mayflower, 201
Melbourne, 5, 9, 19, 20
Millen, Edward, 22
Miller, Horrie, 32, 34, 36
Minerva (car), 248, 251, *image*: 248
Miss America, 239
Moorabbin, 5
　Airport, 275
　primary school, 6
Morgan, Fairfax, 83, 106, 125-6, 142

N
New York *Tribune*, 195
Newcastle UK, 184
Newfoundland
　arrival, 91-6
　Cochrane Hotel, 100-1
　description, 93-5
　Glendenning's Farm, 94, 96, 118, 135, *image*: 97, 110
　Raynham & Morgan, 83, 97, 104-5, 109, 140-142
　residents, 95, 99
　St John's, 95, *image*: 83, 99, 108, 115, 119, 120
　takeoff, 135-7, *image*: 136
Nieuport Goshawk, 228, 253-257, *image*: 254, 257
Norfolk, UK, 205
Northcliffe, Lord, 73, 166-7, 237

P
Paris Peace Conference, 70, 109
Paterson, Banjo, 169
Peaty, Laurence, 161, 163, 165, 177, 251, 259
Peaty, Muriel, 1-4, 37, 39
　parents, 36, 44
　siblings, 37
Pickles, Sidney, 75, 83, 126, 165
Placentia, 92
Platford, Eric, 86, 197, 112, 134
Plymouth, UK, 201
Point Cook, 23
postage stamp, 243, 273, 276, *image*: 273, 276

Q
Queen Alexandra, 186, 221

R
Race Round Britain, 16, 74-6, 231, *image*: 74
Raymor, 83, 109, 111, 140-1, *image*: 116, 141
Raynham, Fred, 26, 47, 83, 105, 111, 115, 118, 126, 166, 204, 245, 277.
Read, Lieutenant Commander 'Putty', 145, 199, 204, *image*: 202, 204
Roosevelt, Franklin D, 131
Royal Aero Club, 66, 81, 191, 202, 204, 210
Royal Air Force, 162, 201
Royal Flying Corps, 38, 54, 108
Royal Naval Air Service, 38
Royal Navy, 5, 38, 80, 162, 179, 276

S
Schneider Cup, 27, 210, 212, 214-6, 228
Seely, Major-General, 201
Shamrock, 83, 98, 116-7
Sigrist, Fred, 15, 41, 114, 177, 245
Sopwith aircraft
　1½ Strutter, 40 *image*: 44; Antelope, 232, 240, image: 233; Atlantic, 81-3, 273, *image*: 87, 100, 111, 135, 168, 272; Camel, 17, 40, 55-6, *image*: 55, 56; Gnu, 203, *image*: 203; Grasshopper, 48; Rainbow, 228, *image*: 228; Schneider, 42, *image*: 211, 215; Scooter, 67, 204, 233, *image*: 67; Scout, 30-1, 232; Snapper, 188; Snipe, 219; Sparrow, 44; Swallow, 49, 203; Tabloid, 17, 18-25, 27-28, *image*: 18, 23, 29
Sopwith Aviation, 14, 40, 62, 67, 71, 85, 105, 246, *image*: 14, 16
Sopwith Aviation and Engineering, 85, 216, 244-5

Sopwith, Beatrix, 164, 187, 195-6
Sopwith, Tommy, 15, 17, 29, 40, 82, 85, 113, 188, 195, 202, 209, 246, 275, *image* 188
Southampton Water, 75, 212-4
St Paul's Church, Hook, 171, 176, 186, *image*: 172
   Reverend Wood, 179, 181
Sunbeam cars, 68, 193, 196, 212, 217-8, 220-2, 235-6, 259 *image*: 69, 201, 225, 256, 259
Sunstedt, Hugo, 83, 94, 117, 121
Sunrise, 84, 98, 117
Surrey Comet, 165, 167, 169, 178, 197
Sydney, 22-3

T
Tait-Cox, Major Leonard, 253
Thurso, 183
transatlantic race
   contenders, 83-4, 97-8, *image*: 78
   Daily Mail prize, 66, 72, 73, 76, 205-6
   start point, 79
Trepassey, 122, 124, 125, 127-8, 131
US Navy, 103, 111, 114, 122-4, 200-1
   C-5 blimp, 128-131, *image*: 128, 130
   Nancies, 123-4, 127-8, 145-6, 161, 199-201, *image*: 124, 200

V
Villacoublay, 41, 54-7, 59

W
Washington Evening Star, 200
Watson, Basil, 3, 44
Webb, Connie, 46, 48
Wellman, Walter, 78
Western District of Victoria, 7
Western Front, 5, 41, 45, 48, 57, 69, 95
Whitten-Brown, Lieutenant Arthur, 84, 125, 205-6
Wood, Major J. C. P., 116-7
Worthing Road State School. *See* Moorabbin: primary school
Wylie, Captain C. C., 116-7

Y
Yaniman, Melvin, 78
York, UK, 184

Z
Zeppelins, 39, 58